AN AMBITIOUS
SECONDARY SCHOOL
CURRICULUM

To order, or for details of our bulk discounts, please go to our website www.criticalpublishing.com or contact our distributor, Ingram Publisher Services (IPS UK), 10 Thornbury Road, Plymouth PL6 7PP, telephone 01752 202301 or email IPSUK.orders@ingramcontent.com.

AN AMBITIOUS
SECONDARY SCHOOL
CURRICULUM

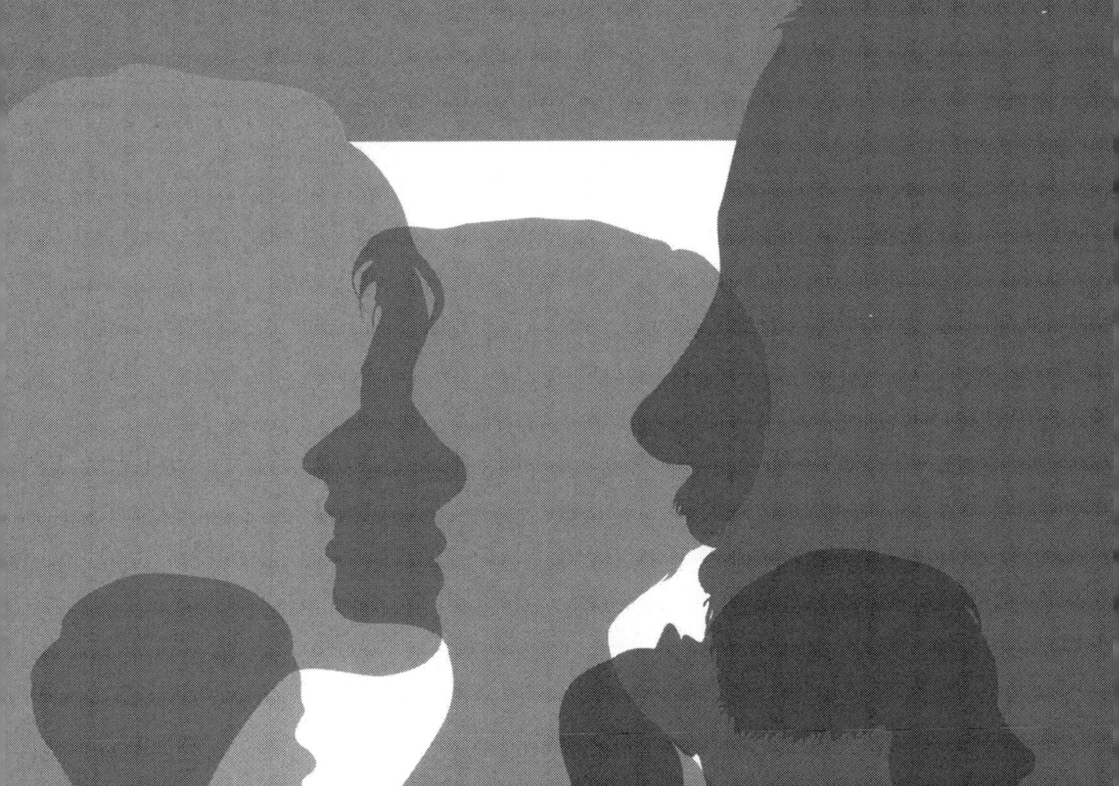

Jonathan Glazzard and Michael Green

First published in 2022 by Critical Publishing Ltd

British Library Cataloguing in Publication Data
A CIP record for this book is available from the British Library

ISBN: 978-1-913453-21-3

This book is also available in the following e-book formats:

EPUB ISBN: 978-1-913453-23-7
Adobe e-book ISBN: 978-1-913453-24-4

Cover and text design by Out of House Limited
Project management by Newgen Publishing UK
Printed and bound in Great Britain by 4edge, Essex

Critical Publishing
3 Connaught Road
St Albans
AL3 5RX

www.criticalpublishing.com

Printed on FSC accredited paper

+ CONTENTS

✛ MEET THE AUTHORS

JONATHAN GLAZZARD

Jonathan Glazzard is Professor of Teacher Education and Head of Department for Children, Education and Communities at Edge Hill University. He is an active researcher and teacher educator as well as a qualified teacher. Jonathan taught in state primary schools for 10 years before moving into higher education. His research addresses issues of inclusion and social justice within education.

MICHAEL GREEN

Michael Green is an experienced educational professional and leader. Until recently, he was one of Her Majesty's Inspectors. Before working for Ofsted, he gained extensive experience in a range of educational settings and roles, including leading initial teacher education in higher education, working as a government adviser, undertaking international advisory work and holding senior leadership positions within primary schools. His areas of expertise also include policy development, English, advising on teacher workload and learning outside the classroom.

✛ **INTRODUCTION**

This book introduces the ambitious curriculum in secondary schools. It will be of interest to trainee teachers, teachers and subject leaders in secondary schools.

We recognise that the term 'ambitious' means different things to different people. It is often associated with the level of challenge, and sometimes it is associated with exceeding the minimum requirements of the national curriculum. Throughout this book, we use this term to mean that the curriculum is designed to enable pupils to achieve the ambitious 'end points' of the national curriculum. We argue that the national curriculum is not a curriculum in the strict sense, as it is not sequenced and it does not break down its ambitious goals into smaller components.

This book uses many terms that may be unfamiliar to some readers. We define 'progress' as knowing more, remembering more and doing more in the subject. Essentially, pupils make progress when they learn the knowledge that is intended in the curriculum. We define curriculum 'intent' as everything that is planned before the curriculum is delivered. This might include the subject vision statement, the curriculum plan that sequences the knowledge that pupils need to learn, and the lesson plans that support lesson delivery. We define curriculum 'implementation' as everything that happens during curriculum delivery. This includes the pedagogical approaches that teachers use in classrooms to teach the intended curriculum, and the use of formative assessment, which provides teachers with information to ascertain whether pupils are in fact learning the intended curriculum. We define 'impact' as knowing, remembering and doing more in the subject. Impact is evaluated according to the extent to which pupils have learned the things they have been taught and therefore whether they go on to achieve the qualifications they are aiming to achieve.

The book covers a range of themes, including: designing a curriculum that provides pupils with cultural capital; relationships, sex and health education (RSHE); and decolonising the curriculum. We emphasise the importance of designing a curriculum that is broad in scope, particularly at Key Stage 3, and we stress that an examination syllabus is not a curriculum.

So, what do we mean by the term 'curriculum'? A curriculum ensures that pupils achieve the broad goals outlined in the national curriculum. These are often meaty statements that are made up of several components. The broad goals of the national curriculum specify the knowledge that pupils need to learn by the end of each key stage. This is sometimes referred to as 'composite knowledge'. However, to learn this knowledge, teachers need to break these goals down into smaller components, often referred to as 'component knowledge'. These components need to be sequenced in a logical way so that foundational concepts are taught before more complex concepts and so that new learning builds on prior learning. The sequencing of the component knowledge is essentially the subject curriculum. This is sometimes a difficult task for subject leaders because while the composite knowledge is specified in the national curriculum, the component knowledge often is not specified, and this is where the process of curriculum design begins.

In addition, the national curriculum sets out the minimum expectations for a secondary curriculum. Schools are required to exceed this minimum requirement by providing a curriculum that is broad and rich. Knowledge that is essential for the advancement of inclusion and social justice is not included in the national curriculum, but is essential to ensure that pupils develop good citizenship skills. All pupils should develop knowledge about disability, race, sexuality and gender. Schools are required by law to teach religious education, but this is not part of the national curriculum. All pupils need to learn about mental health, climate change and environmental sustainability. All pupils need to develop knowledge of careers and develop the skills that will enable them to transition to further education (FE) and higher education (HE), and employment, training and independent living. The school's wider curriculum offer provides pupils with valuable knowledge and experiences that will prepare them for the next stage.

The Office for Standards in Education, Children's Services and Skills (Ofsted) has emphasised that the curriculum is the 'substance' of education. For far too long, schools have prioritised the knowledge that is tested through statutory assessments. This has resulted in a weak and narrow curriculum because pupils have not gained a deep and rich knowledge of the subjects they have studied. Practices such as 'gaming' have resulted in some subjects and subject content being given insufficient attention due to teaching to the test. It is time to reopen the conversation about curriculum. Amanda Spielman (2019) has reassured schools that 'there is no need for anyone to think they must develop a new curriculum, or design everything themselves from scratch, or put themselves through intellectual gymnastics'. There are many excellent curriculum frameworks already available, which simply need to be adapted to specific contexts, and multi-academy trusts are developing trust-wide curriculums that take the load off individual subject leaders. This book is a starting point to support you in that process.

✛ CHAPTER 1

AN AMBITIOUS CURRICULUM FOR THE TWENTY-FIRST CENTURY

CHAPTER OBJECTIVES

After reading this chapter you will understand:

+ the meaning of ambitious end points of the curriculum;

+ the importance of designing a curriculum that provides pupils with cultural capital;

+ the aspects that need to be addressed in a contemporary curriculum.

INTRODUCTION

The *Education Inspection Framework* (Ofsted, 2019b) rightly emphasises the curriculum as the substance of education. The curriculum outlines the essential knowledge that pupils need to learn and is central in determining the quality of education. However, since the 1990s, schools have focused less on the curriculum and placed more emphasis on raising examination results. In some schools, this has resulted in an emphasis on teaching the knowledge that is tested rather than teaching the whole domain of a subject. In addition, the emphasis on improving examination results has resulted in some schools choosing to offer a restricted curriculum in Year 9 rather than providing a broad and balanced curriculum offer. This chapter addresses key aspects of curriculum design that heads of department need to consider when planning the curriculum. It addresses cultural capital and the aspects that should be present in a contemporary curriculum.

CURRICULUM INTENT, IMPLEMENTATION AND IMPACT

The *Education Inspection Framework* uses the terms 'intent', 'implementation' and 'impact' under the category of 'quality of education'. It is therefore important that school leaders have a clear understanding of what these terms mean.

CURRICULUM INTENT

The intent of the curriculum is an outline of what the school curriculum and the subject curriculum is trying to achieve and an overview of how the curriculum will be implemented. It should summarise the essential knowledge, values and attitudes that school leaders intend the curriculum to develop in pupils, rather like a vision statement. It should also clearly outline the knowledge that pupils will learn in the curriculum, and it should demonstrate clearly how this knowledge will be sequenced across and within school years. Simply, curriculum intent is the essential planning that school leaders need to do prior to implementation. To demonstrate intent, schools will need to provide a vision statement for the school curriculum and for each subject. Schools will also need to provide plans to demonstrate when knowledge will be introduced, when it will be revisited and the end points they intend pupils to achieve. Curriculum planning and sequencing is therefore an essential component of curriculum intent.

School leaders will also need to outline the knowledge that they want pupils to learn. The national curriculum and examination syllabi often state the desired end points that pupils need to achieve. However, the national curriculum is not actually a curriculum. It simply states the ambitious end points that pupils need to achieve. An examination syllabus is also not a curriculum. Again, it outlines the end points that pupils need to achieve. School leaders need to break these end points down further into smaller chunks of knowledge that combine to enable pupils to achieve the ambitious end points of the curriculum. It is essential that school leaders do not confuse end points with a curriculum. A curriculum is a more detailed outline of the knowledge that pupils need to learn to achieve the ambitious end points outlined in the national curriculum and in examination syllabi.

It is therefore helpful to think of curriculum intent as the 'what' aspect of the curriculum. It states what the vision of the curriculum is plus what knowledge pupils need to learn and in what order they need to learn it.

CURRICULUM IMPLEMENTATION

Implementation is the 'how' aspect of the curriculum. It focuses on how pupils are taught and supported to learn the intended curriculum. It therefore includes pedagogy and assessment. Implementation is often associated with curriculum delivery. It relates to what happens in classrooms to support pupils to learn the intended curriculum.

The critical aspect of implementation is teacher subject knowledge. Teachers need to demonstrate good subject knowledge to enable pupils to learn. Content knowledge (knowledge of the subject) is a crucial aspect of subject knowledge. Teachers cannot help pupils to learn a subject if they do not have a good grasp of the subject concepts, principles and facts themselves. However, pedagogical content knowledge is also important. This relates to the pedagogical choices that teachers make in the classroom to enable their pupils to effectively learn the subject. Often, different pedagogical strategies are required for different subjects. For example, fieldwork is an essential component of geography, and problem-solving is an essential component of mathematics. However, there are some common pedagogical approaches that we might expect teachers to use in all subjects. These include modelling/demonstration, explanation, questioning and retrieval. Teachers also need to ensure that pupils with special educational needs and disabilities (SEND) and disadvantaged pupils are appropriately supported in lessons to enable them to achieve the same ambitious end points of the curriculum as their peers.

Assessment is also part of implementation. Effective assessment enables pupils to learn. It is through assessment that teachers can identify when pupils have developed misconceptions. Regular use of assessment during a lesson, through observation and questioning, enables teachers to notice and respond to misconceptions. It also enables teachers to address misconceptions before moving on to the next stage of the lesson. Checking that pupils understand something before moving on is a critical aspect of effective teaching. If teachers move on too quickly, before pupils have understood something, pupils will not have the essential knowledge to master the subject content that will be introduced next.

CURRICULUM IMPACT

The impact of a curriculum is measured in various ways – not just through examination results. This is because examinations only assess part of a subject domain. They do not assess the whole subject domain. The curriculum should outline the progression of knowledge that pupils need to learn. Pupils make progress by knowing more and remembering more of the intended curriculum that is set out in the progression map. Knowing and remembering more of the subject is a more reliable indicator of positive impact than examination results are. Pupils might gain good examination results because the teaching has emphasised the subject elements that are tested. They might also gain good examination results because more curriculum time has been allocated to the subjects being tested. These practices result in a narrowed curriculum. The two examples help to illustrate that good examination results do not necessarily indicate that pupils have had a high-quality educational experience, particularly if there are gaps in their subject knowledge. If a curriculum is planned and delivered well, it should lead to good examination results, but good examination results cannot be used as a proxy for an effective curriculum.

Knowing and remembering more of the subject is a reliable indicator of positive impact. An effective curriculum should also ensure that pupils are ready for their next phase of education. For secondary pupils, the curriculum at Key Stage 3 should prepare them for the curriculum at Key Stage 4, and the curriculum at Key Stage 4 should prepare them for the curriculum at Key Stage 5. For primary pupils, the curriculum at Key Stage 2 should prepare them for the curriculum at Key Stage 3. The secondary curriculum should also promote an interest in and love of reading. Reading is an essential skill because it enables pupils to access the whole curriculum. Reading is therefore an essential component of the subject curriculum because it is the key that unlocks the door to knowledge when pupils are learning independently.

Another reliable indicator of impact is the destinations pupils progress to after leaving school. The secondary curriculum should prepare pupils to undertake further qualifications in FE and HE, and qualifications through employment and training.

TYPES OF KNOWLEDGE

Two forms of knowledge are important in the curriculum: composite knowledge and component knowledge.

COMPOSITE KNOWLEDGE

Composite knowledge refers to the ambitious end points of the national curriculum or the end points of subject specifications at Key Stages 4 and 5. The statements in the national curriculum are often broad in scope, and pupils will need to learn several aspects of knowledge before they can demonstrate that they have achieved the ambitious end points of the national curriculum.

Composite knowledge might be the knowledge that pupils need to learn at the end of a unit of work, the end of a year or the end of a key stage. It is rarely the knowledge that pupils are learning in a single lesson. It is the knowledge that is gained from the cumulative knowledge that pupils learn over time.

Let's take the example of learning to drive a car. If your goal (ambitious end point) is to learn to drive a car by the end of the year, the skill of driving the car is the composite knowledge that you need to learn. However, to be able to drive the car, there are smaller bits of knowledge that you need to learn. You need to learn the Highway Code. You need to learn how to use the clutch in a manual car. You need to learn how to check blind spots. You need to learn how to use the gears. You need to learn how to hold the car on the biting point when you are on a hill. In addition, you need to learn how to use your mirrors, how to approach a junction, how to reverse park and how to do a turn in the road. The overall goal is for you to learn to drive the car, but you cannot do all of this at once. You need to learn the smaller pieces of knowledge that will combine to enable you to achieve the composite knowledge. The smaller chunks of knowledge are known as component knowledge. The overall goal of learning to drive requires the composite knowledge. Each driving lesson might focus on a single component of knowledge. Your driving instructor will explain the component knowledge and perhaps model/demonstrate it to you, and then you might spend the remainder of the lesson time practising that specific skill. The more you practise, the better you will get at the skill. Eventually you will be able to perform the skill without thinking. You can perform it to automaticity fluently because you have practised it repeatedly.

It is similar in teaching. The curriculum plan should identify the ambitious end points of the national curriculum. This is the composite knowledge. However, it should also state the components that are required to achieve this composite knowledge. The components should be sequenced in the correct order and there should be opportunities to revisit them. The lessons will provide an opportunity for pupils to learn the component knowledge. Pupils will need to master each component so that they reach fluency and automaticity. This can be supported by having sufficient time to practise and by planning in opportunities to revisit each component in a sequence of teaching. Eventually, the cumulative effect of achieving automaticity in the components is that pupils learn the composite knowledge and achieve the ambitious end points of the curriculum.

COMPONENT KNOWLEDGE

Component knowledge refers to the small chunks of knowledge that combine to enable pupils to achieve the ambitious end points of the curriculum. A curriculum must identify and sequence the components of knowledge. Heads of department need to collaborate with subject teams to work backwards from the end points of the curriculum to identify the components that pupils need to learn in order to learn the composite knowledge. They need to decide how to sequence the components in a logical way so that the learning makes sense to pupils, and pupils will need opportunities for revisiting component knowledge across a sequence of lessons or across a year.

Teachers need to assess the components to ensure that pupils have developed the required knowledge before moving on to the next component. It is not sufficient to design an assessment tool to assess the composite knowledge. Teachers need to assess the components to identify where the misconceptions are. Using the example of driving a car, if we only do an overall assessment of whether someone can drive a car or not (composite knowledge), this does not tell us why some people cannot drive. They might be struggling to drive effectively because one of the components (eg changing gears) is not secure. There might be several components that are not secure. We therefore need to know more about which components are secure and which are not. We need to know if the individual has difficulties just with the gears or if they are struggling with multiple components. An effective assessment system should therefore support teachers to identify where the gaps in learning are in relation to each of the essential components.

CULTURAL CAPITAL

In sociology, the term 'cultural capital' is most commonly associated with Pierre Bourdieu (1930–2002). Broadly speaking, cultural capital can be understood as the resources that enable individuals to access opportunities and to achieve social mobility. Bourdieu (1986) identified three categories of cultural capital (see Figure 4.1):

1. embodied: language, mannerisms and preferences;

2. objectified: cultural goods, books and works of art;

3. institutionalised: qualifications and other education credentials.

Knowledge of vocabulary can support pupils to access further knowledge, because vocabulary knowledge improves reading comprehension. In addition, having a wide repertoire of vocabulary enables individuals to articulate themselves effectively, builds confidence and gives access to opportunities that are denied to others who have a restricted vocabulary. Knowledge of key texts, authors, artists, musicians and significant people and events from the past are all forms of cultural capital. Pupils who have deep and rich knowledge are more likely to be granted opportunities which enable them to achieve social mobility, and arguably this cannot be a bad thing.

The problem lies in the fact that some pupils are disadvantaged by their social background or other circumstances. These pupils are likely to have less cultural capital than pupils from more affluent backgrounds because cultural capital can be purchased. Families that are affluent can afford to purchase books, theatre tickets, and even education. This means that pupils from disadvantaged backgrounds are less likely to benefit from opportunities to advance their social mobility and less likely to read for knowledge and pleasure.

A well-designed curriculum should therefore provide all pupils with cultural capital so that all pupils can access the same opportunities in the future. Ofsted's understanding of cultural capital is informed by the following statement in the national curriculum:

The national curriculum provides pupils with an introduction to the essential knowledge that they need to be educated citizens. It introduces pupils to the best that has been thought and said; and helps engender an appreciation of human creativity and achievement.

(Department for Education [DfE], 2014, para 3.1, p 5)

Cultural capital is therefore sometimes associated with knowledge that is specialist and significant. In science, it might include knowledge of the galaxies or the periodic table. In history, essential knowledge could include knowledge of the Magna Carta or the Enlightenment. In geography, essential knowledge could include knowledge of glaciation. In English, essential knowledge might include knowledge of Shakespeare. In art and design, it could include knowledge of sculpture.

CRITICAL QUESTIONS

+ In your specialist subject, what examples of cultural capital do pupils need to learn?
+ Why is it important to design a curriculum to provide pupils with cultural capital?
+ Is cultural capital a form of traditional knowledge, or can it also be a form of contemporary knowledge?

EXTENDED THINKING

+ To what extent might the emphasis on cultural capital in the curriculum reflect a curriculum model that promotes middle-class values?

+ To what extent is the taught curriculum in schools shaped by politicians who may have privileged backgrounds, and in what ways might this influence what schools are required to teach pupils?

KNOWLEDGE VERSUS SKILLS

In this chapter, and indeed in this book, we do not differentiate between knowledge and skills. We use 'knowledge' to mean the things that pupils need to know and also the things that they need to be able to do. Knowledge and skills have often been unhelpfully separated as though they are two separate entities. To be able to drive a car (skill), we still need to know how to drive (knowledge). The skill of driving therefore requires knowledge. The skill of reading requires knowledge of vocabulary, phonics and concepts about print. Being able to read therefore requires knowledge. These examples illustrate why it is impossible to separate knowledge and skills.

Effective curriculum planning should therefore specify the essential knowledge that pupils need to learn. This will include what pupils need to know, understand and be able to do. Effective curriculum planning enables pupils to deepen their knowledge over time by revisiting key knowledge at specific points in a sequence of learning. Knowledge becomes deeper and richer as pupils progress through their education, and progress should be evaluated on the basis of pupils' ability to demonstrate greater knowledge as they progress through the curriculum. The curriculum is therefore a progression model, and a well-sequenced curriculum that states the cumulative component knowledge pupils need to learn also becomes the assessment framework for evaluating progress. Therefore, curriculum design should not be separated from assessment.

A CURRICULUM FOR THE TWENTY-FIRST CENTURY

The national curriculum is a minimum entitlement. It is not a curriculum in the strict sense because it is not sequenced and does not break knowledge into smaller components. It does identify the ambitious end points that pupils need to achieve, but school leaders need to break this composite knowledge into smaller components and sequence these in a logical way to develop a curriculum. Given that the national curriculum is a minimum entitlement, school leaders need to consider how to design their own curriculum that meets and exceeds the ambition of the national curriculum.

ADDRESSING THE BIG ISSUES IN SOCIETY

The school curriculum should be designed to empower pupils to address societal issues, including mental health and climate change. It should also promote positive attitudes in relation to race, ethnicity, gender, sexual orientation and disability. Education is a powerful tool for addressing societal prejudice, and the curriculum should teach pupils to respect people's different identities and beliefs. Through addressing issues of inclusion and social justice, pupils are prepared for adult life. They will be required to study, work and live alongside people who are different. Heads of department and subject teams also have an ethical and moral responsibility to decolonise the subject curriculum at Key Stages 3, 4 and 5.

CRITICAL QUESTIONS

Think about your specialist subject and answer the following questions.

+ Which significant women might you introduce into the subject curriculum?

+ How might you integrate lesbian, gay, bisexual, trans or queer (LGBTQ+) identities and experiences into the subject curriculum?

+ How might you decolonise the subject curriculum?

+ Who are the significant individuals with minority identities who have shaped the development of your subject?

EXTENDED THINKING

+ To what extent can the curriculum address social problems?

+ Does the national curriculum promote social justice? Justify your response.

AN AMBITIOUS CURRICULUM FOR PUPILS WITH SEND

Pupils with SEND are entitled to an ambitious curriculum so that they can access the same opportunities as their peers. Too often, pupils with SEND are placed in low-ability classes and provided with tasks that lack challenge. This widens the ability gap between pupils with and without SEND and results in underachievement among pupils with SEND. This can have a serious long-term detrimental effect for these pupils. Far too many pupils with SEND underachieve at school and consequently are disadvantaged. As a result, many do not enter FE or HE and are denied access to employment and training opportunities.

All pupils have an entitlement to an ambitious curriculum that enables them to develop good subject knowledge. Pupils with SEND should be supported to work towards the same ambitious end points of the curriculum that pupils without SEND are working towards. They need to be on the same trajectory, though some pupils with SEND will be working on foundational components of knowledge. Of course, through adaptive teaching, many pupils with SEND can achieve the ambitious end points of the national curriculum. However, some pupils with complex needs may need a tailored curriculum that further breaks down the component knowledge. Pupils with highly complex needs may require a sensory curriculum to enable them to learn more effectively. Teachers should always start with the mindset that pupils can achieve a goal, rather than simply assuming that they will be unable to achieve the goals other pupils are working towards.

Providing pupils with SEND with a lower level of challenge should not be the default way teachers think when they are planning classroom tasks. Teachers should consider ways of enabling pupils with SEND to access the same curriculum as their peers by building in access strategies to remove barriers to learning. Pupils with cognition and learning difficulties can achieve the same end points of the curriculum as their peers over a longer period of time. However, teachers may need to build in specific strategies to enable them to access the curriculum. Examples include the use of additional adult support, breaking curriculum content down into smaller chunks, use of technology to overcome barriers to learning, pre-teaching subject-specific concepts or vocabulary, and opportunities for overlearning.

CASE STUDY

CURRICULUM DESIGN FOR PUPILS WITH SEND

WHOLE SCHOOL

School leaders wanted to design a curriculum for pupils with SEND in mind from the outset. This meant that the needs of pupils with SEND were addressed through the process of curriculum design, as opposed to designing a curriculum for most pupils and then subsequently adapting it for pupils with SEND. Curriculum design ensured that knowledge was broken down into small components of knowledge. Each component of knowledge was to be learned to automaticity before moving on to the next component, and effective curriculum design addressed the principles of spaced or distributed practice. This ensured that knowledge is revisited after a gap to embed knowledge into pupils' long-term memories.

CRITICAL QUESTIONS

+ What other ways might you address the needs of pupils with SEND from the outset in curriculum design?

+ How does organising knowledge into smaller components support the reduction of cognitive load?

THE ROLE OF TECHNOLOGY IN THE CURRICULUM

The curriculum for the twenty-first century needs to ensure that pupils have the knowledge, skills and attitudes required to be digital citizens. The pace of technological development in recent decades has been nothing short of remarkable. Technology is now a central component of everyone's life. It is central to the modern workplace, and it plays a vital role in facilitating communication and knowledge exchange across the global community. It is a key component not only in people's homes and workplaces but also in the outdoor environment. Although we cannot predict what the future will look like, we can be certain that technological development will continue to advance and that technology will play an even greater role in people's lives as we progress through the twenty-first century.

The curriculum for the twenty-first century needs to be designed to ensure that pupils develop a wide repertoire of digital skills. This will enable them to be confident users of technology. It should ensure that they develop automaticity in a range of skills and can confidently use hardware and software, including computers and mobile devices. The curriculum should be designed so that pupils become confident in the use of Web 3.0 technologies as these are already playing a significant role in people's lives. In addition, the digital curriculum should ensure that pupils know how to keep themselves safe online and support them in critically evaluating content they see online. It should also ensure that pupils understand the importance of digital citizenship. As digital citizens, pupils have a responsibility to treat other people with respect online. They also have a responsibility to challenge and report online abuse. Pupils need to understand their rights and responsibilities as digital citizens and, in particular, their responsibilities towards other people.

CASE STUDY

CURRICULUM DESIGN

WHOLE SCHOOL

A secondary school developed a subject curriculum that met the requirements of the national curriculum. School leaders then identified additional knowledge that they wanted pupils to learn. They wanted pupils to learn about disabled hate crime, historical treatment of disabled people in society and changing attitudes to disability. They also wanted pupils to learn about British imperialism, race and racism. Finally, they wanted pupils to learn about climate change. The school leaders then decided in which subjects this content could be delivered in, and where content did not easily fit into subjects, they organised themed events to address the content.

15

CRITICAL QUESTIONS

+ Why might this content be considered ambitious?

+ What content might you include in a curriculum that is additional to the content in the national curriculum?

SUMMARY

This chapter addressed the concept of the ambitious secondary curriculum. It emphasised that, first and foremost, the subject curriculum must enable pupils to achieve the ambitious end points of the national curriculum. In addition, an ambitious curriculum should address the major problems in society that need to be solved, including racism, homophobia, disability hate crime and climate change. Finally, the ambitious curriculum is outward-looking and also relevant to pupils' daily lives. It enables pupils to view themselves as global citizens, but at the same time it considers the local community.

CHECKLIST

+ An ambitious curriculum supports pupils to achieve the ambitious goals in the national curriculum.

+ An ambitious curriculum introduces content that is not identified in the national curriculum.

+ When the curriculum is designed for pupils with SEND in mind, this reduces the necessity to adapt the curriculum.

+ An ambitious curriculum provides pupils with the knowledge that they need in the twenty-first century.

+ An ambitious curriculum ensures that all pupils are challenged.

FURTHER READING

Demie, F (2021) Transforming the Secondary Curriculum. British Educational Research Association. [online] Available at: www.bera.ac.uk/blog/transforming-the-secondary-curriculum (accessed 19 August 2022).

Fearne, H and Keay, J (2021) Curriculum: Keeping It Simple. [online] Available at: https://educationinspection.blog.gov.uk/2021/12/08/curriculum-keeping-it-simple/ (accessed 19 August 2022).

Singh, H (2019) Designing a Secondary School Curriculum that Prepares Pupils for the World. [online] Available at: https://teaching.blog.gov.uk/2019/07/15/designing-a-secondary-school-curriculum-that-prepares-pupils-for-the-world/ (accessed 19 August 2022).

✚ CHAPTER 2
ADDRESSING DISADVANTAGE

CHAPTER OBJECTIVES

After reading this chapter you will understand:

+ the impact of disadvantage on outcomes for pupils;
+ ways in which schools can counter the effects of disadvantage.

INTRODUCTION

Schools cannot solve all the problems that exist in society. Teachers are being asked to perform an increasingly demanding role. Not only must they design an ambitious curriculum that enables pupils to achieve qualifications, they are also required to address a broader range of issues including, but not limited to, mental health, climate change and poverty. There is only so much that schools can reasonably be expected to do, but addressing the effects of disadvantage is one priority worth committing to.

It is a fact that pupils from more affluent backgrounds tend to achieve more. They get off to a better start in school, achieve higher qualifications, go to more prestigious universities and access higher-paid employment. This is clearly unfair and is not something we should resign ourselves to. The political system in England perhaps best illustrates how advantage and disadvantage play out. Many politicians are born into affluent families, receive private education, attend Oxford or Cambridge universities, and then end up in politics! This is not by accident. It is the effects of a system that privileges those who have access to social and cultural capital. Politicians from working-class backgrounds appear to be exceptions rather than the norm, and despite their significant achievements, they are sometimes criticised by their peers because of the way they speak.

Young people from areas of social disadvantage do less well in school. They may lack the financial capital to access FE or HE, and their opportunities may be restricted due to caring responsibilities or the need to earn an income. This is a devastating loss of talent and opportunity.

Schools can, and do, play a crucial role in improving long-term outcomes for pupils who are disadvantaged. There is no reason why pupils from poorer backgrounds should not have the same opportunities as their more affluent peers. They are not less intelligent. They are not less hard-working. They are not less worthy. All pupils have a right to equality of opportunity. Some pupils may need more academic support or more encouragement, and some may need help with raising their aspirations. However, life chances should not be determined by a person's postcode, their income, their accent, the clothes they wear and the type of house that they live in. Opportunities should be available for all.

This chapter addresses disadvantage and provides some practical strategies for schools to support them in addressing disadvantage.

DISADVANTAGE

When people use the term 'disadvantage', they often immediately think of social disadvantage. This is one form of disadvantage. However, it might reasonably be argued that pupils who have experienced adverse childhood experiences, including bereavement or other trauma, and those with minority identities are disadvantaged by their experiences. Therefore, those from affluent backgrounds can also be disadvantaged.

ADDRESSING SOCIAL DISADVANTAGE THROUGH THE CURRICULUM

Schools can play a significant role in reducing the attainment gap between disadvantaged pupils and their non-disadvantaged peers by providing access to a broad and rich curriculum that provides pupils with 'powerful knowledge'. Michael Young offers several definitions of powerful knowledge.

Powerful knowledge refers to what the knowledge can do or what intellectual power it gives to those who have access to it. Powerful knowledge provides more reliable explanations and new ways of thinking about the world and ... can provide learners with a language for engaging in political, moral, and other kinds of debates.

(Young, 2008, p 14)

'Powerful knowledge' is powerful because it provides the best understanding of the natural and social worlds that we have and helps us go beyond our individual experiences.

(Young, 2013, p 196)

Knowledge is 'powerful' if it predicts, if it explains, if it enables you to envisage alternatives.

(Young, 2014, p 74)

Schools can create opportunities for pupils by providing them with experiences that they otherwise would not get. Disadvantaged pupils may have less cultural capital than their non-disadvantaged peers. The relationship between cultural capital and good life outcomes is clear – cultural capital provides access to social, cultural and economic opportunities and increases social mobility. Through developing a school curriculum that embeds cultural capital, the curriculum then serves as a leveller by minimising the effects of disadvantage and creating equality of opportunity. The school curriculum should provide access to knowledge that takes pupils beyond their immediate experiences.

Back in 2013, Michael Gove stated: '*The acquisition of cultural capital – the acquisition of knowledge – is the key to social mobility*' (Walker, 2013). Cultural capital prepares pupils well to compete economically in a global society.

However, there is a fine balancing act to be achieved. The curriculum should develop pupils' knowledge of places and cultures beyond their immediate locality. It should extend their vocabularies and provide pupils with opportunities to learn specialist and deep knowledge. Para 163 of the *School Inspection Handbook* defines this as '*the essential knowledge that pupils need to be educated citizens, introducing them to the **best that has been thought and said** and helping to engender an appreciation of human creativity and achievement*' (Ofsted, 2022, our emphasis). It should confront prejudices head on and provide pupils with rich experiences that extend their cultural and linguistic knowledge. At the same time, the curriculum should reflect pupils' backgrounds and experiences so that they know these are recognised, valued and respected. Research demonstrates that many working-class pupils experience a sense of powerlessness and educational worthlessness as well as feeling that they are not really valued and respected within education (Reay, 2017). A culturally responsive pedagogy is premised on the idea that valuing the cultural worlds of pupils is central to learning. Teachers should understand the sociocultural worlds of their pupils, listen to them, value them and incorporate their cultural identities and histories within the curriculum. A culturally responsive pedagogy nourishes them intellectually, socially, emotionally and politically, and prepares them for a contemporary multicultural and multiracial world (Lucas and Villegas, 2013; Nieto, 2000; Sleeter, 2011). A culturally responsive pedagogy also enhances pupils' cognitive development and self-esteem, which enables them to express their own cultural identities and be proud of them.

CRITICAL QUESTIONS

+ How can a school's wider curriculum address cultural capital?
+ How can the subject curriculum address cultural capital? Think through specific subjects and consider how the curriculum can provide pupils with cultural capital.
+ How does social deprivation impact on vocabulary, and how can the subject curriculum in secondary schools address this?

EXTENDED THINKING

+ Who decides which knowledge should be included in the curriculum?
+ Is cultural capital a way of providing pupils with a middle-class curriculum or a way of levelling up?

CASE STUDY

THE SCHOOL'S WIDER CURRICULUM

WHOLE SCHOOL

A school's wider curriculum offer attempted to address disadvantage and provide pupils with cultural capital. The offer included the following:

+ support services for pupils provided within school, including therapeutic services;
+ homework clubs;
+ reading clubs, book clubs and debating societies;
+ visits to the theatre;
+ visits to museums;
+ visits to coastal regions;
+ additional classes for disadvantaged children;
+ sporting and cultural enrichment activities, including chess, music and cricket;
+ support services for parents, including adult literacy classes;
+ activities targeted at the wider community.

EVIDENCE-BASED PRACTICE

In a study in 2019, Hutchinson et al (2020) found the following.

+ At the end of primary school, the attainment gap between pupils from a disadvantaged household (those who have been eligible for free school meals at any point in the last six years) and their peers was 9.3 months on average.

+ At secondary school, by the time they took their GCSEs, disadvantaged pupils were on average 18.1 months of learning behind their peers in English and mathematics. This gap is the same as it was in 2014.

+ Pupils with a high persistence of poverty (those on free school meals for at least 80 per cent of their time at school) had a learning gap of 22.7 months – twice that of pupils with a low persistence of poverty (those on free school meals for less than 20 per cent of their time at school), who had a learning gap of 11.3 months.

+ Large disadvantage gaps remained well-established in several regions in England, but were particularly acute in the north, West Midlands and parts of the south.

+ In some areas, poorer pupils were over two full years of education behind their peers by the time they took their GCSEs. These areas were Blackpool (26.3 months), Knowsley (24.7 months) and Plymouth (24.5 months).

+ In contrast, there were very low GCSE disadvantage gaps in parts of London, including Ealing (4.6 months), Redbridge (2.7 months) and Westminster (0.5 months).

POVERTY

This section focuses on the role of poverty in creating educational disadvantage. However, it also addresses broader aspects of inclusion, specifically LGBTQ+ inclusion in secondary schools. Poverty impacts detrimentally on educational and life outcomes. Schools cannot compensate for the effects of disadvantage, but they can reduce the effects. The National Education Union (NEU) states that '*our education system does not have to mirror the society and economy within which it is situated'* (2021, p 8). Through the curriculum, schools can show pupils an alternative future. Just because someone is born disadvantaged, this does not mean that they need to remain disadvantaged for the rest of their lives. The curriculum should empower pupils by supporting them to recognise what they can achieve and that they can go on to have fulfilling and rewarding careers.

EVIDENCE-BASED PRACTICE

The NEU (2021) has produced a synthesis of key research. Some key points are given below.

+ *Poverty is the strongest statistical predictor of how well a child will achieve at school.* (p 6)

+ *[By Year 6] pupils living in poverty are often over nine months behind their peers in reading, writing and maths.* (p 6)

+ *The attainment gap persists for pupils throughout secondary school. Students eligible for free school meals are half as likely to achieve a good pass at GCSE in English and Maths in comparison to other students.* (p 6)

+ *Students living in poverty are four times more likely to be permanently excluded from school than their peers.* (p 6)

+ *Even with the same qualifications disadvantaged students are 50 per cent more likely to be Not in Education, Employment, or Training [after leaving school].* (p 6)

+ *Lone parents are more likely to experience poverty than those in a couple.* (p 13)

+ *People from Black and Ethnic Minority groups are also more likely to live in poverty.* (p 13)

+ *There is a strong stigma attached to poverty and children living in poverty are often bullied at school. A lot of children who are entitled to free school meals don't actually take them, and poorer families will often go without other items to protect their children from this stigma.* (p 7)

CASE STUDY

POVERTY

YEAR 8

Pupils had a lesson on poverty. The purpose of the lesson was to challenge stereotypes. Pupils were given a range of cards with statements, including those below.

+ People who are poor are lazy.

+ People claim benefits because they don't want to work.

+ Many people in our country live in poverty even if they have a job, because they still don't earn enough money.

+ Sometimes people can't work – for example, if they have to care for someone.

Pupils worked in groups and discussed each statement. Each statement had to be categorised as true or false.

ADVERSE CHILDHOOD EXPERIENCES

Adverse childhood experiences may include abuse, parental separation, parental conflict or bereavement. This is a limited list; there are many more examples of adverse childhood experiences. Children who have experienced these are more likely to experience mental ill health and social and emotional problems, and they are more likely to underachieve. They are disadvantaged by their experiences.

CRITICAL QUESTIONS

+ What are the advantages and disadvantages of nurture groups (small informal groups designed to support the development of social and emotional regulation skills) to support pupils who have had adverse childhood experiences?

+ How might the subject curriculum, particularly RSHE, address adverse childhood experiences in a sensitive way?

MINORITY IDENTITIES

Pupils with minority identities are often exposed to additional stressors because of experiencing prejudice, discrimination and harassment. In addition, internal stressors can arise when individuals with minority identities start to internalise the stigma they experience. This can impact detrimentally on overall self-esteem and result in poor mental health and educational disadvantage.

RACE AND ETHNICITY

Race and ethnicity impact on pupils' experience of education in a way that can perpetuate inequalities and, in some cases, create poverty. An unrepresentative curriculum and racism contribute to the systemic exclusion of young Black and minority ethnic (BAME) people. BAME pupils are disadvantaged not only by poverty, but also by the curriculum and exposure to minority stress (Meyer, 2003). Specific groups of BAME pupils are more likely to underachieve, resulting in poor long-term outcomes. This prevents them from escaping the cycle of poverty. Some key facts are given below (NEU, 2021).

+ Child poverty rates are 60 per cent and 54 per cent, respectively, for children from Bangladeshi and Pakistani families.

+ BAME people are more likely to be in low-paid employment.

+ BAME households are more likely to include larger families.

PUPILS WITH SEND

Children and young people with SEND are more likely to be bullied, may find it harder to make friends and are more likely to be permanently excluded. Long-term outcomes are poor. Far too many do not achieve good qualifications or gain entry to employment, training, FE and HE. This traps them in a cycle of poverty. Some key facts are outlined below (Joesph Rowntree Foundation, 2020).

+ In the UK in 2019/20, 31 per cent of people with disabilities were living in poverty, compared to 20 per cent of people without disabilities.

+ In the same period, 26 per cent of families with a child with disabilities were living in poverty.

REFUGEES AND MIGRANT PUPILS

Refugees, migrants and those with no recourse to public funds are often trapped in a cycle of poverty. Children and young people who are refugees or migrants, or whose families have no recourse to public funds, experience disruption to their education. They often have inadequate and insecure housing as well as lack of knowledge of the English education system. Evidence also suggests that many migrant children take on additional caring responsibilities that teachers do not always know about (NEU, 2021).

LGBTQ+ PUPILS

Pupils who are LGBTQ+ experience educational disadvantage. This is because they are more likely than non-LGBTQ+ pupils to experience poor mental health due to exposure to bullying, prejudice and discrimination. Key statistics from a study conducted in 2016/17 are presented below.

+ *Nearly half of lesbian, gay, bi and trans pupils (45 per cent) – including 64 per cent of trans pupils – are bullied for being LGBT at school. (p 6)*

+ *Half of LGBT pupils (52 per cent) hear homophobic language 'frequently' or 'often' at school. (p 6)*

+ *The majority of LGBT pupils – 86 per cent – regularly hear phrases such as 'that's so gay' or 'you're so gay' in school. (p 6)*

+ *Nearly one in ten trans pupils (9 per cent) are subjected to death threats at school. (p 6)*

+ *More than four in five trans young people (84 per cent) have self-harmed. For lesbian, gay and bi young people who aren't trans, three in five (61 per cent) have self-harmed. (p 7)*

+ *More than two in five trans young people (45 per cent) have attempted to take their own life. For lesbian, gay and bi young people who aren't trans, one in five (22 per cent) have attempted to take their own life. (p 7)*

(Bradlow et al, 2017)

Pupils must learn about LGBTQ+ content as part of relationships, sex and health education (RSHE) in secondary schools. It is not adequate for schools to only address prejudice-based bullying. The Equality Act 2010 places a duty on schools to promote good relations between those with and without protected characteristics. Sexual orientation, race, gender reassignment and disability are examples of protected characteristics. Schools cannot meet their statutory duties if different identities are not visible in the curriculum and if pupils are not taught to respect those with different identities. Social justice and inclusion should be at the heart of school improvement. Gorard argues that 'schools, in their structure and organisation, can do more than simply reflect the society we have; they can try to be the precursor of the kind of society that we wish to have' (2010, p 15). The best way of addressing this is to provide pupils with a curriculum that promotes social justice.

INTERSECTIONALITY

This chapter has addressed different categories of identities. It is important to emphasise that pupils may have intersecting identities. A pupil may have SEND, be LGBTQ+ and be living in poverty. This is only one example, but it serves to illustrate that young people may be exposed to multiple forms of disadvantage. This can impact negatively on attainment, mental health and long-term outcomes.

EVIDENCE-BASED PRACTICE

Hutchinson et al's (2020) study provides the following findings for 2019.

+ Gypsy/Roma pupils were almost three years (34 months) behind white British pupils at GCSE level. In contrast, Chinese pupils were two whole years (23.9 months) ahead of white British pupils.

+ Some ethnic groups have experienced growing inequalities over recent years. Black Caribbean pupils were 6.5 months behind white British pupils in 2011, but this gap increased to 10.9 months in 2019, meaning that the gap for Black Caribbean pupils widened by over four months in this eight-year period.

ENHANCING SELF-ESTEEM

Disadvantage can have an impact on self-esteem. Pupils might have low self-esteem if they are surrounded by adults who have low self-esteem. In addition, for pupils with minority identities, the experience of discrimination can also impact detrimentally on self-esteem.

Effective teachers protect and nurture pupils' self-esteem. Self-esteem is made up of two components.

1. Self-worth: This is the view we have of ourselves – for example, we might think we are a worthy person. Our self-worth is shaped by the views of other people, including parents, teachers and peers. These people can enhance or reduce our self-worth.

2. Self-competence: This is how well we perform when completing a task. This is sometimes known as self-efficacy.

Being positive with pupils will improve their self-worth. In addition, setting pupils appropriate learning challenges which are pitched at exactly the right level will ensure that pupils are able to achieve those challenges. Pupils can fall into one of the quadrants shown in Figure 2.1.

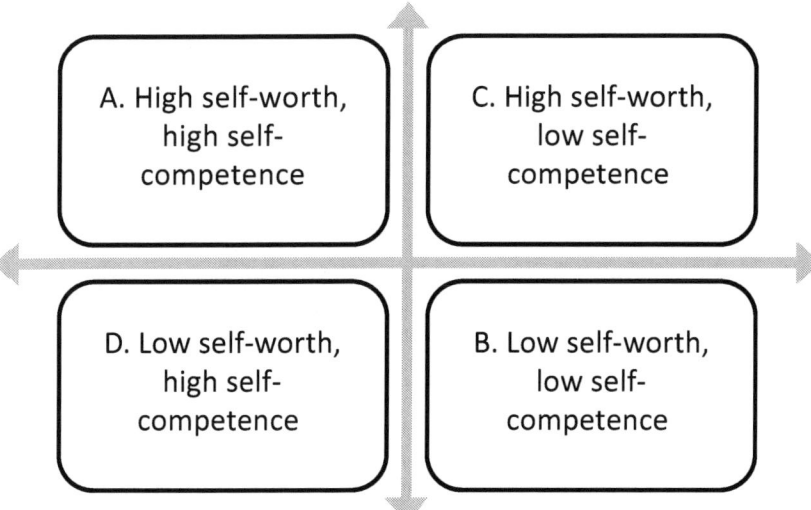

Figure 2.1 Self-worth and self-competence. Adapted from Mruk (1999)

Pupil A has overall high self-esteem. Pupil B has overall low self-esteem. Pupil C and pupil D have defensive self-esteem. In the case of pupil C, their high self-worth is not matched when they complete tasks; when they complete a task, they struggle despite having overall high self-worth. Pupil D has low self-worth, but they perform well when they complete tasks. Pupils C and D might become frustrated, which can result in disengagement. This model demonstrates that high self-worth alone does not result in overall high self-esteem; pupils also need to achieve (self-competence) for overall self-esteem to be high. Telling someone they are brilliant may improve a person's self-worth, but when this is not matched by their ability to complete tasks correctly, this can be damaging.

CRITICAL QUESTIONS

+ What factors influence pupils' self-esteem?

+ Where would you position yourself on the quadrant in Figure 2.1?

+ What factors can change a pupil's self-esteem?

EXTENDED THINKING

+ How might disadvantage impact on self-esteem?

+ What does disadvantage mean to you?

SUMMARY

Schools can address the effects of disadvantage. By providing a full curriculum for all, as opposed to a reduced curriculum for some pupils, schools can ensure that pupils have equity of experience. The curriculum should connect learning with pupils' lives and contexts outside schools. Valuing the knowledge and experiences of all pupils can be transformative and helps pupils to see how the curriculum aligns with their own lived experiences.

CHECKLIST

+ Disadvantage is broader than poverty.

+ Poverty can impact detrimentally on long-term outcomes for pupils, and therefore schools must ensure that expectations are kept high.

+ Children in poverty often experience multiple forms of disadvantage.

+ Poverty can impact detrimentally on self-esteem.

FURTHER READING

The Black Curriculum (nd) Re-imagining the Future of Education through Black British History. [online] Available at: https://theblackcurriculum.com/ (accessed 19 August 2022).

+ CHAPTER 3

SUBSTANTIVE AND DISCIPLINARY KNOWLEDGE

CHAPTER OBJECTIVES

After reading this chapter you will understand:

+ the difference between substantive and disciplinary knowledge;

+ the difference between component and composite knowledge;

+ the curriculum as the progression framework.

INTRODUCTION

Good subject knowledge is an essential part of effective teaching. It is important that teachers know and understand subject-specific concepts, laws, principles and facts. This will enable them to explain and demonstrate subject content clearly to their pupils. However, having subject knowledge is not sufficient on its own. Teachers need to know how to transmit that content effectively so that pupils can learn it. There are some general pedagogical approaches that can be used in all subjects. These include, but are not limited to, modelling, explanations and questioning. In addition to these general pedagogical approaches, there are also pedagogical approaches that can be utilised in specific subjects. In science, pupils will benefit by working scientifically. Pupils learn how scientists work and start to develop knowledge of the scientific approach. In history, pupils need to learn how historians investigate the past. In design and technology, pupils need to learn about the process of designing and making products. In English, the teacher might support pupils to improve their writing using the techniques of shared composition and oral rehearsal.

These examples illustrate that pedagogical approaches are sometimes tied to specific subjects. Teachers do not just impart information to learners who sit passively in the classroom. Pupils need to be actively engaged in the process of learning so that they get to experience what it is like to be a biologist, an artist, a writer and a historian. We can all remember highly knowledgeable teachers who knew their subjects well but were not capable of teaching it because they did not know how to support their pupils to learn the subject content. In addition, you might be able to recall a teacher who used the correct pedagogical approaches in the classroom but, when questioned by pupils about the subject content, they could not answer the questions and could not explain the subject content adequately.

This chapter addresses different types of subject knowledge. Case studies are provided to illustrate good practice, and research is included to provide underpinning evidence.

SUBSTANTIVE KNOWLEDGE

Substantive knowledge refers to the knowledge of the subject, its concepts, laws, principles and facts. It is the 'substance' of the subject. Each subject has its own distinctive body of knowledge. As pupils progress through the subject curriculum, their knowledge of the subject should deepen. Pupils make progress by knowing more, remembering more and being able to do more of the subject. Secondary teachers are generally subject experts. Typically, they have studied their subject to degree level, and they may also be members of subject associations. Substantive knowledge is made up of the building blocks that reflect the central concepts in a discipline and how they connect with one another.

It is important that pupils learn that a subject is not static. Researchers continually carry out research within subjects, and new knowledge is developed from the latest research. Although some subject content never changes, it is important that pupils learn that knowledge is always tentative. New research adds to the body of knowledge within a subject and sometimes our existing knowledge is modified by the latest research.

It is important that pupils view themselves as members of the subject community. Teachers should introduce pupils to resources from subject associations, including providing pupils with access to the latest research. Some teachers capitalise on visits to universities so that pupils can listen to leading academics within specific disciplines. They may also provide opportunities for pupils to attend and participate in national subject conferences.

Although it is valuable to make cross-curricular links when teaching, each subject has its own body of knowledge that pupils need to learn. This is what makes each subject distinctive. Pupils need to learn the knowledge, skills, concepts, laws, facts, principles and theories that make each subject unique. The secondary curriculum should be designed to provide frequent opportunities for pupils to revisit and deepen their knowledge as they progress through the subject curriculum.

DISCIPLINARY KNOWLEDGE

Disciplinary knowledge is the knowledge of how subject experts work within the discipline. In science, disciplinary knowledge might mean knowing how to formulate and test hypotheses. Scientists work scientifically by designing scientific investigations, collecting and interpreting data, and drawing conclusions. They understand about variables and controls. This knowledge of how scientists work is an example of disciplinary knowledge. In history, historians ask questions about the past. They investigate a range of historical sources, detect bias and use the sources to answer historical questions. They explore cause and effect. In history, disciplinary knowledge might mean using evidence to construct a claim about the past. Disciplinary knowledge therefore provides pupils with the knowledge that they need to work within a discipline.

CRITICAL QUESTIONS

+ What is an example of substantive knowledge in geography?
+ What is an example of disciplinary knowledge in geography?

EXTENDED THINKING

+ Which type of knowledge is the most important – substantive or disciplinary knowledge? Justify your answer.

THE IMPORTANCE OF SUBJECT KNOWLEDGE

Effective teachers must have good subject knowledge to enable pupils to learn. Broadly, subject knowledge can be categorised as content knowledge, pedagogical knowledge and pedagogical content knowledge.

+ Content knowledge refers to knowledge of a subject's facts, concepts, principles and laws. It is the substance of the subject curriculum and is an essential component of effective teaching.
+ Pedagogical knowledge refers to knowledge of pedagogical approaches that teachers use in classrooms, including modelling, questioning, explanations and practical activities.
+ Pedagogical content knowledge refers to knowledge of the pedagogical approaches that teachers must select to enable pupils to learn the content knowledge of the subject.

Content knowledge is critical. If teachers do not know the subject content, they will not be able to transfer this knowledge to pupils. However, content knowledge alone is insufficient. Everyone can probably recall a teacher who was knowledgeable in a subject but did not know how to transmit this knowledge to their pupils effectively. Teachers' knowledge of effective teaching approaches within a subject is essential so that pupils can be best supported to know, understand and apply the content knowledge. However, teachers' knowledge of pedagogical approaches in the absence of content knowledge is insufficient because pupils will not learn the substantive curriculum knowledge that underpins the subject. It is only when content knowledge is linked with pedagogical knowledge (pedagogical content knowledge) that the conditions for effective learning are created. The most effective teachers know their subjects, but they also know *when* and *how* to introduce content knowledge to pupils.

EVIDENCE-BASED PRACTICE

In October 2014, a review of educational research (Coe et al, 2014) was conducted by Durham University and The Sutton Trust. The review outlines six components of great teaching as indicated by extensive research. The six components are listed in order of '*how strong the evidence is in showing that focusing on them can improve student outcomes*'. The strongest aspect was content knowledge. The review states that the '*most effective teachers have deep knowledge of the subjects they teach*'. Significantly, the review continues that '*when teachers' knowledge falls below a certain level it is a significant impediment to students' learning*' (Coe et al, 2014, p 2).

THE IMPORTANCE OF CURRICULUM SEQUENCING

The importance of logical curriculum sequencing cannot be overstated, given its emphasis in the *Education Inspection Framework*. Subject-specific concepts need to be sequenced appropriately so that pupils can link new learning to prior learning. In history, understanding of the concept of 'kingdom' will support pupils' understanding of 'empire', and therefore it is beneficial to introduce pupils to kingdoms before they move on to learn about empires. Subject leaders therefore need to consider where to position subject content in the curriculum so that pupils can build on their existing schema.

The national curriculum offers some broad guidance in relation to the subject content which must be taught at Key Stages 3 and 4. However, it is essential to recognise that the programmes of study in the national curriculum are the ambitious end goals that pupils must achieve at the end of the respective key stages. This knowledge is often referred to as composite knowledge. Subject leaders must break down the subject curriculum into smaller components, referred to as component knowledge. Each component must be positioned at an appropriate point in the curriculum plan so that it connects with pupils' prior learning, and there should be opportunities for pupils to revisit components so that their knowledge becomes automatic. The national curriculum does not identify component knowledge. It focuses on the composite knowledge that pupils need to achieve at the end of Key Stages 3 and 4. Through accurate sequencing of components, new learning can usually be assimilated into existing schemas. Sometimes, new learning results in the original schema being modified. This occurs when the new learning cannot be assimilated into the existing schema and the schema needs to be modified to accommodate the new learning. Regardless, accurate sequencing of component knowledge will enable pupils to link new learning more effectively to prior learning.

REVISITING SUBJECT CONTENT

Revisiting subject content in lessons and over time is an important way of ensuring that pupils know, understand and can apply the intended curriculum. Spaced or distributed practice is where subject content is spaced out over time, with gaps in between to allow pupils to almost forget the content, then revisited. This supports knowledge retention. Alternative approaches to curriculum design, including clustered practice – where content is taught in blocks and not revisited – is likely to be less effective in generating gains in knowledge. Repetition is an effective way of consolidating knowledge. Through the process of revisiting component knowledge, pupils develop fluency, mastery and automaticity. If subject content is never revisited, it is stored in the long-term memory and forgotten. However, if content is revisited and consolidated, the knowledge that is stored in the long-term memory from the prior learning is retrieved and reprocessed in the working memory. This process of retrieval strengthens fluency and automaticity because it ensures that pupils process the content rather than storing it away.

DEVELOPING AUTOMATICITY

When we learn to drive a car, the more driving practice we get, the greater proficiency we develop in the skill of driving. It is the same in the classroom. The more practice pupils have, the greater their proficiency will be. We know that learning to play a musical instrument takes a significant amount of practice. Learning to speak another language also requires a significant amount of practice. Developing proficiency in a specific aspect of mathematics also requires practice. Time for pupils to practice is therefore an essential component of effective teaching.

Some lessons might appear, on the surface, to be repetitious. In a languages lesson, for example, pupils might be asked to repeat French words or phrases over and over again after the teacher. By the end of the lesson, the amount of repetition has resulted in pupils knowing those words or phrases. This is an effective pedagogical approach because it enables pupils to learn the intended curriculum. Regular ongoing formative assessment by the teacher during the lesson ensures that misconceptions are addressed, and by the end of the lesson, the pupils can use the correct French words or phrases.

In recent years, teachers have often focused on pedagogy rather than curriculum. They have focused on developing a range of interesting activities within their teaching to motivate and engage pupils. Although motivation and engagement are clearly important, it is crucial to recognise that while some activities are engaging, they might not support pupils in learning the intended curriculum. The pedagogical approaches that are selected must therefore enable pupils to learn the intended curriculum so that they develop the knowledge laid out in the curriculum. An overemphasis on pedagogy at the expense of knowledge is therefore unhelpful, and teachers should select pedagogical approaches that best enable their pupils to learn the knowledge specified in the curriculum plan.

CRITICAL QUESTION

+ Why is it important to learn knowledge to automaticity?

EXTENDED THINKING

+ What factors might support or hinder the development of automaticity?

COMPONENT KNOWLEDGE

Component knowledge (see Chapter 1) refers to the small 'chunks' of knowledge that pupils need to learn before they can learn the broader goals that the curriculum intends them to learn. For example, if we want pupils in Key Stage 3 to understand respiration in living organisms, there are some smaller components of knowledge they need to learn. These include:

1. aerobic respiration in living organisms;

2. anaerobic respiration in living organisms;

3. the breakdown of organic molecules to enable chemical processes necessary for life;

4. anaerobic respiration in humans and other organisms, including fermentation;

5. the differences between aerobic and anaerobic respiration in terms of the reactants, the products formed and the implications for the organism.

Each of the points above is component knowledge that enables pupils to achieve the overall goal of understanding respiration. It is important that curriculum plans identify the component knowledge because this supports teachers in understanding the steps towards supporting pupils to achieve a broader curriculum goal.

CRITICAL QUESTIONS

+ Why is it important to sequence the components correctly?

+ How does effective curriculum design support assessment?

EXTENDED THINKING

+ Some schools do not design subject curriculums from scratch. Subject leaders might adopt a scheme of work that has already been published. What aspects might subject leaders need to consider when adopting and using a scheme of work that has been published?

COMPOSITE KNOWLEDGE

Composite knowledge (see Chapter 1) is the broader aspects of knowledge that we want pupils to know, remember and be able to do. In the above example, understanding respiration is an example of composite knowledge. Composite knowledge might typically be the ambitious goals in the national curriculum that pupils are required to achieve at the end of Key Stage 3 or Key Stage 4. Composite knowledge might also be the overall knowledge that teachers want pupils to learn at the end of a unit of work. Composite knowledge is typically made up of several smaller components.

ASSESSING KNOWLEDGE

In the above example, it is not helpful to assess whether pupils understand respiration. If they do not understand and we only assess the composite knowledge, then we will not know which components the pupils know and which they do not know, and are therefore impeding their understanding of respiration. It is more helpful to assess the components, because teachers can then identify which components have not been understood. Teachers can then provide additional intervention for the components that are not secure to enable pupils to achieve the composite knowledge.

EVIDENCE-BASED PRACTICE

Sadler and Sonnert (2016) investigated science teachers' subject knowledge. Science students and teachers sat a subject knowledge test, and the teachers also completed a test that asked them to identify the scientific misconceptions they thought their pupils hold. In the study, teachers whose own subject knowledge was weak commonly selected the dominant pupil misconceptions as the 'correct' answers on their own subject knowledge tests. This shows that a teacher with weak subject knowledge may teach the concept incorrectly, and pupils may end up with the same incorrect understanding as their teacher.

TYPES OF SUBJECT KNOWLEDGE

The Ofsted curriculum reviews carried out in 2021 and 2022 are a useful starting point for teachers because they specify the specific types of subject knowledge that make up each subject. Broadly, subject knowledge can be categorised into substantive and disciplinary knowledge. Substantive knowledge refers to knowledge of the subject content (also known as content knowledge) – its facts, concepts, principles and laws. Disciplinary knowledge refers to the knowledge that subject experts need in order to work within their discipline. The following sections provide examples.

SUBJECT KNOWLEDGE IN HISTORY

In history, substantive knowledge is knowledge of the past, including knowledge of subject-specific concepts like class, democracy, parliament, invasion, monarchy, tax, trade, peasantry, revolution and empire. It also includes chronological knowledge and knowledge of continuity and change, cause and consequence, similarity, difference and significance. Disciplinary knowledge relates to knowledge of how historians investigate the past, including the type of questions that historians ask and the sources of evidence they use. Pupils need to learn how evidence is used rigorously to make historical claims and discern how and why contrasting arguments and interpretations of the past have been constructed.

SUBJECT KNOWLEDGE IN SCIENCE

In science, substantive knowledge refers to knowledge of scientific concepts, laws, theories, models and principles. It is the knowledge related to biology, chemistry and physics. Disciplinary knowledge is the knowledge of how scientific knowledge is generated and is built on. It relates to the 'working scientifically' strand of the national curriculum. Disciplinary knowledge includes knowledge of the methods that scientists use, knowledge of the apparatus and techniques that scientists use, knowledge of data analysis and knowledge of how evidence is used to develop scientific explanations.

SUBJECT KNOWLEDGE IN GEOGRAPHY

In geography, substantive knowledge relates to knowledge of location and place as well as human, physical and environmental processes. It includes knowledge of important geographical concepts, such as 'scale' and 'space'. Location knowledge relates to the naming and positioning of locations. Place knowledge relates to the connection between location and physical and human processes via personal experience. Human, physical and environmental processes include, respectively, migration, glaciation and climate change. Disciplinary knowledge relates to the practices of geographers. Knowledge of geographical skills and fieldwork includes knowledge of maps, globes and collecting first-hand evidence. Through developing disciplinary knowledge, pupils learn and begin to adopt these practices.

SUBJECT KNOWLEDGE IN MUSIC

Broadly, through music, pupils develop tacit knowledge as well as procedural and declarative knowledge. Tacit knowledge is the knowledge gained through exposure to music and through the experience of participating in music. One example of this is the knowledge that a particular piece of music includes an element of tension. Procedural knowledge relates to knowing how to perform a musical task, including how to play a musical instrument. Declarative knowledge is the knowledge of musical facts, eras, styles, composers, performers and musical notation, keys and chords.

Teachers need to break procedural knowledge down into smaller components. For example, learning how to play a musical instrument is an ambitious end goal, and to achieve this, pupils need to gain knowledge of several components. They might need to know about musical notation, the location of notes or keys on the instrument, and which fingers to use to produce specific sounds. Teachers should focus on assessing pupils' proficiency in each of the components that need to be mastered before they can successfully play the instrument rather than assessing the composite knowledge (ie can they play the instrument?). Assessing the composite knowledge does not provide teachers with enough diagnostic information. It simply identifies whether the pupil can play the instrument; but if they pupil cannot play the instrument, an assessment of the composite knowledge will not identify which components have not been mastered.

SUBJECT KNOWLEDGE IN MATHEMATICS

Subject knowledge in mathematics is broadly divided into three categories:

1. declarative knowledge – *I know that*;
2. procedural knowledge – *I know how*;
3. conditional knowledge – *I know when*.

Declarative knowledge relates to knowledge of mathematical facts and formulae. Procedural knowledge relates to knowledge of mathematical methods. Conditional knowledge relates to knowledge of when to use specific mathematical strategies.

SUBJECT KNOWLEDGE IN RELIGIOUS EDUCATION

Substantive knowledge in religious education relates to knowledge of religious and non-religious traditions, and knowledge of religious artefacts and texts. It also relates to knowledge of religious concepts, including incarnation, sacrifice, ritual, prayer and redemption. Subject leaders will need to identify these subject concepts and make curriculum decisions about where they need to be positioned in the curriculum plan. Another type of subject knowledge is 'ways of knowing'. This relates to knowledge of modes of inquiry within the subject, including knowledge of source materials and asking questions about religious claims. The third type of knowledge that pupils must develop in religious education is 'personal knowledge'. This relates to supporting pupils to develop their own viewpoint in relation to the substantive knowledge that is introduced in the curriculum. It is important to teach religion from an impartial perspective so that pupils are not indoctrinated into a particular religious perspective. It is also important in secondary schools to engage pupils in contemporary debates – for example, by exploring specific faith perspectives on sexuality. In this example, the faith perspective on sexuality can be taught but it must not be presented to pupils as a claim of truth. Teachers must make it clear to pupils that they are presenting a particular faith perspective and that alternative perspectives exist. It is therefore acceptable to introduce a faith perspective providing that pupils have an opportunity to debate that perspective and explore alternatives. Presenting a faith perspective as a truth is not acceptable. It is also important for teachers to establish a culture of respect for beliefs that differ from one's own. This is essential because pupils need to learn that they may not always agree with the beliefs of other people and that people are entitled to their beliefs and have a right to be respected. Pupils will study, live and work alongside people with various religious and non-religious beliefs, so to best prepare them for life in modern Britain, it is important that they learn during their education to respect different beliefs.

SUBJECT KNOWLEDGE IN PHYSICAL EDUCATION

In recent years, examination pressures (Progress 8 and EBacc) have led to a reduction in curriculum time for physical education in secondary schools, and this is a significant concern. An ambitious physical education curriculum should ensure that all pupils, including those with SEND and those who are socially disadvantaged, can benefit from physical activity.

Subject knowledge in physical education is broadly divided into declarative and procedural knowledge. Declarative knowledge is the factual knowledge that pupils need to develop in relation to movement, rules, tactics, strategies and healthy living. Procedural knowledge is how to apply declarative knowledge to practical situations. All procedural knowledge begins as declarative knowledge. For example, to play a game of football (procedural knowledge), pupils need knowledge of the rules and tactics of the game (declarative knowledge). It is also important to recognise that the aims of the national curriculum in physical education cannot be met by only playing games or other competitive activities.

There should be opportunities for pupils to revisit knowledge within a well-sequenced curriculum. For example, the skill of ball possession can be introduced in a unit on football and revisited in another unit that focuses on a different game.

Effective curriculum planning should identify both component and composite knowledge. Knowledge of how to use a range of tactics and strategies to overcome opponents in direct competition in football is a broad programme of study taken from the national curriculum. It is composite knowledge that pupils need to develop. However, this composite knowledge should be broken down further so that specific tactics and strategies are taught. Each strategy or tactic is a component of knowledge that pupils need to know and practise to automaticity. Assessment of the composite knowledge (ie can they use a range of tactics and strategies to overcome opponents?) is insufficient because this does not identify which specific tactics and strategies are not secure. Teachers therefore need to provide enough opportunities for pupils to develop proficiency in the component knowledge and then assess each of those components to see whether the pupil can demonstrate it to automaticity. Teachers should limit the number of components that they introduce at one time, and in many cases it is more effective to introduce one component and practise it to automaticity before moving on to the next component. Teachers should support pupils to learn component knowledge through powerful demonstrations. This ensures that the skills pupils need to learn are expertly modelled. In physical education, 50–80 per cent of the lesson time should involve pupils in activity, and pupils need ample opportunity to practise a skill. Pupils with SEND are often denied opportunities to participate in physical education lessons. Teachers therefore need to ensure that all pupils can fully participate in all lessons.

SUBJECT KNOWLEDGE IN ENGLISH

It is particularly important that all secondary schools promote a reading culture. The ability to read fluently enables pupils to access knowledge right across the curriculum. Pupils do not improve in their reading comprehension skills by doing additional reading comprehension practice. Pupils' reading comprehension skills improve by having a broad and a rich vocabulary, and vocabulary knowledge supports subsequent reading success. All subjects should ensure that subject-specific vocabulary is explicitly taught and that vocabulary is not just viewed as a component of English. Pupils must be encouraged to read widely and in depth. Teachers of English need to ensure that pupils study whole texts rather than extracts of texts, and they should read aloud to pupils as often as possible in lessons. Secondary schools also need to develop a strategy to promote reading for pleasure. Developing prizes such as certificates and other awards can be unhelpful because they can promote extrinsic motivation and surface-level reading.

Spoken language, reading and writing are the three interrelated components of a curriculum for English. Knowledge of vocabulary improves pupils' spoken language and provides them with linguistic capital, which will enable them to access opportunities in the future. Vocabulary knowledge also improves reading comprehension and the overall quality of pupils' writing. It is well-established in research that pupils from areas of social deprivation know fewer words than their more affluent peers, and this is one of the reasons why they do not achieve as well in school. Vocabulary knowledge supports pupils learning across the curriculum and should therefore be a focus for all secondary schools. Pupils also need to

45

know how to use registers of speech in their spoken language. They need to be able to select the most appropriate register to suit the audience and purpose, and they specifically need to be taught about when to use a more formal register. This will enable them to access opportunities in the future because it provides them with linguistic capital.

It is not uncommon now for secondary schools to provide pupils with reading interventions. If the intervention is focusing on developing the skill of decoding (word recognition), schools must use a systematic programme of synthetic phonics to develop pupils' knowledge of the alphabetic code and the skills of blending phonemes for word recognition and segmenting words into phonemes and representing these as graphemes for spelling. If pupils cannot read, they are disadvantaged for life, and they will not be able to access knowledge in the rest of the curriculum. Reading is fundamental to most, if not all, subjects in the secondary curriculum, and therefore developing the skill of accurate and fluent word recognition must be a priority if pupils cannot read.

CASE STUDY

SYSTEMATIC SYNTHETIC PHONICS

YEAR 7

A school identified a group of pupils who are not reading at an age-appropriate level. The reason for this was that the skill of accurate word recognition had not been developed, and this was impacting fluency and comprehension. The school designed a systematic programme of synthetic phonics that introduces pupils to the simple and complex alphabetic code. Reading books are age-appropriate but matched to the sounds that pupils are taught. Pupils are explicitly taught the skills of decoding and segmenting for writing, and daily dictation of sentences supports the development of accurate spelling.

SUPPORTING PUPILS' PERSONAL DEVELOPMENT

Personal development is a distinct strand of the *Education Inspection Framework* and is graded separately to denote its importance.

It includes citizenship, character development, British values, inclusion and equality of opportunity, careers information, education, advice and guidance, including opportunities to participate in work experience and spiritual, moral, social and cultural (SMSC) development.

This strand also includes RSHE, and schools should follow the statutory guidance (DfE, 2019b) to teach this aspect of the curriculum. Fundamentally, schools must ensure that pupils can distinguish between healthy and unhealthy relationships. They must ensure that pupils understand about consent, and they must provide inclusive RSHE by not making the assumption that all pupils are heterosexual. Schools will need to decide when to teach pupils about pornography, but given that some pupils are now viewing pornography from the age of 11, it is clearly too late to start in Year 11. Schools must provide pupils with safe spaces to discuss topics they find difficult – for example, the sharing of nude images. It is important to recognise that children of the same age may be at very different stages developmentally, and therefore schools will need to consider how best to deliver some of this content. Schools must provide pupils with a range of opportunities, including lunchtime and after-school clubs, and educational visits. These opportunities provide pupils with cultural capital and are particularly important for pupils who experience social deprivation.

TEACHING SENSITIVE TOPICS

In secondary schools, pupils will learn about sexuality, gender, abortion and contraception in RSHE. They also cover these topics in religious education. Schools are allowed to teach specific faith perspectives in relation to these topics. However, they must clearly signal that this is a faith perspective and offer balance by including opposing views. They must also ensure that pupils are given all the information they need to make informed decisions and stay safe. Pupils should be informed about UK law, including the Equality Act 2010. Schools are not allowed to promote partisan political views in any subject. It is unlawful for schools to promote non-democratic governments or extremist positions, such as opposing freedom of speech or endorsing racist and antisemitic attitudes. For example, schools are allowed to teach pupils about Extinction Rebellion, but they must approach this by also teaching different points of view. The secondary curriculum must address all protected characteristics that are listed in the Equality Act.

CASE STUDY

LGBTQ+ INCLUSION

YEAR 8

A faith school teaches pupils the faith perspective on LGBTQ+. The curriculum explicitly teaches pupils that this is only one perspective, and pupils are given the opportunity to debate the content. The teacher discusses the Equality Act 2010 and specifically refers to the protected characteristics of sexual orientation and gender reassignment. Pupils learn about the legislation that underpins same-sex marriage in England as well as their responsibilities to LGBTQ+ people in school, college, university and the workplace.

SUMMARY

This chapter has outlined the difference between substantive and disciplinary knowledge. It has also outlined the difference between component and composite knowledge. It has provided examples of different types of knowledge in specific subjects, and it has emphasised the importance of assessing components to check that they are secure.

CHECKLIST

+ Component knowledge refers to small chunks of knowledge that support pupils to learn the broader goals of the national curriculum.

+ Composite knowledge refers to the broader ambitious goals that pupils need to learn.

+ Substantive knowledge is the knowledge of the subject, its concepts, principles, theories, laws and facts.

+ Disciplinary knowledge is the knowledge of how to work within the subject.

+ Good subject knowledge is an essential element of effective teaching.

FURTHER READING

Ofsted (2021–22) Curriculum Research Reviews. [online] Available at: www.gov.uk/government/collections/curriculum-research-reviews (accessed 19 August 2022)

✚ CHAPTER 4

BUILDING CULTURAL CAPITAL INTO THE CURRICULUM

CHAPTER OBJECTIVES

After reading this chapter you will understand:

+ the key aspects of cultural capital;

+ the importance of embedding cultural capital into the curriculum;

+ how to develop pupils' linguistic capital;

+ how to build cultural capital into specific subjects;

+ the role of the co-curriculum in relation to cultural capital.

INTRODUCTION

This chapter draws on Pierre Bourdieu's (1986) conceptualisation of cultural capital within the context of equality. It outlines Bourdieu's understanding of the role of the family in relation to cultural capital, and it explores the association between cultural capital, social class and social mobility. The three forms of cultural capital are then outlined and examples of each are discussed. This discussion is summarised in order to provide you with a broad and holistic understanding of the concept of cultural capital. The chapter also explores how opportunities for pupils to participate in the arts, literature and music can differ according to socio-economic background and how this can affect educational outcomes and prospects for career progression. In doing so, it emphasises the importance of embedding cultural capital into the curriculum in order to close the gap and ensure that forms of cultural capital are available to all pupils, regardless of their social background. Research is outlined to demonstrate the relationship between language learning and socio-economic status, and practical guidance is offered to support you to embed cultural capital in a range of subject areas. Finally, we discuss the importance of extracurricular activities within the context of the co-curriculum, and we highlight how schools can compensate for disadvantage by providing these activities.

WHAT IS CULTURAL CAPITAL?

Pierre Bourdieu was interested in how cultural capital is a source of inequality. He defined cultural capital as familiarity with what might be referred to as 'high culture'. According to Bourdieu, the family plays a critical role in transmitting cultural capital through immersing pupils in dance and music, visiting theatres, galleries and historic sites, and introducing them to literature and art. Cultural capital has traditionally been associated with social class. The more cultural capital a person possesses, the greater chance they have of achieving social mobility.

According to Bourdieu, cultural capital exists in three forms: embodied, objectified and institutionalised (Figure 4.1).

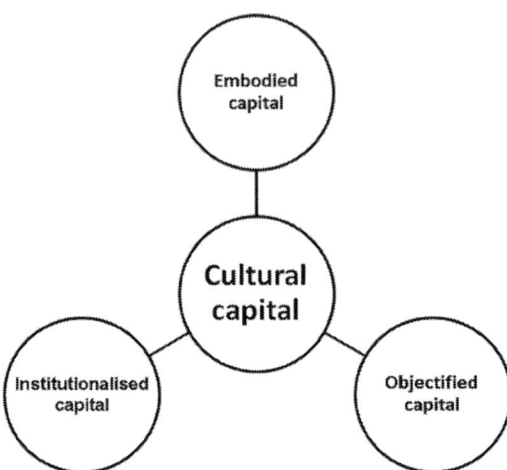

Figure 4.1 Cultural capital

Embodied cultural capital is acquired over time through a process of socialisation, for example accent. A person's accent can restrict or support their chances of achieving social mobility. Another example is vocabulary. The more advanced one's vocabulary, the greater the chances of achieving social mobility. Individuals are socialised into specific ways of thinking or behaving to fit in with the social norms and expectations of a specific social group.

Objectified cultural capital is demonstrated through a person's possessions, which can be exchanged for economic capital. This form of cultural capital can therefore be exchanged for economic capital.

Institutional cultural capital is related to the type of school someone attends or their qualifications. Someone with a degree possesses more cultural capital than someone without a degree, and someone with a postgraduate degree holds more cultural capital than someone with an undergraduate degree. Someone who attends an independent school holds more cultural capital than someone who attends a state school. The former is more likely to enter Russell Group universities than the latter. This form of cultural capital can be exchanged for economic capital after leaving education.

Broadly, cultural capital is the accumulation of knowledge, attitudes, habits, language and possessions that should enable individuals to demonstrate their cultural competence and social status. It can be demonstrated through social interests as people with more cultural capital may develop different social interests from those with less cultural capital.

CRITICAL QUESTIONS

+ Do you agree with the argument that cultural capital is a rejection of working-class cultures and values? Justify your response.

+ Why do you think cultural capital plays an important role in achieving social mobility?

OFSTED'S TAKE ON CULTURAL CAPITAL

Ofsted has used the following statement from the national curriculum to inform their understanding of cultural capital (see Chapter 1):

the essential knowledge that they need to be educated citizens. It introduces pupils to the best that has been thought and said; and helps engender an appreciation of human creativity and achievement.

(DfE, 2014, para 3.1, p 5)

Schools have a responsibility to teach pupils the essential knowledge they need to be able to make the most of opportunities in adult life. Cultural capital can be understood as 'powerful knowledge' that enables pupils to access opportunities and, for some, achieve social mobility. However, deciding which knowledge is powerful and which knowledge is less powerful is not straightforward, and these decisions are influenced by personal experiences and values. This raises critical questions about which knowledge is privileged and who decides this.

POWERFUL KNOWLEDGE

If cultural capital is linked to powerful knowledge, it is important to understand exactly what this means (see Chapter 2). Young and Lambert (2014) identify some important features of powerful knowledge. These are listed below.

+ It is the best knowledge within a subject and is valued by specialist subject communities.

+ It is specialised knowledge.

+ It is generated by research in universities and other research organisations.

+ It takes the form of academic subjects.

Young (2020) argues that teachers and pupils need to view themselves as members of subject communities. The teaching of subjects in school should not be divorced from the subject communities that generate research which informs the substantive knowledge in a subject. Knowledge is therefore always in a state of flux as new knowledge is created to build on existing knowledge, and this may even result in existing knowledge being displaced.

Powerful knowledge is taught by a subject expert, not by individuals without subject expertise. This is due to its specialist nature. It may require specialist teaching rooms, such as laboratories, gymnasiums or workshops. Reid (2020) emphasises that powerful knowledge should take pupils beyond their immediate experience. The aim of a school curriculum should be to empower pupils to reach outwards into the global community they are part of. It should enable pupils 'to envisage alternatives' (Reid, 2020, p 45) – for example, learning about the cultures and empires across Eurasia, Africa and the Americas as well as learning about Britain (Reid, 2020).

Claire Sealy (2020) writes about how, until very recently, the discourse in education focused very heavily on *how* to teach rather than *what* to teach. The *what* aspect became diluted because teachers often focused on teaching content that was assessed in statutory tests rather than designing a subject curriculum which increased the depth of pupils' knowledge. The emphasis has now shifted to curriculum design and curriculum content, and subject leaders need to give greater attention to designing a curriculum which deepens pupils' knowledge across the subject domain. The emphasis on subject knowledge provides schools with an opportunity to develop a knowledge-based curriculum that is well sequenced and builds pupils' knowledge of the subject as they progress through the curriculum. The curriculum is the progression map. As pupils progress through the curriculum, they should know more about the subject, and the curriculum sequence is also then the basis for assessment.

WHY IS CULTURAL CAPITAL IMPORTANT?

Pupils from higher socio-economic backgrounds benefit significantly from the cultural capital transmitted to them by their families (see Addressing social disadvantage through the curriculum in Chapter 2). They have more opportunities to participate in the arts, literature and music because economic capital can enable families to purchase cultural capital. Pupils from more affluent backgrounds have greater opportunities, often benefit from private tuition and are more likely to attend a good school. This means that pupils from lower socio-economic backgrounds are less likely to experience these opportunities because their families do not have the economic capital needed to purchase these forms of capital. This disadvantages them because they are then less likely to achieve the same educational outcomes as their more affluent peers and, therefore, are less likely to attend a good university and enter a high-salaried profession in the future.

Embedding cultural capital into the curriculum is a way of closing the gap by ensuring that forms of cultural capital are available to all pupils, irrespective of their social background. All pupils should have the same opportunities in society to achieve their full potential. Pupils' life chances should not be determined by their socio-economic background. Their futures should not be determined by the families and communities that they are born into. If cultural capital increases the likelihood of future success, then this must be made available to everyone and not just to the few.

All pupils should have the same opportunities to develop a rich vocabulary. All deserve to learn about the arts, history and literature. Every pupil should have an equal opportunity to learn to play a musical instrument. All pupils should have the same chance of achieving good educational outcomes. Pupils should not be disadvantaged because their families have not been able to purchase cultural capital. Regardless of social background, all pupils should have the same opportunity to attend a good university, where they can gain qualifications that enable them to access top professions, including medicine, law, politics, science and teaching. Building cultural capital into the curriculum is a way of compensating for the disadvantage that may result from pupils being born into lower socio-economic backgrounds.

EVIDENCE-BASED PRACTICE

Research has found that social background influences levels of parental interest and participation in education. Financial capital can be exchanged for cultural capital, with parents from higher socio-economic groups being able to purchase forms of cultural capital for their children. A study of parental resources and children's education found significant inequalities in the power of parents to enhance the educational success of their children (Montacute and Cullinane, 2018). This shows that parents in higher socio-economic groups are more likely to:

+ use a variety of strategies to make sure their children go to their preferred schools;

+ research potential schools thoroughly before making a choice for their children;

+ send their children had received private tuition;

+ become school governors or trustees of multi-academy trusts.

CRITICAL QUESTIONS

+ How do the effects of social disadvantage affect pupils' life chances?

+ How far can schools compensate for the effects of social disadvantage?

EXTENDED THINKING

+ How does social deprivation impact on vocabulary development?

+ How does social deprivation impact on health, cognition and social and emotional development?

CASE STUDY

CULTURAL CAPITAL

WHOLE SCHOOL

A secondary school focused on developing pupils' cultural capital. School leaders required all subject leaders to identify opportunities for developing pupils' cultural capital through their subjects. They stated that educational visits and other types of enrichment could not be a 'bolt-on' to the subject curriculum, but had to be planned so that they connected seamlessly with the curriculum. They identified a range of opportunities for developing cultural capital. These included visits to museums, galleries, historical sites, significant cities and towns, theatre and concerts.

LINGUISTIC CAPITAL

Research has, for a long time, demonstrated the relationship between language learning and socio-economic status. The following are findings from a study on early language ability (Fernald et al, 2013).

+ Children from disadvantaged families start school with lower language and cognitive skills than those from more advantaged families.

+ Parents who experience stress provide less adequate social and cognitive stimulation, thus reducing the quality of parent–child interaction.

+ Significant differences in both vocabulary learning and language processing efficiency are already present by 18 months.

+ By 24 months, there is a six-month gap emerging between toddlers in families with higher and lower socio-economic status.

+ Deficiency in language learning can result in potentially important long-term consequences.

Language development underpins development in reading and writing. In addition, it impacts on pupils' cognitive development because pupils with impaired linguistic comprehension are disadvantaged in understanding language use across the curriculum. Pupils with speech and language difficulties may need a structured intervention programme to support their speech, language and communication skills. They may also need a structured programme to support their vocabulary development. All pupils will greatly benefit from the explicit teaching of vocabulary in all subjects. Teachers should introduce pupils to an extensive range of sophisticated vocabulary so that they can communicate with a range of people in both formal and informal contexts.

It is sadly the case that society makes judgements on people based on their use of vocabulary and skills in articulation and pronunciation. Incorrect associations are made between people's use of vocabulary and their general intelligence. This can result in people with restricted vocabularies being disadvantaged from opportunities that people with more extensive vocabularies benefit from. In addition, vocabulary use can also lead to social exclusion in that people with more restricted vocabularies may be excluded from social networks, which can also limit their opportunities. Schools can compensate for the vocabulary gap by explicitly introducing pupils to more complex sophisticated vocabulary so that they can fully comprehend what they hear and read and so that they can interact with people from different social backgrounds.

BUILDING CULTURAL CAPITAL THROUGH SUBJECT CURRICULUMS

Subject curriculums can address pupils' cultural capital in various ways.

BUILDING CULTURAL CAPITAL INTO ENGLISH

Figure 4.2 provides ideas to support you to develop pupils' cultural capital through English.

A well-designed English curriculum should introduce pupils to seminal texts. Pupils need to know the works of Shakespeare, Dickens, Brontë and Hardy. However, as argued by Reid (2020), they should also be introduced to *Wide Sargasso Sea* (Rhys, 2000). Some pupils will come from social backgrounds where they are immersed in literature, film and theatre. Their social backgrounds provide them with a high level of cultural capital. They come to school with knowledge of playscripts,

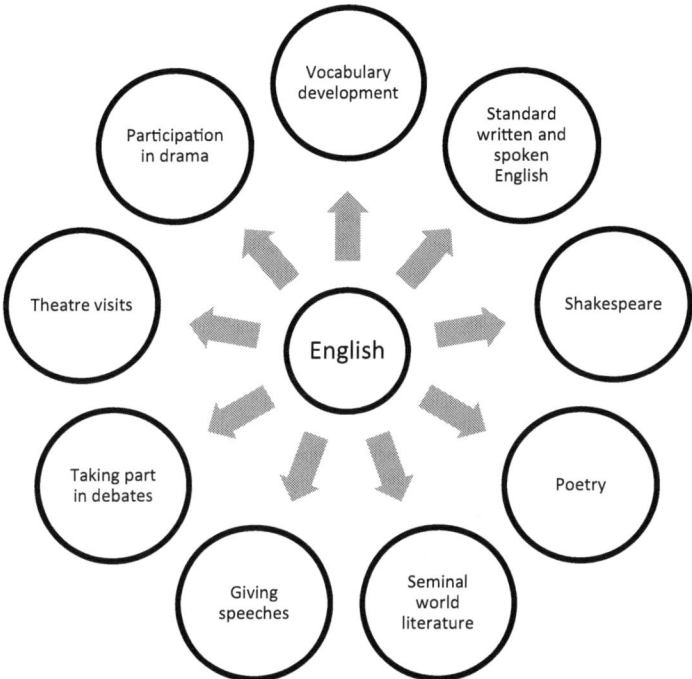

Figure 4.2 Developing cultural capital through English

significant writers and theatre. Some pupils are disadvantaged by their social backgrounds, and therefore schools must ensure that there is a co-curriculum offer that provides disadvantaged pupils with this knowledge.

CASE STUDY

ENGLISH

WHOLE SCHOOL

Subject leaders in a secondary school wanted to introduce a wider range of literature for pupils to read. Following an analysis of current texts, they identified that many of the authors were white and male. They identified Black authors, female authors and disabled authors, and texts that provided pupils with more of a global perspective.

CRITICAL QUESTION

✦ What other ways can cultural capital be developed through English?

BUILDING CULTURAL CAPITAL INTO MATHEMATICS

Figure 4.3 shows ideas to support you to develop pupils' cultural capital through mathematics.

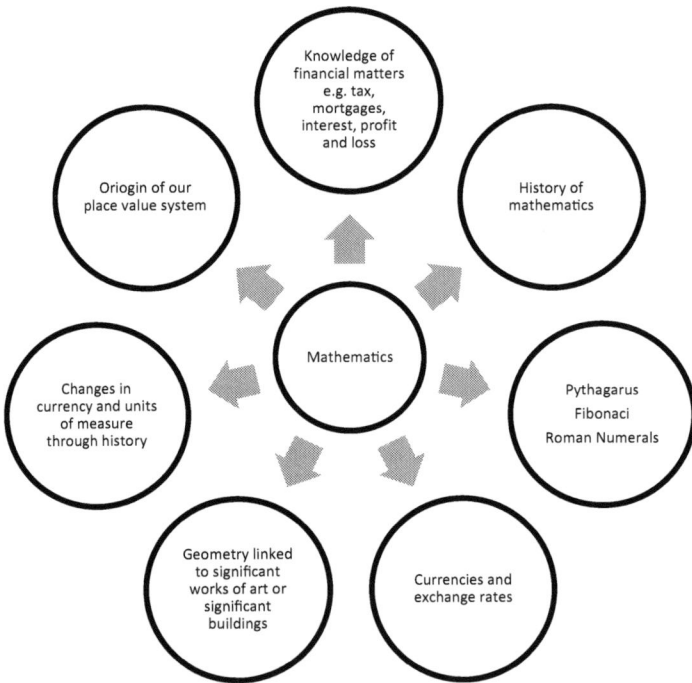

Figure 4.3 Developing cultural capital through mathematics

CRITICAL QUESTION

✦ What other ways can cultural capital be developed through mathematics?

BUILDING CULTURAL CAPITAL INTO SCIENCE

The ideas in Figure 4.4 can support you to develop pupils' cultural capital through science.

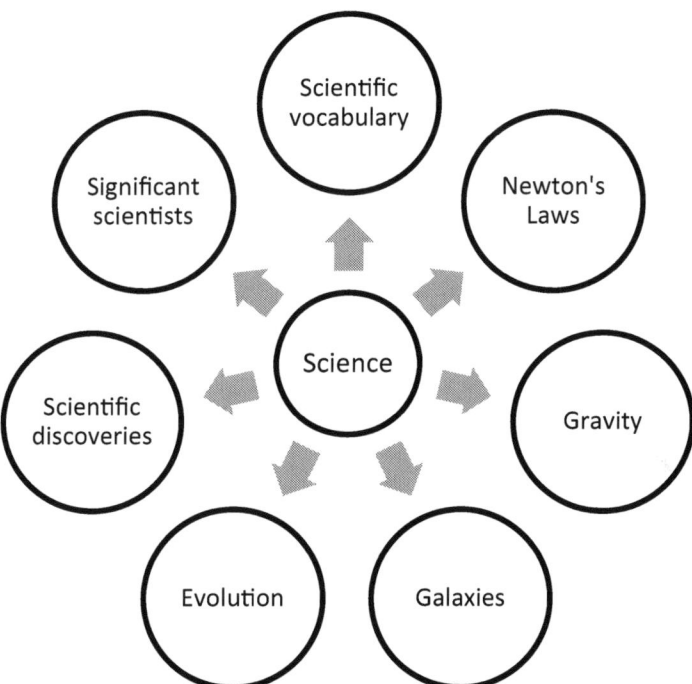

Figure 4.4 Developing cultural capital through science

CRITICAL QUESTION

+ What other ways can cultural capital be developed through science?

BUILDING CULTURAL CAPITAL INTO HISTORY

Figure 4.5 shows ideas to support you to develop pupils' cultural capital through history.

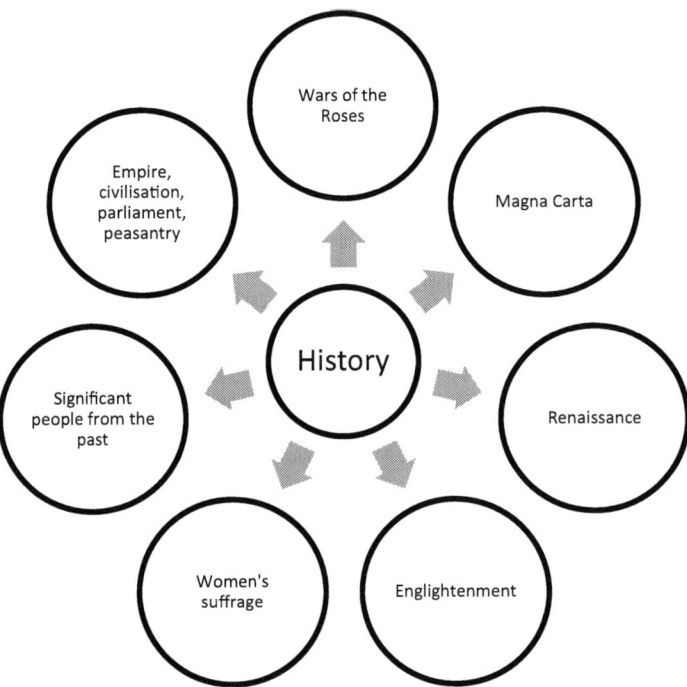

Figure 4.5 Developing cultural capital through history

CRITICAL QUESTIONS

+ What other ways can cultural capital be developed through history?

+ What aspects of history would you class as powerful knowledge?

BUILDING CULTURAL CAPITAL INTO GEOGRAPHY

The ideas shown in Figure 4.6 can support you to develop pupils' cultural capital through geography.

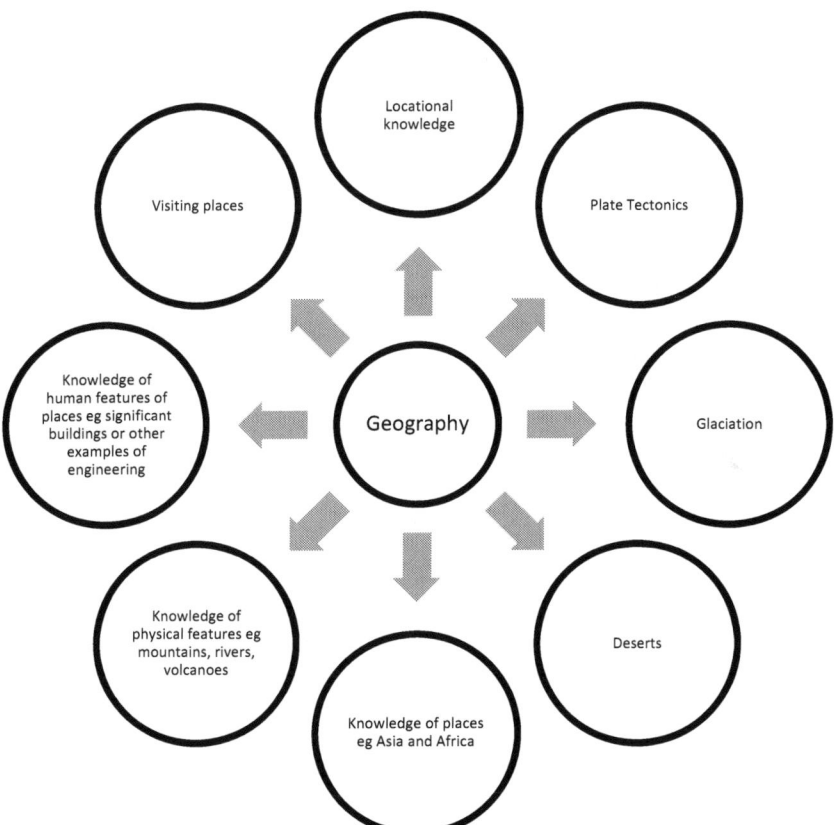

Figure 4.6 Developing cultural capital through geography

CRITICAL QUESTION

+ What other ways can cultural capital be developed through geography?

BUILDING CULTURAL CAPITAL INTO MUSIC

The ideas in Figure 4.7 can support you to develop pupils' cultural capital through music.

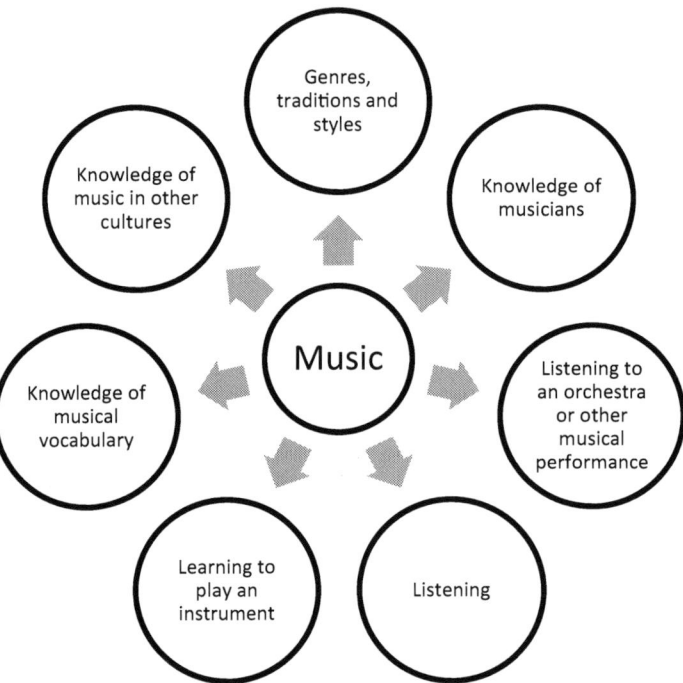

Figure 4.7 Developing cultural capital through music

CRITICAL QUESTION

+ What other ways can cultural capital be developed through music?

BUILDING CULTURAL CAPITAL INTO ART AND DESIGN

Figure 4.8 has ideas that can support you to develop pupils' cultural capital through art and design.

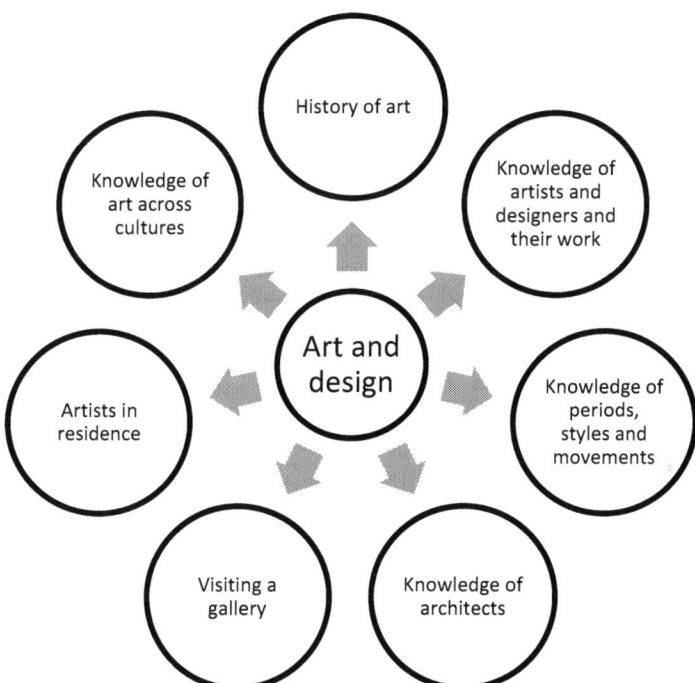

Figure 4.8 Developing cultural capital through art and design

CRITICAL QUESTION

+ What other ways can cultural capital be developed through art and design?

BUILDING CULTURAL CAPITAL INTO DESIGN AND TECHNOLOGY

The ideas in Figure 4.9 can support you to develop pupils' cultural capital through design and technology.

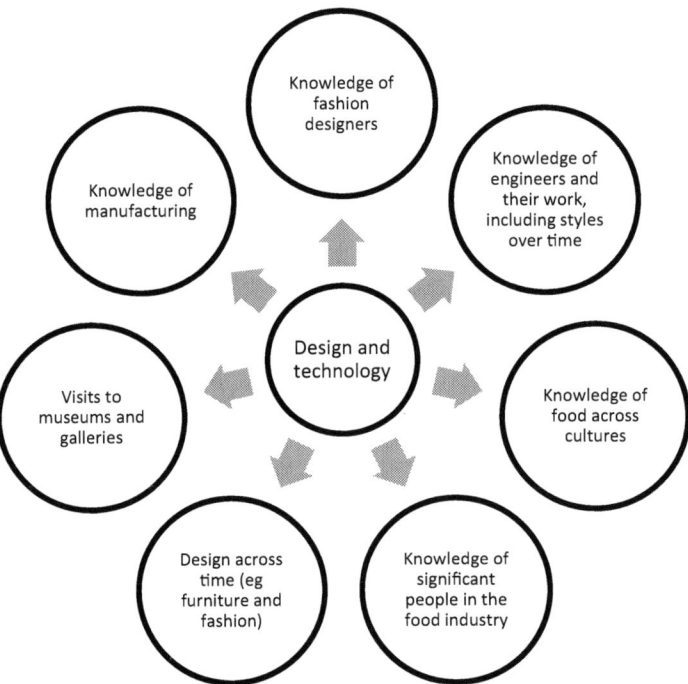

Figure 4.9 Developing cultural capital through design and technology

CRITICAL QUESTION

+ What other ways can cultural capital be developed through design and technology?

BUILDING CULTURAL CAPITAL INTO PHYSICAL EDUCATION

Figure 4.10 shows ideas to support you to develop pupils' cultural capital through physical education.

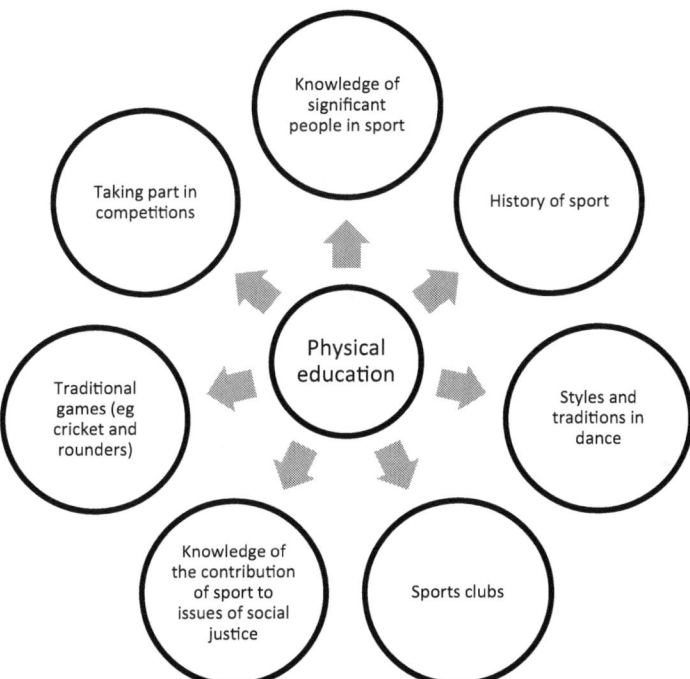

Figure 4.10 Developing cultural capital through physical education

CRITICAL QUESTION

+ What other ways can cultural capital be developed through physical education?

BUILDING CULTURAL CAPITAL INTO LANGUAGES

The ideas in Figure 4.11 can support you to develop pupils' cultural capital through languages.

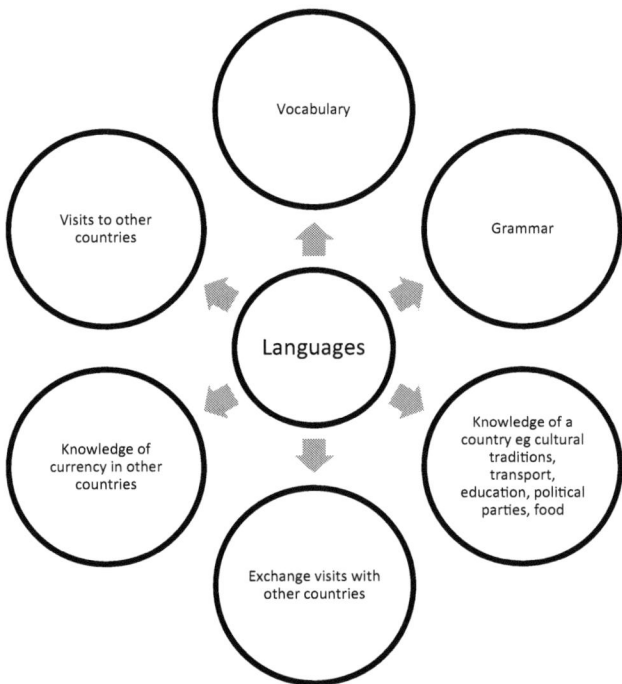

Figure 4.11 Developing cultural capital through languages

CRITICAL QUESTION

+ What other ways can cultural capital be developed through languages?

BUILDING CULTURAL CAPITAL INTO CITIZENSHIP

Figure 4.12 has ideas that can support you to develop pupils' cultural capital through citizenship.

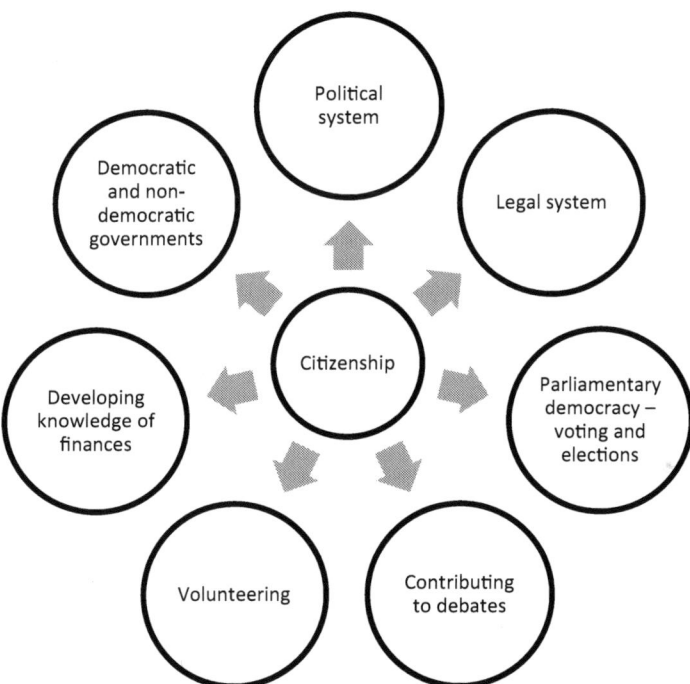

Figure 4.12 Developing cultural capital through citizenship

CRITICAL QUESTION

+ What other ways can cultural capital be developed through citizenship?

BUILDING CULTURAL CAPITAL INTO THE CO-CURRICULUM

The ideas in Figure 4.13 can support you to develop pupils' cultural capital through the co-curriculum.

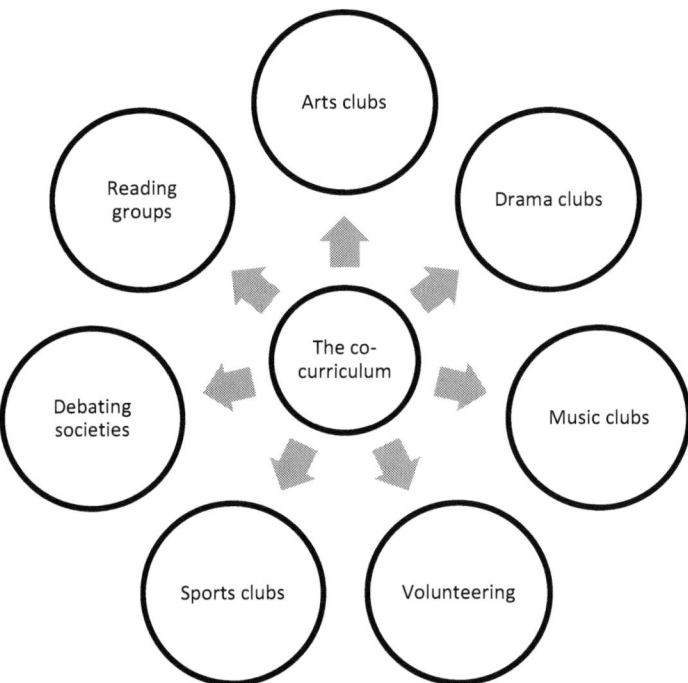

Figure 4.13 Developing cultural capital through a co-curriculum

CRITICAL QUESTIONS

+ What other ways can cultural capital be developed through the co-curriculum?

+ What are the advantages of a co-curriculum offer?

+ What are the practical considerations for schools when providing a co-curriculum?

Research demonstrates that participation in extracurricular activities can increase pupils' connectedness and sense of belonging to their school (Martinez et al, 2016). In addition, research shows how participation in arts activities or academic societies or clubs results in improved academic outcomes and a better sense of connection to the school (Girls Education Challenge, 2018).

The co-curriculum should provide pupils with a rich variety of activities that they normally would not have the opportunity to access. Pupils from higher socio-economic backgrounds are more likely to participate in a range of activities outside of school because parents can exchange economic capital for cultural capital. Pupils from lower socio-economic backgrounds may not benefit from the same opportunities due to lack of financial capital. Schools can compensate for disadvantage by providing pupils with activities to boost their cultural capital.

CRITICAL QUESTIONS

+ Should one of the aims of education be to support pupils to achieve social mobility?

+ What other aims should the secondary curriculum promote?

EVIDENCE-BASED PRACTICE

Bernstein's (1971) seminal research identifies two types of language use: restricted code and elaborated code. Restricted code is less formal with shorter phrases and is used in situations where there is 'taken for granted' knowledge. In contrast, elaborated code uses longer and more complex sentence structures. Restricted code does not refer to restricted vocabulary. Elaborated code does not refer to better, more sophisticated language use.

Bernstein made a correlation between social class and language codes. He reported that people from working-class backgrounds tended to use restricted code, whereas people from middle-class backgrounds use both restricted code and elaborated code.

CRITICAL QUESTIONS

+ What are the implications of Bernstein's research?

+ What criticisms can you make of Bernstein's research?

SUMMARY

This chapter emphasised the importance of cultural capital and outlined the associations between equality, social class and social mobility. It highlighted the role of the family in relation to cultural capital, and it explained the concept of cultural capital and its three separate forms. Examples of each were offered to support your understanding. The chapter also outlined the importance of participation in the arts, literature and music, and it demonstrated how socio-economic background can influence educational outcomes and career progression prospects. Throughout the chapter, subject-specific examples were provided to support your curriculum planning and ensure that forms of cultural capital are available to all pupils, regardless of their social background. Research was presented to demonstrate the relationship between language learning and socio-economic status, and the importance of offering extracurricular activities within the context of the co-curriculum was emphasised. In doing so, schools can close the gap in cultural capital and compensate for disadvantage, to support the life chances of all.

CHECKLIST

+ Individuals who have lots of cultural capital are more advantaged than those who do not.

+ Cultural capital can improve long-term outcomes for pupils.

+ Cultural capital is the essential knowledge that pupils need to thrive in the twenty-first century.

+ Pupils from disadvantaged communities may have less cultural capital than their more affluent peers.

+ Vocabulary is also a form of cultural capital.

FURTHER READING

Didau, D (nd) Where We're Getting Cultural Capital Wrong. [online] Available at: https://learningspy.co.uk/curriculum/where-were-getting-cultural-capital-wrong/ (accessed 19 August 2022).

K Leaders (2022) 'Cultural Capital': Expanding Narrow Definitions. [online] Available at: https://schoolleaders.thekeysupport.com/school-evaluation-and-improvement/inspection/whole-school-inspection-criteria/how-to-avoid-narrow-definitions-of-cultural-capital/ (accessed 19 August 2022).

Oxford History Team (2019) How to Boost Cultural Capital as a History Teacher. [online] Available at: https://educationblog.oup.com/secondary/cultural-capital (accessed 19 August 2022).

+ CHAPTER 5

CURRICULUM DESIGN

CHAPTER OBJECTIVES

After reading this chapter you will understand:

+ the factors to consider in curriculum design;

+ the importance of identifying composite and component knowledge.

INTRODUCTION

This chapter introduces the factors to consider in curriculum design. Designing a curriculum is not an easy task, and teachers do not have complete freedom to design the curriculum as they wish. They must ensure that the subject curriculum addresses the minimum expectations of the national curriculum and other statutory frameworks. However, beyond this there is scope to be innovative. This chapter addresses a range of factors, but from the outset it is important to see SEND and disadvantaged pupils as golden threads. Curriculum design should therefore start with these pupils in mind. This requires subject leaders to ensure that the curriculum develops pupils' cultural capital and to design a curriculum that breaks knowledge down into manageable bite-sized chunks.

THE IMPORTANCE OF SUBJECT KNOWLEDGE

The curriculum is the heart of education, and subjects are the heart of the curriculum by Ofsted (2019a) (see Chapter 3, p 35). Subject knowledge for teaching includes:

+ content knowledge: knowledge of subject-specific concepts and facts;

+ pedagogical knowledge: knowledge of effective teaching approaches;

+ pedagogical content knowledge: knowledge of how to teach a subject.

Research has found that teachers with greater content knowledge have higher levels of pedagogical content knowledge (Baumert et al, 2010), which increases cognitive activation in pupils. This is due to the use of strategies such as effective questioning and summarising, which enhance learning. However, research into the relationship between content knowledge and attainment is inconclusive. While some studies show a positive relationship (Clotfelter et al, 2010), others show no effect (Darling-Hammond, 2000). Research has found a much stronger relationship between pedagogical content knowledge and pupils' progress (Baumert et al, 2010).

APPROACHES TO CURRICULUM DESIGN

Research carried out by Ofsted (2019a) shows that schools adopt different approaches to curriculum design.

+ Knowledge-rich schools: These schools focus curriculum design on subject-specific knowledge that learners need to acquire. There is an emphasis on subject-specific facts and concepts that are essential to subject mastery.

+ Knowledge-engaged schools: In these schools the curriculum is designed to enable learners to acquire relevant subject knowledge which underpins the application of skills that learners also need to develop. In these schools there is no perceived tension between knowledge and skills because knowledge supports skills acquisition and skills support knowledge acquisition. An example of this is where pupils acquire knowledge of the alphabetic code (phonics) to support the skills of reading acquisition. Fluency in reading then supports pupils to gain knowledge.

+ Skills-led curriculum design: In these schools the curriculum is designed to support the development of critical skills such as resilience.

CRITICAL QUESTIONS

+ Should knowledge and skills be equally balanced in the curriculum?
+ Why do pupils need to learn knowledge in school when knowledge is now easily accessible on the internet?

THE NATIONAL CURRICULUM AS A STARTING POINT

The national curriculum specifies the ambitious end points that pupils need to achieve at the end of Key Stage 3 and Key Stage 4. It is not a curriculum per se because teachers need to break these goals down into smaller components that essentially form the basis of the subject curriculum. Subject leaders need to be confident that the subject curriculum enables pupils to achieve the ambitious goals in the national curriculum.

COMPOSITE KNOWLEDGE

The ambitious end points in the national curriculum specify the composite knowledge that pupils need to learn. These are often broad in scope and are underpinned by several aspects of knowledge.

COMPONENT KNOWLEDGE AND CHUNKING

When subject leaders break down the national curriculum goals into smaller components, this makes learning more manageable. The working memory is limited in capacity, and pupils can only process a limited amount of subject content in a single lesson. The components of knowledge combine to enable pupils to learn the composite knowledge that is specified in the national curriculum. The process of breaking composite knowledge down into smaller components is often referred to as 'chunking'.

SEQUENCING COMPONENTS

Once subject leaders have identified the components of knowledge that underpin the composite knowledge, the components must be sequenced in a logical way so that learning makes sense to pupils. Pupils progress through the subject curriculum from developing foundational knowledge to developing more advanced knowledge. As they learn the components of knowledge, each component should build on the previous component so that pupils can deepen their understanding of the subject content. Sometimes it is necessary to spend a longer time on a specific component so that pupils learn that knowledge to automaticity. Therefore, time spent practising specific content is not wasted time if it enables pupils to achieve fluency with a specific aspect of content.

SCHEMAS

Schemas are mental representations that are formed when pupils learn something. In chemistry, for example, pupils might develop mental representations of an atom. They learn that an atom has

77

a circular structure with a central nucleus surrounded by orbits of electrons. As pupils progress through the subject curriculum, they develop a more advanced understanding and the original schema (or mental representation) that they formed no longer works. The schema therefore must be modified to accommodate their more advanced understanding.

INSIGHTS FROM COGNITIVE SCIENCE

The Education Endowment Foundation (EEF) identifies a range of insights from cognitive science that can support curriculum design:

+ *spaced learning—distributing learning and retrieval opportunities over a longer period of time rather than concentrating them in 'massed' practice;*

+ *interleaving—switching between different types of problem or different ideas within the same lesson or study session;*

+ *retrieval practice—using a variety of strategies to recall information from memory, for example flash cards, practice tests or quizzing, or mind-mapping;*

+ *dual coding—using both verbal and non-verbal information (such as words and pictures) to teach concepts; dual coding forms one part of a wider theory known as the cognitive theory of multimedia learning.*

(EEF, 2021, p 5)

Interleaving, dual coding and retrieval practice support the process of curriculum design in lessons. Spaced learning can also be used within lessons, but it is more commonly applied when designing the subject curriculum over time. It is the practice of revisiting subject content after a gap in time. In this process, pupils almost forget the subject content, but the revisiting of that content after a gap in time activates the long-term memory. Pupils are supported to retrieve the knowledge from the long-term memory and work with that subject content again. Teachers then develop pupils' knowledge further by exploring the subject content in greater depth.

DESIGNING A CURRICULUM FOR PUPILS WITH SEND

Designing a subject curriculum with SEND pupils in mind from the outset benefits all pupils. This means that subject leaders should break down the ambitious end points of the national curriculum into small aspects of component knowledge. Pupils learn one component before progressing to the next component. Each component is practised to automaticity before progressing onto the next component. This approach benefits all pupils.

Pupils with SEND are entitled to an ambitious curriculum so that they have the same opportunities as their peers. Too often, pupils with SEND are placed in low-ability groups and provided with tasks that lack challenge. This widens the ability gap between those pupils with and without SEND and results in underachievement. This can have a serious long-term detrimental effect. Far too many pupils with SEND underachieve at school and consequently are disadvantaged. As a result, many do not enter FE or HE and are denied access to employment and training opportunities.

All pupils have an entitlement to an ambitious curriculum which enables them to develop good subject knowledge and transferable skills. Like all pupils, those with SEND should be supported to develop literacy and numeracy skills. With the right kind of teaching and support, many pupils with SEND can learn to read, write and become numerate. Some pupils with highly complex needs may need a tailored curriculum that supports them to develop specific skills. However, this should be the exception rather than the norm, and generally all pupils should follow the same subject curriculum so that they are working towards the same ambitious end points of the national curriculum.

Providing pupils with SEND with a lower-level task should not be the default position. Teachers should consider ways of enabling pupils with SEND to access the same curriculum as their peers by building in access strategies to remove barriers to learning. Pupils with complex needs may require a highly personalised curriculum that focuses on the development of specific skills, and some may require a sensory curriculum to enable them to learn. Pupils with moderate and specific learning difficulties can access the same curriculum as their peers, but teachers may need to build in specific strategies to support them to do so.

Examples include the use of additional adult support, the breaking down of curriculum content into small steps and the use of technology to assist learners.

DESIGNING A CURRICULUM FOR DISADVANTAGED PUPILS

Pupils from disadvantaged backgrounds may have less cultural capital than those from more affluent backgrounds, although this is not always the case. They may have a restricted vocabulary, and they may not have had the rich experiences that financial capital provides access to. Limiting pupils' social and cultural experiences can have an impact on vocabulary development, social and emotional development and the development of pupils' knowledge and imagination. This can impact not only on pupils' literacy development but also on their development in a range of academic subjects.

To compensate for disadvantage, the curriculum should be designed so that it is ambitious for all pupils. It should provide pupils with the cultural capital they may have been denied as a result of their social background. The curriculum should expose pupils to a range of texts that capture their imagination and provide cognitive challenge. It should provide them with experiences they have not had access to, including opportunities to participate in sport, drama, dance, music and art and to learn a foreign language. The curriculum should ensure that pupils have opportunities to visit localities that contrast with where they live. It should promote a love of reading and poetry and ignite pupils' imaginations. It should provide pupils with opportunities to visit museums, galleries and places of worship, and it should promote a connection with the landscape, including developing a sense of awe and wonder in relation to the land, oceans, lakes, rivers and space. The curriculum should promote an interest in architecture and engineering. It should provide pupils with knowledge of our rich social, political and cultural history. These are all examples of ways in which the curriculum can compensate for disadvantage. You will be able to think of many more examples. However, the key point is that pupils' futures should not be defined by their social backgrounds. Their backgrounds may limit their exposure to all these forms of cultural capital, but the curriculum can be designed to ensure that all pupils have opportunities to broaden their interests, knowledge, skills and imaginations.

GOING BEYOND THE NATIONAL CURRICULUM

Knowledge provides pupils with cultural capital. It enables them to reason and debate from an informed perspective. The national curriculum identifies the minimum level of knowledge that pupils need. School leaders will need to decide what additional knowledge pupils may need to serve them well in the future. Pupils *should* know about the history of race and racism, even though it is not specified in the national curriculum. They should know about the treatment of disabled people in the past. They should know about climate change and the damage that humans have caused to the planet, including the damage of single-use plastics to the environment. They should know how to grow their own food, and they should know about the importance of saving money for the future. They should know the name of the local river and about significant events in history that may have had an impact on their community. These are examples of aspects of knowledge that may fall outside the specified knowledge in the national curriculum, but which are nonetheless important.

PROMOTING PERSONAL DEVELOPMENT

A curriculum for personal development is a curriculum that addresses the needs of the whole pupil. This includes their intellectual, moral, spiritual, cultural, physical and mental development. The *Education Inspection Framework* (Ofsted, 2019b) identifies 'personal development' as a separate strand that inspectors evaluate. Inspectors evaluate the extent to which schools meet the criteria listed below.

+ *The curriculum extends beyond the academic, technical or vocational and provides for learners' broader development, enabling them to develop and discover their interests and talents.*

+ *The curriculum and the provider's wider work support learners to develop their character – including their resilience, confidence and independence – and help them know how to keep physically and mentally healthy.*

+ *At each stage of education, the provider prepares learners for future success in their next steps.*

+ *The provider prepares learners for life in modern Britain by: equipping them to be responsible, respectful, active citizens who contribute positively to society; developing their understanding of fundamental British values; developing their understanding and appreciation of diversity; celebrating what we have in common and promoting respect for the different protected characteristics as defined in law.*

(Ofsted, 2019b, p 37)

PROMOTING INTELLECTUAL DEVELOPMENT

An effective curriculum promotes intellectual development. It enables pupils to learn the knowledge and skills they need to be able to succeed in life. A carefully sequenced curriculum enables pupils to develop higher-order thinking skills, including the ability to apply, analyse and synthesise information. Although facts are important, an effective curriculum goes beyond the transmission of information. It empowers pupils to think, reason, debate, challenge, evaluate and question. These are fundamental aspects of intellectual development that provide pupils with the tools they need to succeed in subsequent stages of their education and in life.

PROMOTING MORAL DEVELOPMENT

The curriculum should promote pupils' understanding of what is right and what is wrong. This includes promoting an awareness of the importance of respecting others, their values and beliefs, and their differences. In addition, moral development includes promoting an awareness of the rule of law and the ability to make judgements about what is morally acceptable and unacceptable within society. The following is from Ofsted's *School Inspection Handbook*.

Provision for the moral development of pupils includes developing their:

+ *ability to recognise the difference between right and wrong and to readily apply this understanding in their own lives, and to recognise legal boundaries and, in doing so, respect the civil and criminal law of England*

+ *understanding of the consequences of their behaviour and actions*

+ *interest in investigating and offering reasoned views about moral and ethical issues and ability to understand and appreciate the viewpoints of others on these issues*

(Ofsted, 2022)

It is important to recognise that some pupils live in families and communities that do not support them to understand what is right and what is wrong. The curriculum should provide all pupils with a clear message about what is socially, morally and legally acceptable, regardless of the values that are promoted within pupils' homes and communities. The curriculum is therefore a vehicle for breaking a negative cycle of disadvantage. It demonstrates to pupils that there is a different path they can take. In RSHE, pupils learn how to treat other people, including friends and family members. If pupils are exposed to unhealthy relationships in the home, it may take them longer to understand how to treat others. The curriculum should also support pupils to understand that although specific behaviours may be tolerated or promoted at home, these will not necessarily be tolerated within school or within society. Pupils need to learn how to treat people in positions of authority with respect, and the curriculum should help them to recognise that bullying, prejudice and discrimination are morally unacceptable. Providing pupils with a curriculum that addresses race, disability, sexual orientation, age and gender equality will enable them to recognise the importance of treating everyone with respect, regardless of people's differences.

PROMOTING SPIRITUAL DEVELOPMENT

Spiritual development is not just about understanding religions. It goes beyond this. Ofsted's *School Inspection Handbook* includes the following.

Provision for the spiritual development of pupils includes developing their:

+ *ability to be reflective about their own beliefs (religious or otherwise) and perspective on life*

+ *knowledge of, and respect for, different people's faiths, feelings and values*

+ *sense of enjoyment and fascination in learning about themselves, others and the world around them*

+ *use of imagination and creativity in their learning*

+ *willingness to reflect on their experiences*

(Ofsted, 2022)

Embedding frequent opportunities into the curriculum for promoting self-reflection is one way of promoting spiritual development. Developing a rich curriculum that provides opportunities for pupils to become immersed in deep learning through problem-solving, investigation and collaborative learning helps to develop pupils' enjoyment in and fascination for learning. Activities that enable pupils to take risks and those which promote engagement with the natural environment can also promote intrinsic motivation and a sense of awe and wonder. Providing pupils with opportunities to become immersed in one task or project for an extended length of time can also promote enjoyment and fascination.

Too often, pupils are expected to race through the curriculum at speed. There are limited opportunities for pupils to become absorbed in learning, and, unfortunately, in many secondary schools, the structure of the school day now mirrors a secondary school timetable. This means that pupils move quickly from one lesson to the next, without any opportunity to engage deeply with a task. It is time for secondary schools to reclaim the curriculum. Moving pupils on too quickly from one aspect of content to the next limits exposure to deep and rich learning experiences that pupils will remember.

CRITICAL QUESTIONS

+ How are opportunities for promoting self-reflection embedded throughout your curriculum?

+ What knowledge and skills do pupils need to be able to succeed in life?

PROMOTING SOCIAL DEVELOPMENT

A curriculum for social development supports pupils to understand the importance of adjusting their behaviour in different contexts, and it also supports pupils to regulate their behaviours in different social situations.

Ofsted's *School Inspection Handbook* includes the following.

Provision for the social development of pupils includes developing their:

+ *use of a range of social skills in different contexts, for example working and socialising with other pupils, including those from different religious, ethnic and socio-economic backgrounds*

+ *willingness to participate in a variety of communities and social settings, including by volunteering, cooperating well with others and being able to resolve conflicts effectively*

+ *acceptance and engagement with the fundamental British values of democracy, the rule of law, individual liberty and mutual respect and tolerance of those with different faiths and beliefs. They will develop and demonstrate skills and attitudes that will allow them to participate fully in and contribute positively to life in modern Britain.*

(Ofsted, 2022)

Schools can build opportunities for collaborative learning into the curriculum to support pupils in developing important social skills. These include turn-taking, listening to others, showing respect towards other people and sharing. Fundamental British values should be promoted through the curriculum in addition to being taught in personal, social and health education (PSHE). Subject leaders should identify links to these in curriculum planning.

PROMOTING CULTURAL DEVELOPMENT

Cultural development is not just about teaching pupils about different cultures, although this is a key part of it. It also includes developing an awareness of different socio-economic backgrounds. The following is from Ofsted's *School Inspection Handbook*.

Provision for the cultural development of pupils includes developing their:

+ *understanding and appreciation of the wide range of cultural influences that have shaped their own heritage and that of others*

+ *understanding and appreciation of the range of different cultures in the school and further afield as an essential element of their preparation for life in modern Britain*

+ *ability to recognise, and value, the things we share in common across cultural, religious, ethnic and socio-economic communities*

+ *knowledge of Britain's democratic Parliamentary system and its central role in shaping our history and values, and in continuing to develop Britain*

+ *willingness to participate in and respond positively to artistic, musical, sporting and cultural opportunities*

+ *interest in exploring, improving understanding of and showing respect for different faiths and cultural diversity and the extent to which they understand, accept, respect and celebrate diversity. This is shown by their respect and attitudes towards different religious, ethnic and socio-economic groups in the local, national and global communities*

(Ofsted, 2022)

PROMOTING PHYSICAL DEVELOPMENT

Physical development is an essential aspect of healthy development. Pupils need to be physically active so that they can be healthy and strong. Physical activity also promotes good mental health. Pupils need frequent opportunities for movement, and therefore physical education is an essential component of the curriculum.

PROMOTING GOOD MENTAL HEALTH

The curriculum should support pupils to be aware of the importance not only of physical health but also of mental health. In the early stages of pupils' education, the curriculum should develop their understanding of a range of emotions. It is important that pupils can name the different emotions they experience and that they know it is normal for everyone to experience these different emotions. The curriculum should also provide pupils with strategies to enable them to regulate their emotions.

The mental health curriculum needs to be age appropriate. Schools will need to decide when to start introducing pupils to specific mental health conditions. The curriculum should help pupils to understand the importance of talking to others about their feelings, and it should provide them with a range of strategies for managing their own mental health. It should also ensure that pupils know how to seek support for their mental health.

CASE STUDY

MENTAL HEALTH

YEAR 8

Subject leaders in a secondary school designed a mental health curriculum for pupils in Year 8. The curriculum introduced pupils to a range of themes. These included different types of mental ill health, how to look after your mental health, how to seek support and changing attitudes in relation to mental health. When the pupils completed the curriculum, they could differentiate between low mood and depression, and they could also discuss the benefits and harmful effects of stress. Pupils could also articulate the impact of gender on willingness to seek help, and they challenged the harmful gender stereotypes that lead to this.

CRITICAL QUESTIONS

+ If you had to design a mental health curriculum, what themes might you address?

+ Is Year 8 the right age to introduce this curriculum? Explain your answer.

PREPARING PUPILS FOR LIFE IN MODERN BRITAIN

Schools are legally required to teach fundamental British values, including the law. This teaching should prepare pupils for life in modern Britain by demonstrating the importance of respect for other people, regardless of belief or identity. The curriculum should also support pupils to acquire an understanding of the need for individual liberty, mutual respect, and tolerance of those with different faiths and beliefs. Pupils must understand that mutual respect for difference is one of the fundamental British values. The curriculum plays an important role in teaching pupils that difference takes many forms, including, but not restricted to, physical appearance, personality, social background, cultural diversity, disability, sexual orientation, sex, gender, age and religion or belief. Above all, the curriculum must support pupils to know and understand that they have a responsibility to respect other people irrespective of any differences. This principle helps pupils' development as good citizens and also contributes to the development of an inclusive society.

PROMOTING CHARACTER

Although character education is not identified as a separate strand within the statutory guidance (DfE, 2019a), it is embedded within specific themes. Within 'caring friendships', specific character traits are addressed. Character traits include belief in achieving goals and persevering with tasks, as well as personal attributes such as honesty, integrity, courage, humility, kindness, generosity, trustworthiness and a sense of justice, underpinned by an understanding of the importance of self-respect and self-worth. Character education is part of RSHE in secondary schools.

The statutory guidance states: *'A growing ability to form strong and positive relationships with others depends on the deliberate cultivation of character traits and positive personal attributes, (sometimes referred to as "virtues") in the individual'* (DfE, 2019a, p 20).

Character is a complex concept and multifaceted. According to the DfE (2019a), important aspects include:

+ the ability to stay motivated by long-term goals, including the ability to invest effort and persevere with something despite setbacks;

+ the development of moral attributes or virtues;

+ the acquisition of social confidence, including the ability to make persuasive arguments, listen to others and demonstrate good manners and courtesy toward others;

+ the ability to appreciate the importance of long-term commitments – for example, by demonstrating commitment to a relationship, a vocation, a faith or world view or the local community.

The *Education Inspection Framework* (Ofsted, 2019b) embeds character education within the strand of 'personal development'. Inspectors evaluate the school's curriculum and the work done in supporting learners to develop their character, including their resilience, confidence and independence.

CRITICAL QUESTIONS

+ How can resilience be embedded into the curriculum?

+ How can the curriculum be designed so that it fosters intrinsic motivation?

EVIDENCE-BASED PRACTICE

Evidence suggests that character education supports the development of a positive school culture and leads to a more conducive learning environment and improved behaviour, attendance and motivation (OECD, 2015; Walker et al, 2017). It also leads to positive long-term outcomes, including access to HE (Walker et al, 2017) and good mental well-being (DfE, 2019a; Taylor et al, 2017). Research suggests that character education drives equality and social mobility (Chanfreau et al, 2016).

PROMOTING COMMITMENT THROUGH THE CURRICULUM

The curriculum should prepare pupils for the challenges that they will face in their next stage of learning as well as in later life. It is crucial that the curriculum provides experiences for pupils to engage in and commit to their own learning with the confidence to think independently and take responsibility for their own learning.

Offering pupils activities and opportunities they can commit to is one way that the curriculum can be used to promote a sense of commitment. This allows pupils to reflect on the commitments they have. If pupils express an interest in quitting or giving up on a commitment, then you should explain why it is important to be resilient and persevere. This modelling of commitment can support character development and help pupils to recognise values and priorities in a positive way.

EVIDENCE-BASED PRACTICE

Research has found that specific character traits are associated with positive outcomes. Gutman and Schoon's (2013) findings are summarised below.

+ High self-efficacy is associated with better performance and greater persistence and motivation.

+ High levels of intrinsic motivation are associated with greater persistence and achievement.

+ Good self-regulation, including the ability to delay gratification, is associated with greater attainment.

+ High levels of resilience are associated with greater well-being.

+ Mindsets are malleable, and supporting pupils to develop a growth mindset may result in small to medium improvements in performance.

Another study shows that the ability to self-regulate is a significant predictor of attainment (Moffitt et al, 2011). There is also evidence that teaching pupils to develop appropriate social behaviour improves attainment (Durlak et al, 2011).

DEVELOPING THE CO-CURRICULUM

As part of the character education curriculum, schools should ensure that there is strong provision for co-curricular activities. A well-planned co-curriculum can build social confidence, raise self-esteem and improve motivation, attendance and academic outcomes for pupils (DfE, 2019a). Research demonstrates that participation in outdoor adventure programmes has positive effects on the psychological, behavioural, physical and academic outcomes of young people (Gutman and Schoon, 2013).

Activities may include access to sporting or other physical activities, theatre performances, the arts, volunteering, debating, cooking and participation in service. This is not an exhaustive list. The critical point is that schools should ensure that all pupils can participate in the co-curriculum, including those pupils who are the most disadvantaged. Barriers to participation include the cost of activities, and to address this schools should subsidise activities to prevent financial constraints becoming a barrier to equal opportunities. The co-curriculum should be designed to enable pupils to compete and perform. These opportunities improve social confidence and self-esteem.

DEVELOPING AND PROMOTING THE VALUE OF VOLUNTEERING

Volunteering empowers pupils by enabling them to make a positive contribution to their local community. It helps pupils to develop a civic mindset and provides them with an opportunity to engage in meaningful work. Pupils can participate in a range of volunteering opportunities. These may include fundraising activities for local and national organisations, protecting the environment and providing services to elderly people in the local community. Research findings suggest that volunteering produces moderate effects for academic outcomes and small effects for noncognitive outcomes, including social skills, self-perception and motivation (Gutman and Schoon, 2013).

PROMOTING READING

There is increasing evidence showing the importance of reading for pleasure for both educational purposes and personal development (Clark and Rumbold, 2006). Research demonstrates that there is a positive relationship between reading frequency, reading enjoyment and attainment (Clark, 2011; Clark and Douglas, 2011). Reading for pleasure has been reported as more important for pupils' educational success than their family's socio-economic status (Kirsch et al, 2002). There is consistent evidence that age affects attitudes to reading, with pupils getting less enjoyment from reading as they get older (Topping, 2010; Clark and Osborne, 2008; Clark and Douglas, 2011). However, some evidence suggests that while frequency of reading declines with age for young people, when they do read, the length of time spent reading increases with age (Clark, 2011).

Several studies have shown that boys enjoy reading less than girls and that pupils from lower socio-economic backgrounds are less likely than pupils from higher socio-economic backgrounds to read for enjoyment (Clark and Rumbold, 2006; Clark and Douglas, 2011). Having access to cultural capital, such as books and other literacy resources, impacts positively on pupils' attainment. There is a positive relationship between the number of books in the home and attainment (Clark, 2011). Pupils who have books of their own enjoy reading for pleasure and read more frequently (Clark and Poulton, 2011).

EXTENDED THINKING

+ What factors might lead to boys demonstrating less enjoyment of reading than girls?

+ Why does social deprivation impact on attitudes to literacy?

CASE STUDY

ADDRESSING THEMES IN THE CURRICULUM

WHOLE SCHOOL

School leaders in a secondary school asked subject leaders to consider ways of addressing themes such as resilience, character and mental health in the secondary subject curriculum. Some subjects had strong links to some themes, and it was important not to make tenuous links. For example, in physical education, the subject curriculum was adapted to include stronger links to mental health. In history, mental health was addressed at Key Stage 3 by exploring historical attitudes to mental illness. The music curriculum was adapted in Key Stage 3 to include links to resilience.

CRITICAL QUESTIONS

+ What are the dangers of making links between subjects and themes in this way?
+ How might SMSC be developed through the subject curriculum?

SUMMARY

This chapter emphasised the essential components of a secondary curriculum including SMSC, mental health, resilience and character. It also emphasised the need to design a secondary curriculum for pupils with SEND in mind from the outset, and it highlighted the different types of knowledge that the secondary curriculum needs to address.

CHECKLIST

+ The curriculum should enable pupils to achieve the ambitious goals of the national curriculum.

+ Composite knowledge is often understood as the broad goals that pupils need to achieve.

+ Component knowledge is often understood as smaller chunks of knowledge that pupils learn. The components of knowledge combine to enable pupils to learn the composite knowledge.

+ The secondary curriculum must also address broader aspects, including resilience, mental and physical health, character, and SMSC development.

FURTHER READING

Bawden, M (2016) Embedding Character in the Curriculum. [online] Available at: www.sec-ed.co.uk/best-practice/character-and-the-curriculum/ (accessed 19 August 2022).

English-Speaking Union Scotland (nd) Community Resilience: Debating Resource Pack for Secondary Schools. [online] Available at: https://education.gov.scot/Documents/SecondaryResilienceDebatingResource.pdf (accessed 19 August 2022).

Mentally Healthy Schools (nd) Mental Health on the Curriculum in England. [online] Available at: www.mentallyhealthyschools.org.uk/whole-school-approach/england/mental-health-on-the-curriculum-in-england/ (accessed 19 August 2022).

SMSC (nd) What is SMSC? [online] Available at: www.smscqualitymark.org.uk/what-is-smsc/ (accessed 19 August 2022).

+ CHAPTER 6
TEACHING THE CURRICULUM

CHAPTER OBJECTIVES

After reading this chapter you will understand:

+ the role of explicit direct instruction in promoting learning;

+ the role of modelling, scaffolding and fading in teaching;

+ the function of the memory and strategies for reducing cognitive load.

INTRODUCTION

This chapter addresses the role of explicit direct instruction and associated strategies in teaching. From the outset, we wish to emphasise that this does not mean pupils should be learning passively through rote learning. Explicit direct instruction, when done well, engages learners and maximises their participation in the process of learning. It is also important to stress from the start that inquiry-based approaches to learning do play an important role in the classroom. However, it is critical that pupils have been taught the essential knowledge and skills they need before they are required to undertake inquiry. Pupils do not get better at solving mathematical problems by doing more problems. They improve by mastering the mathematical concepts and skills that are required to enable them to solve mathematical problems. We highlight the importance of modelling, scaffolding and fading as essential components of explicit direct instruction. We also highlight the processes involved in supporting the development of metacognitive skills and the role of assessment in teaching.

THE IMPORTANCE OF DIRECT AND EXPLICIT INSTRUCTION

Various terms are used to describe this approach to teaching. These include 'explicit teaching, explicit instruction, teacher-led instruction and direct instruction' (Ashman, 2019, p 29). The approach generally involves chunking content into smaller components, guiding pupils' initial attempts at working, and gradually releasing more control to pupils as they develop mastery of the content (Ashman, 2019). It is usefully summarised in the following way.

+ I do: the teacher models the subject content.

+ We do: the teacher supports the pupils to work with the subject content or pupils support each other to work with the content.

+ You do: pupils work independently on the subject content.

According to Ashman, 'the principles of explicit teaching directly contradict those of inquiry-based learning' (2019, p 31). Through inquiry-based approaches, pupils are often required to discover knowledge for themselves or to figure things out. However, the research evidence suggests that inquiry-based learning approaches are less effective than direct teaching (Kirschner et al, 2006), and evidence therefore broadly supports direct instruction (Coe et al, 2014).

Clearly, teachers want pupils to be able to use the knowledge that they provide in some meaningful way. However, pupils cannot think critically about a topic unless they have the knowledge of the subject content (Willingham, 2007). One of the risks of inquiry-based approaches is that pupils might in fact develop misconceptions. In addition, leaving pupils to discover things for themselves can lead to cognitive load because pupils might not have the substantive subject knowledge to understand fully what they are being asked to do. There is also a misconception that pupils should be actively engaged by 'doing things' in lessons. In fact, teachers can promote active engagement by promoting active thinking. Pupils need to be actively engaging with the subject content by thinking about it deeply. There is little value in asking pupils to complete practical tasks if those tasks do not promote thinking. It therefore follows that teachers can promote thinking without asking pupils to complete practical tasks.

Explicit direct instruction is associated with breaking down subject content into manageable chunks, maintaining a brisk pace and using worked examples. It is also associated with retrieval practice and spaced or distributed learning, both of which are supported by experimental research (Dunlosky et al, 2013).

THE ROLE OF MODELLING, SCAFFOLDING AND FADING

The approaches to direct and explicit instruction are discussed here.

MODELLING

Pupils learn more effectively when teachers demonstrate the subject content explicitly. Modelling can be supported with teacher explanations and questioning, but these are not sufficient. Through modelling, teachers explicitly demonstrate processes, subject concepts or principles in various ways. One strategy that is particularly effective is the use of worked examples in teaching to demonstrate a process, skill or technique (Engelmann and Carnine, 1982). Another modelling technique is teachers drawing diagrams on the board to illustrate the subject content they are explaining to pupils. This technique of combining verbal explanations with visual information is an application of 'dual coding'. Teachers are using modelling when they demonstrate:

+ how to work through a series of steps in a problem in order to solve the problem;

+ how to construct an effective answer to a question;

+ how to use subject specialist equipment;

+ how to execute a skill;

+ good examples of writing;

+ thinking aloud – modelling their thought processes very explicitly as they perform a task in front of the pupils.

CRITICAL QUESTIONS

+ How might you use modelling in your subject?

+ What are the advantages and disadvantages of modelling?

SCAFFOLDING

The term 'scaffolding' is often associated with Jermone Bruner. However, the concept was introduced by Wood, Bruner and Ross in 1976. The term was initially used to describe how adults interact with pre-school children to support them in completing a task. However, the process is now used across all age groups. Initially the teacher models the subject content ('I do'). Before pupils are required to work independently on the subject content, the next phase in a learning sequence involves the teacher supporting pupils to master the subject content they have just modelled – this is done through the use of scaffolding ('we do'). In a mathematics lesson, a teacher might model a strategy for solving a mathematical problem. The teacher might then provide pupils with another mathematical problem and ask them to solve the problem with the teacher. The role of the teacher is to support the pupils at this stage. The teacher is therefore scaffolding the pupils' learning. It is often useful to think of scaffolding as a process of providing support, similar to the way in which scaffolding supports buildings when they are being erected. Eventually the scaffolding can be removed when the building is strong enough to stand on its own. Alternatively, the teacher might model a mathematical problem to the pupils and then provide a second problem, which the pupils are asked to solve in pairs. In this strategy, the pupils are being asked to scaffold the learning of their peers (peer scaffolding).

The key point is that scaffolding supports pupils to become confident with the subject content before they are asked to work independently on that content. Teachers can also scaffold pupils' thinking by asking questions that support them to understand the subject content. Pupils' learning can also be scaffolded through the use of templates or graphic organisers, which help them to document their thinking in a structured way. Examples include mind maps and writing frames.

FADING

Fading is the gradual removal of scaffolding. This ensures that pupils have opportunities to demonstrate mastery and fluency of the subject content. Teachers need to decide when to fade out the support, ensuring that pupils have an opportunity to demonstrate what they know and can do. If the support is faded out too soon, pupils might not be confident with the subject content. If the support is faded out too late, this restricts pupil achievement.

When pupils are learning new subject content, the working memory is, at that point, working to full capacity (Cullen, 2019). This is because pupils are trying to process the subject content. At this stage, either the new learning is assimilated into existing schemas because it fits in with what pupils already know (assimilation), or existing schemas have to be modified to accommodate the new learning when the existing schemas no longer work (accommodation). It is at this stage of the lesson that pupils will need the most support from a teacher (Cullen, 2019), and therefore scaffolding is critical. At the point when pupils have understood the subject content, the teacher should fade out the support or risk pupils becoming dependent on scaffolding rather than becoming autonomous. Fisher and Frey (2010) describe this as the moment when teachers must relinquish control. The key to effective scaffolding is that it is gradually dismantled (Dixon et al, 1993) rather than suddenly removed.

EVIDENCE-BASED PRACTICE

Rosenshine (2010; 2012) developed ten principles of effective instruction. These are listed below.

+ *Begin a lesson with a short review of previous learning.*

+ *Present new material in small steps with student practice after each step.*

+ *Ask a large number of questions and check the responses of all students.*

+ *Provide models.*

+ *Guide student practice.*

+ *Check for student understanding.*

+ *Obtain a high success rate.*

+ *Provide scaffolds for difficult tasks.*

+ *Require and monitor independent practice.*

+ *Engage students in weekly and monthly review.*

(Rosenshine, 2012, p 12)

It is clear that explicit direct instruction is embedded into Rosenshine's principles – for example, chunking content into small components, guiding pupils' initial attempts at working, and gradually releasing more control to pupils so that they develop mastery and fluency.

METACOGNITION

Metacognition is the process of learning how to learn. It involves the skills of identifying goals, planning how to achieve these, self-monitoring, and evaluating learning in order to achieve the best possible outcomes. Effective learners use these metacognitive strategies all the time and they are lifelong skills. Teachers can model metacognitive strategies by showing how to:

+ check the accuracy of tasks that have been attempted;

+ use checklists (success criteria) to monitor the quality of work during completion of a task;

+ edit work to improve it;

+ self-evaluate work against the success criteria;

+ plan how to approach a specific task.

This is not an exhaustive list. The key point is that effective learners are strategic learners. They can use the skills of goal setting, planning, monitoring and evaluating to meet deadlines and achieve goals and to improve the quality of their work. Teachers need to explicitly model these strategies because they are not always intuitive. One crucial meta-cognitive skill is for pupils to use self-monitoring strategies. Effective learners monitor their progress towards achieving their learning goals using strategies such as self-checking as they complete a task so that any necessary changes can be made. For example, pupils might check the accuracy of their answers to questions during a task and make corrections where necessary.

WORKING MEMORY AND LONG-TERM MEMORY

To understand how pupils acquire knowledge, it is important to know about the role of the memory in the learning process. The memory is made up of the working memory and the long-term memory.

WORKING MEMORY

When we take in new knowledge, the information is processed by the working memory. We also use the working memory to complete a task. When we are performing any task (eg writing, solving a mathematical calculation, walking, reading, watching television), the working memory helps us to complete the task.

The problem with the working memory is that it is limited in capacity. It can only process a limited amount of information at any one time. On average, the working memory can process seven pieces of information, although this varies across individuals. The working memory quickly becomes overloaded when it is trying to process too much information. Information transfers from the working memory into the long-term memory. This frees up space (capacity) in the working memory to enable it to process new information.

The working memory is made up of four components, shown in Figure 6.1.

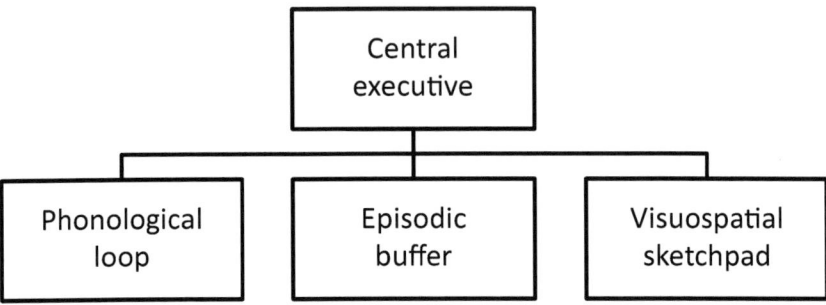

Figure 6.1 Components of working memory

CENTRAL EXECUTIVE

The central executive is the driver. It controls all the other aspects of the working memory. The working memory processes different types of information. Information processing takes place in the sub-systems of the working memory. The central executive filters the information received by the working memory and directs different types of information to different sub-systems.

PHONOLOGICAL LOOP

The phonological loop is a sub-system of the working memory. When the working memory is trying to process spoken language (eg following spoken instructions) or other language-based tasks, including reading and writing, the information is processed in the phonological loop. When we listen to music or to information on the radio or even when we listen to the television, we process what we hear in the phonological loop.

VISUOSPATIAL SKETCHPAD

The visuospatial sketchpad is a sub-system of the working memory. This is the part of the working memory that helps us to process visual or spatial information. If we are driving a car, we must visually process what we see in front of us and we must have a good sense of direction.

We are processing this task in the visuospatial sketchpad. If we are visually processing a diagram or a photograph, this will take place in the visuospatial sketchpad.

EPISODIC BUFFER

The episodic buffer is a temporary storage system in the working memory. Once the information has been processed in the phonological loop and the visuospatial sketchpad, the episodic buffer can hold information before it is transferred to the long-term memory. This part of the working memory was a later addition to the model of the working memory.

LONG-TERM MEMORY

Information processed in the sub-systems of the working memory are transferred to the long-term memory. Information can be held in the long-term memory indefinitely. However, to remember information and for knowledge to become fluent, information needs to be retrieved regularly from the long-term memory. The more we retrieve information, the more automatic the knowledge becomes.

We can use the example of learning to drive a car. When we first learn to drive a car there is a lot of new information (knowledge) to process. This processing takes place in the working memory. Learning to drive places a heavy burden on the working memory because there are many things to remember. The information is then transferred from the working memory to the long-term memory. Every time we repeat the task of driving, the information is constantly being retrieved from the long-term memory. Eventually, we can perform the task of driving with very little thinking. This is because the constant retrieval (ie using the knowledge through practising driving) means that the knowledge becomes automatic. We can drive through towns, cities and villages and on motorways without consciously having to think about what we are doing because the knowledge is fluent.

When pupils are learning new subject content, the working memory is working to full capacity to process the information. There is a risk that pupils might experience cognitive load if they are given too much information to process at any one time. It is crucial therefore that teachers break down the subject content into small, manageable chunks. This process is known as chunking.

The long-term memory has much greater capacity than the working memory. Knowledge that is stored in the long-term memory is organised into categories. It can sometimes be helpful to think of the long-term memory as a filing cabinet with lots of separate folders that group information together to store related content. However, if we store information in folders and never revisit that information, we forget that information. The information is still stored, but because we do not revisit it, we cannot fluently recall the information. Pupils become fluent with subject content when they retrieve that content regularly and work with it. Information therefore transfers from the working memory to the long-term memory, but when it is retrieved from the long-term memory it is transferred from the long-term memory back into the working memory and reprocessed. Revisiting knowledge regularly through purposeful practice helps pupils to develop automaticity with the subject content. Regularly revisiting subject content that they have already learned helps pupils to develop 'fingertip' knowledge. The knowledge begins to 'stick'. It becomes automatic and pupils can start to work with subject content fluently and automatically.

SCHEMAS

Schemas are mental representations that are formed in the brain (see Chapter 5). Young children may form a mental representation of a car. They associate a car as an object with four wheels. Initially they see one type of car and learn that it is a car. They then see different models and colours of cars, but the schema still works (they all have four wheels) and they can therefore attach the label of 'car' to multiple cars. This process is known as 'assimilation'. The new learning fits in with the existing learning, and the schema does not need to be modified. Then they are introduced to a car with three wheels (a Reliant Robin) and learn that this is also a car. The original mental representation (schema) of car now needs to be modified to include vehicles with three wheels as well as those with four wheels. This results in cognitive dissonance because initially the new learning does not make sense given the previous learning. The new knowledge must be accommodated, and the schema must be modified so that the category of 'car' now includes vehicles with three wheels and vehicles with four wheels. This process is known as 'accommodation'.

Now let's consider how this applies to teaching and learning the secondary curriculum. Schemas do not just apply to young children. In chemistry, pupils might form a mental representation of an atom. They learn that an atom is a circular structure with a central nucleus surrounded by orbits of electrons. If they study the subject at a more advanced level, pupils learn that atoms have a more complex structure. They must modify their original mental representation of atom (schema) to accommodate their new knowledge of atomic structure (see Chapter 9).

CRITICAL QUESTIONS

+ What challenges might pupils have when they are experiencing a schema modification?

+ How do you think the processes of assimilation and accommodation affect working memory capacity?

COGNITIVE LOAD

When pupils are learning new subject content, that content needs to be processed in the working memory before being transferred to the long-term memory. It is easy for the working memory to become quickly overloaded, particularly if the processing is taking place in the same sub-system of the working memory. An example of this might be when a teacher provides pupils with multiple instructions at the same time. Each instruction will need to be processed in the phonological loop, the chamber that processes spoken language. If multiple instructions are presented, the phonological loop can quickly become overloaded, and this reduces its efficiency. It is more effective to chunk the information that is presented so that the working memory can process a limited amount of information at any one time. Sometimes, teachers might provide pupils with verbal explanations and support these with visual information – for example, by displaying a diagram. Interestingly, although information is being presented in several formats, this does not result in cognitive load because the information is being processed in separate sub-systems of the working memory. The verbal instructions are processed in the phonological loop and the diagram is processed in the visuo-spatial sketchpad. These sub-systems can process separate types of information concurrently without interfering with each other – a form of dual coding.

Cognitive interference occurs when a single sub-system is required to process several pieces of different information. Think about how this works in everyday life. It is difficult to follow a conversation with a friend if you are listening to the background noise of the television. Both tasks require the working memory to process spoken language, and therefore the processing takes place in the phonological loop. The effect is that the phonological loop quickly becomes overloaded because the tasks conflict. There are three main types of cognitive load: intrinsic load, extraneous load and germane load.

INTRINSIC LOAD

Intrinsic load occurs when pupils are introduced to new subject content. When pupils are asked to think about something new, the working memory must work at full capacity to process the new information. If pupils are asked to think about too many new concepts, principles or facts, this places a burden on the working memory and reduces its capacity to process subject content. The solution to increasing the capacity of the working memory is to reduce the amount of new subject content pupils are asked to think about in a lesson.

CASE STUDY

REDUCING COGNITIVE LOAD

WHOLE SCHOOL

Subject leaders in a secondary school noticed that pupils were not remembering the knowledge they had been taught. Following a series of lesson visits, leaders noticed that teachers were introducing pupils to too many concepts during lessons. This was mainly due to the fact that there was too much to cover in the curriculum and not enough time. Leaders asked subject teams to identify content that could be displaced so that there was less to cover. Leaders asked teachers to focus in lessons on introducing one, or a maximum of two, concepts and then provide pupils with an opportunity to practise working with this subject content.

CRITICAL QUESTIONS

+ What are the advantages of this approach?
+ Identify and note down any potential disadvantages.

EXTRANEOUS LOAD

Extraneous load occurs when pupils are introduced to interesting but irrelevant material in a lesson. This is when teachers introduce content which is not relevant or essential to the core learning. This additional 'froth' reduces the capacity of the working memory to process the core information, and this results in cognitive load.

GERMANE LOAD

Germane load occurs when there is a modification of a schema. When schemas are modified in some way, this results in deep and trans-formative learning, because pupils' thinking is altered in some way. An example of this is when pupils progress from a basic understanding of an aspect of subject content to a more advanced understanding of that same subject content. Their understanding deepens, and they displace their basic understandings of the content because they have developed a more sophisticated understanding. Teachers should therefore aim to increase germane load in lessons as this results in a shift in thinking.

CRITICAL QUESTIONS

+ What are the implications of working memory for planning lessons?
+ What are the implications of long-term memory for curriculum planning?

EXTENDED THINKING

+ Take one aspect of subject content in your specialist subject. Consider how pupils progress from a basic understanding of this content to a more advanced and sophisticated understanding of this content.
+ What strategies might you use in this example to support pupils to think in a more advanced way about this subject content?

RETRIEVAL PRACTICE

Learning does not just 'sink in'. It requires conscious effort, determination and some practice (Sherrington, 2019). A useful definition of retrieval practice is provided by Kate Jones: *'Retrieval practice refers to the act of recalling learned information from memory (with little or no support) and every time that information is retrieved, or an answer is generated, it changes the original memory to make it stronger'* (Jones, 2019, p 15). Jones (2019) reminds us that retrieval practice is a powerful learning tool. It is intended to be low-stakes or no-stakes, and the focus is not on recording marks or grades. The act of retrieving content that is stored in the long-term memory supports understanding and automaticity. The seminal work of Peterson and Peterson (1959) demonstrated that information stored in the working memory is lost within 18 to 30 seconds if it is not rehearsed. Once information has been rehearsed in the working memory, it is stored in the long-term memory, but it will be forgotten quickly if it is not retrieved or rehearsed (Jones, 2019). Retrieval practice is a central element of Rosenshine's (2010; 2012) principles of effective instruction. Examples of retrieval practice include the following:

+ low-stakes quizzes or tests;

+ labelling diagrams;

+ completing mind maps or retrieval grids;

+ writing a list;

+ asking pupils to write a summary.

SPACED OR DISTRIBUTED PRACTICE

Spaced practice is when subject content is taught over time with gaps in between so that learners almost forget the content (see Chapter 7). Content is then revisited at a subsequent point in the teaching sequence, retrieved and built on. This means that content is not just covered once, but is revisited multiple times, perhaps over a single term of teaching or across an academic year. Retrieval is deliberately built in to the process so that content that has previously been learned and committed to the long-term memory is then reprocessed in the working memory. This supports both fluency and automaticity.

CASE STUDY

RETRIEVAL PRACTICE

WHOLE SCHOOL

Subject leaders in a secondary school noticed that pupils were not remembering the curriculum they had been taught. When they investigated this further, they noticed that the design of the curriculum did not provide opportunities for pupils to revisit the knowledge they had been taught. The curriculum was crowded with content, and pupils were not being given opportunities to revisit content they had stored in their long-term memories. Teachers were asked to develop a range of retrieval practices. A retrieval activity was planned for each lesson to support pupils to revisit content from the previous lesson. During a unit of work, retrieval tasks were planned to allow pupils to revisit content from the previous lessons. Retrieval tasks were also planned for various points during the academic year, to support pupils to revisit knowledge that they had been taught earlier in the year.

CRITICAL QUESTIONS

+ What are the advantages of retrieval tasks?

+ What types of retrieval tasks might you use?

EVIDENCE-BASED PRACTICE

Direct instruction is particularly effective in supporting lower-attaining pupils to improve (Coombe and Martin, 2019). For mastery and fluency of subject content, evidence suggests that pupils need five times more practice than most teachers expect (Engelmann, 1992). Direct instruction can improve motivation because it leads directly to academic achievement, and academic achievement is a predictor of motivation (Garon-Carrier et al, 2016).

SUMMARY

This chapter addressed the concept of cognitive load and described the different types of cognitive load. It covered some essential pedagogical approaches, including modelling, scaffolding and fading. It addressed the principles of spaced or distributed practice.

CHECKLIST

+ Cognitive load is reduced by chunking knowledge.

+ Modelling, scaffolding and fading are components of direct instruction.

+ Direct instruction benefits all pupils.

+ Pupils need time to practise working on subject content. This leads to automaticity.

+ Curriculum design that reflects spaced practice supports long-term retention of knowledge.

FURTHER READING

Benjamin, Z and Main, P (nd) Cognitive Load Theory: A Teacher's Guide. [online] Available at: www.structural-learning.com/post/cognitive-load-theory-a-teachers-guide (accessed 28 August 2022).

Karpicke, J D (2017) Retrieval-based Learning: A Decade of Progress. In Wixted, J T (ed) *Cognitive Psychology of Memory, Vol 2 of Learning and Memory: A Comprehensive Reference* (pp 487–514). Oxford: Academic Press.

Muijs, D (2019) Developing the Education Inspection Framework: How We Used Cognitive Load Theory. [online] Available at: https://educationinspection.blog.gov.uk/2019/02/13/developing-the-education-inspection-framework-how-we-used-cognitive-load-theory/ (accessed 28 August 2022).

Pastötter, B and Bäuml, K-H T (2019) Testing Enhances Subsequent Learning in Older Adults. *Psychology and Aging*, 34(3): 242–50.

Roediger, H L, III and Karpicke, J D (2006) Test-enhanced Learning: Taking Memory Tests Improves Long-term Retention. *Psychological Science*, 17(3): 249–55.

✚ CHAPTER 7

ADAPTIVE TEACHING
IN THE CURRICULUM

CHAPTER OBJECTIVES

After reading this chapter you will understand:

+ the SEND Code of Practice;

+ the meaning of adaptive teaching;

+ adaptive teaching strategies to use in the classroom.

INTRODUCTION

Adaptive teaching is a key aspect of the Initial Teacher Training Core Content Framework and the Early Career Framework. This chapter introduces you to the principles that underpin adaptive teaching. It provides an overview of adaptive teaching strategies that you can use in the classroom to support learners with SEND. It introduces the principles of the SEND Code of Practice (DfE, 2015) and provides a brief overview of the graduated approach, which is used for pupils with SEND. The chapter also outlines some strategies for supporting pupils who have English as an additional language (EAL). From the outset, we emphasise that we are not automatically linking EAL with SEND. However, some pupils with EAL may require some adaptations to support them in their learning regardless of whether they have SEND.

RESPONSIBILITIES OF SCHOOLS FOR PUPILS WITH SEND

This section introduces the key statutory responsibilities of schools as set out in the SEND Code of Practice and describes the graduated approach.

SEND CODE OF PRACTICE

The SEND Code of Practice states that local authorities and schools must have regard to:

+ *the views, wishes and feelings of the child or young person, and the child's parents*

+ *the importance of the child or young person, and the child's parents, participating as fully as possible in decisions, and being provided with the information and support necessary to enable participation in those decisions*

+ *the need to support the young person, and the child's parents, in order to facilitate the development of the child or young person and to help them achieve the best possible educational and other outcomes, preparing them effectively for adulthood*

(DfE, 2015, para 1.1, p 19)

These principles are designed to ensure high-quality provision for learners with SEND through the early identification of needs, effective early intervention to address these needs and more effective collaboration between education, health and social care services. The principles are also designed to ensure that young people and their parents take an increased role in decision-making processes and that they have greater choice.

The code provides:

+ a much clearer focus on the participation of young people and parents;

+ a 0–25 framework for supporting young people into adulthood;

+ an increased emphasis on the need for schools and teachers to have high aspirations for all learners, including those with SEND;

+ an increased emphasis on outcomes (including achievement/ attainment/levels of independence/employment/access to FE) for learners with SEND;

+ an increased emphasis on collaboration between services through the introduction of 0–25 Education, Health and Care plans which replace Statements of Special Educational Need;

+ increased choice in decision-making for parents through the introduction of personal budgets for learners with Education, Health and Care plans.

For those learners who are formally identified as needing SEND support, schools are required to operate a four-part cycle. This is known as a 'graduated approach'. According to the Code of Practice (see DfE, 2015), as part of this process, schools should:

+ assess pupils' needs through the analysis of assessment data and consultation with pupils, parents and other services where applicable;

+ plan appropriate interventions to address pupils' needs both in school and at home;

+ do interventions to address pupils' needs;

+ review the effectiveness of interventions on pupils' progress in a timely manner.

Parents, carers and pupils should be involved fully at each stage of the graduated approach. Effective interventions improve outcomes for pupils.

Thus, it is vital that teachers monitor the impact that specific interventions have on pupils' progress. This can only be achieved if there is a clear baseline assessment prior to the pupil being placed on an intervention. If an intervention appears not to be improving outcomes for learners, then it should be discontinued and a more effective intervention should be implemented. Regular review of pupils' progress and other outcomes throughout the duration of an intervention should ensure that teachers are able to identify whether that intervention is effective. According to the Code of Practice:

The class or subject teacher should remain responsible for working with the child on a daily basis. Where the interventions involve group or one-to-one teaching away from the main class or subject teacher, they should still retain responsibility for the pupil. They should work closely with any teaching assistants or specialist staff involved, to plan and assess the impact of support and interventions and how they can be linked to class-room teaching.

(DfE, 2015, para 6.52, p 101)

There is a clear expectation in the code that:

The first response ... should be high quality teaching targeted at [the child's] areas of weakness. Where progress continues to be less than expected the class or subject teacher, working with the SENCO [Special Educational Needs Co-ordinator], should assess whether the child has SEN [special educational needs]. While informally gathering evidence (including the views of the pupil and their parents) schools should not delay in putting in place extra teaching or other rigorous interventions designed to secure better progress, where required. The pupil's response to such support can help identify their particular needs.

(DfE, 2015, para 6.19, p 95)

GRADUATED APPROACH

The graduated approach is a cycle of intervention that schools must follow when pupils are first identified as having SEND (see Figure 7.1).

114

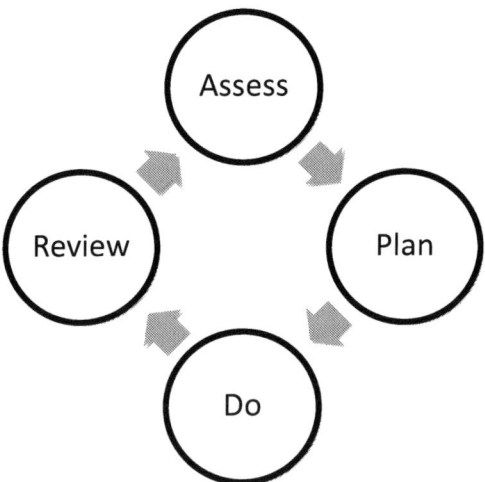

Figure 7.1 The graduated approach

ASSESS

Schools should ensure that:

+ there is a clear process for identifying pupils with SEND;

+ pupils are involved in the assessment process;

+ parents are involved in the assessment process;

+ subsequent planning and teaching is informed by assessments.

PLAN

Schools should ensure that:

+ expectations of the pupil remain high;

+ they have high aspirations for the pupil and that the pupil shares these;

+ access to high-quality adaptive teaching for individual pupils;

+ the SENCO supports class or subject teachers in planning to meet the needs of the pupil;

+ all colleagues who work with the pupil are aware of their specific needs;

+ parents are consulted and included in the planning process;

+ pupils are consulted and included in the planning process;

+ class and subject teachers remain accountable for planning to meet the needs of the pupil;

+ skills and knowledge developed during intervention sessions are subsequently applied in the classroom when the intervention is not taking place;

+ class and subject teachers are fully aware of the progress a pupil is making during an intervention and take account of this in their daily planning;

+ those interventions are fully evaluated according to the extent to which they address the needs of the pupil and accelerate achievement. There is no expectation that schools will plan in a particular way to meet the needs of individual pupils. Some schools will continue to use individual education plans, but there is no legal requirement to do so and schools should adopt innovative approaches that best meet the needs of specific pupils.

DO

It is important that the planned actions to address the specific need are implemented. The SENCO will play an important role in ensuring that planned interventions take place and that the impact of these interventions is evaluated. All pupils deserve to be taught by a qualified teacher, and it is important that class and subject teachers continue to teach pupils with SEND. Subject teachers remain accountable for pupils' progress, and teachers' involvement in teaching pupils with SEND is critical to successful outcomes

In cases where teaching assistants are responsible for delivering interventions for addressing specific areas of need, the teaching assistant:

+ must have the knowledge, skills and training to deliver the intervention;

+ should have received up-to-date training in the intervention;

+ should know how to use an intervention flexibly to meet the specific needs of pupils.

REVIEW

It is important that schools do not wait for formal reviews to evaluate the impact of the provision offered for pupils with SEND. The SEND provision should be reviewed regularly and adaptations should be made to the teaching to ensure that pupils get the opportunity to catch up. When reviewing the quality of provision, SENCOs and class and subject teachers need to consider the following points.

+ Are the pupils on track to achieve their targets?

+ Is the gap narrowing between pupils with and without SEND?

+ Is the provision enabling learners with SEND to make progress?

+ What are the views of support staff?

+ What are the views of the pupil?

+ What are the views of the parent?

Interventions that are not successful and are not having a desired impact on pupil progress should be discontinued and replaced with more effective interventions. Additionally, interventions need to be time-limited rather than permanent. The aim of an intervention is to address gaps in learning so that the pupil can catch up with their peers.

CRITICAL QUESTIONS

+ Why is it important that teachers take responsibility for planning and teaching pupils with SEND?

+ How can subject teachers support teaching assistants so that they are better prepared for supporting pupils with SEND in lessons?

WHAT IS ADAPTIVE TEACHING?

Adaptive teaching is both a mindset and a practice. In relation to the former, it requires teachers to have high expectations of all pupils and to believe that all pupils have an entitlement to work towards achieving the ambitious end points stated in the national curriculum. Adaptive teaching requires teachers to displace traditional practices associated with 'differentiation'. Grouping pupils into ability groups and designing tasks that require different levels of challenge are practices often associated with differentiation. The problem with differentiation is that the practices associated with it limit pupil achievement by creating artificial 'ceilings' for pupils to reach. These practices serve to widen attainment gaps between pupils with SEND and those without SEND as the pupils who are subjected to the lowest level of challenge are often pupils with SEND.

Adaptive teaching requires teachers to adopt the mindset that most pupils can learn the same component knowledge identified in the curriculum plan. Some pupils may require specific adaptations to enable them to learn that component knowledge to a state of automaticity, and they may also need to overlearn specific components of knowledge through additional practice and consolidation. Adaptive teaching therefore requires teachers to assume that most pupils can follow the same trajectory in learning. Some pupils will achieve automaticity with some components at different rates, but the ambitious end points of the curriculum are relevant to most pupils.

Allowing pupils to follow alternative learning trajectories should be the exception, though it may be justified for pupils with complex SEND – for example, pupils who have profound and multiple learning disabilities. In the case of pupils with highly complex needs, the national curriculum end points might not be appropriate, and these pupils may need to follow an alternative curriculum.

CRITICAL QUESTIONS

+ What practices are associated with differentiation?
+ What practices are associated with adaptive teaching?
+ Why do you think the focus is shifting away from the principles of differentiation to adaptive teaching?

EVIDENCE-BASED PRACTICE

According to Davis and Florian (2004), there is little evidence to support the use of distinctive teaching approaches for children with specific learning difficulties, although responding to individual differences is crucial. In-class differentiation, using different tasks or different resources for specific pupils, *'has generally not been shown to have much impact on pupils' attainment'* (Ofsted, 2019a, p 17). In Scheerens and Bosker's (1997) meta-analysis of research on school effectiveness, differentiation showed a null or a very weak relationship with pupils' outcomes.

Evidence on the effects of grouping by ability suggests that it makes very little difference to pupil achievement (Higgins et al, 2013). Although it is claimed that ability grouping can allow teachers to target pupils' specific needs, it can also create an exaggerated sense of within-group homogeneity and between-group heterogeneity in the teacher's mind (Stipek, 2010). This can result in teachers failing to respond to children's individual needs by assuming that all pupils within a group have the same needs. Ability grouping can also result in teachers going too fast with high-ability groups and too slow with low-ability groups.

ADAPTIVE TEACHING STRATEGIES

This section outlines some pedagogical approaches that you can use in the classroom to support adaptive teaching. The list is not exhaustive.

CHUNKING

Chunking is the practice of breaking down curriculum content into smaller, manageable components of knowledge rather than teaching too many subject concepts or facts at the same time. This is an effective strategy for all pupils because if pupils are given too much information in a lesson, this results in cognitive load. The working memory has a limited capacity and can only process a small amount of information at any one time. This is because when pupils learn new subject content for the first time, the working memory must work to full capacity to process that new learning. If pupils are asked to process too much spoken or written language, the phonological loop in the working memory quickly becomes overloaded. If pupils are asked to process too much new visual information in a lesson, the visuospatial sketchpad becomes overloaded. Limiting the number of instructions and reducing the number of subject facts, concepts and principles that are introduced in a single lesson are all examples of chunking content so that the working memory is only required to process a limited amount of new information. You will have heard the phrase 'less is more!'

WORKED EXAMPLES AND GOOD EXAMPLES

While many pupils benefit from seeing worked examples, these are extremely helpful for pupils with SEND and those with EAL. Worked examples typically include steps. In physics, pupils might be provided with a worked example of how to solve an equation with the steps through the problem clearly outlined. In mathematics, teachers can use worked examples to demonstrate the steps through a mathematical problem. Good examples might not include steps, but typically exemplify the features that pupils are required to demonstrate. In English, teachers might provide pupils with a good example of a well-constructed persuasive response that includes the structural and grammatical features of persuasive texts. Seeing good examples and worked examples provides pupils with security and improves outcomes.

PRE-TEACHING

Pre-teaching is an excellent pedagogical approach. It is particularly effective when teachers can identify specific pupils who might struggle with the subject content in a specific lesson. In pre-teaching, pupils are taught the subject content prior to the lesson. This provides them with an additional opportunity to master the content so that they can make better progress in the lesson. Pre-teaching can be used to introduce pupils to subject vocabulary, concepts, laws or facts that they might find difficult. When pupils are introduced to the subject content a second time in the actual lesson, their working memory does not have to work as hard to process the content because they are already familiar with it. Pre-teaching is also useful if you are introducing pupils to a specific resource, such as a key text, in a lesson. It enables pupils to develop familiarity with the resource so that when they are in the lesson, their working memory does not need to work as hard.

CRITICAL QUESTIONS

+ How can subject teachers in secondary schools realistically provide opportunities for pre-teaching?
+ What are the advantages and disadvantages of pre-teaching?

GRAPHIC ORGANISERS

A range of graphic organisers might be useful to help pupils organise their ideas when they are recording them through writing. For example, a mind map can effectively support pupils with dyslexia to organise their notes.

TECHNOLOGY

Technology (hardware and software) can be used effectively to support pupils who have specific barriers to learning. Pupils with dyslexia may benefit from using a laptop in the lesson so that they can record their learning using word processing software. Electronic spell checkers are also helpful if spelling is a specific barrier for some pupils. Some pupils with literacy difficulties might benefit from speech-to-text software or a voice recorder if they struggle to make notes at speed.

CRITICAL QUESTIONS

+ What technological adaptations have you seen being used in schools?
+ Can you identify other technological adaptations that could be used in the classroom?

OVERLEARNING

Some pupils might need longer to achieve automaticity with specific components of knowledge. They might need to practise a specific component of knowledge more than other pupils and have regular opportunities to revisit and consolidate their learning. Through repeated practice (overlearning) pupils will eventually achieve automaticity in the component and be able to move on to the next component.

CRITICAL QUESTIONS

+ Can you identify aspects of knowledge that you have had to overlearn to achieve automaticity?

+ How can secondary teachers realistically provide opportunities for overlearning?

DUAL CODING

Dual coding essentially refers to the practice of presenting information to pupils in different formats. An example of this is when teachers use explanations in lessons to explain subject content but then support their explanations with visual information, such as a diagram. In this example, the diagram can support the pupils' understanding of the teacher's explanations. This can be a useful strategy for all pupils, but it is particularly useful for pupils with SEND because information can then be processed through different channels. Dual coding is more effective when information presented in one format supports the information presented in another format. It does not result in cognitive load because the spoken explanations and the visual information (diagram) are processed in separate sub-systems of the working memory. Spoken language is processed in the phonological loop and visual information is processed in the visuospatial sketchpad. Both slave systems can operate concurrently, and there is therefore no conflict. However, if visual information does not link directly to spoken explanations, the visual information can distract learners from the explanations that the teacher is providing in the lessons. When this happens, this can result in cognitive load.

CASE STUDY

DUAL CODING

WHOLE SCHOOL

During a series of lesson visits, subject leaders noticed that teachers were relying on spoken language to provide pupils with explanations of subject content. In some cases, pupils were struggling to process the information. Leaders introduced the concept of dual coding to teachers during a staff development session. Teachers were asked to consider supporting their verbal explanations with diagrams, pictures and other forms of visual information. The teachers noticed that this strategy helped pupils to process the lesson content. They had initially thought that introducing visual materials in lessons to support verbal explanations would result in cognitive load. However, following the training they now knew that the working memory can process visual information and spoken language concurrently, thus not resulting in cognitive load.

CRITICAL QUESTIONS

+ When might this strategy be useful?

+ When might this strategy be less effective?

SPACED OR DISTRIBUTED LEARNING

Spacing learning out over time improves long-term retention. When teachers use this strategy, subject content is taught and then revisited later in a teaching sequence after a gap in time. This provides an opportunity for pupils to almost forget the content. When the content is revisited, teachers support pupils to retrieve the knowledge from their long-term memory and then build on it further to deepen the knowledge. The teaching sequence might be represented as shown in Figure 7.2. The letters in the figure represent curriculum content.

Figure 7.2 A teaching sequence

Curriculum design that reflects spaced or distributed learning is beneficial to all pupils because it ensures that subject content is revisited and therefore transferred from the long-term memory to the working memory. However, pupils with SEND might need to practise one component of knowledge (eg content X) several times by overlearning it before moving on to the next component of knowledge (content Y).

EVIDENCE-BASED PRACTICE

Spaced or distributed practice is the practice of spacing learning out over time. Subject content is taught and then interspersed with different subject content before being revisited. Evidence suggests that although this approach to curriculum planning makes learning more difficult (EEF, 2021), it is likely to lead to long-term retention of subject content. This is because it challenges children to revisit information that has been almost forgotten, thus activating the long-term memory. Long-term retention of knowledge is supported if learning is spread out with gaps in between to allow forgetting. This 'is one of the most general and robust effects from across the entire history of experimental research on learning and memory' (Bjork and Bjork, 2011, p 59).

SUPPORTING PUPILS WITH EAL

Pupils with EAL do not necessarily have SEND. Their difficulties in learning may arise because they are in the process of learning another language rather than due to an underlying difficulty. They will benefit from being immersed in a social and communication-rich environment. They may also benefit from a structured language and communication intervention. Pre-teaching vocabulary and texts is a useful strategy to maximise their participation during lessons. Aim to support your explanations and modelling with visual cues, manipulatives and other resources. Provide concrete manipulative resources to support their learning and allow them to code-switch between English and their first language if they cannot identify the word in English.

Cummins' (1980) model of bilingualism demonstrates that pupils will draw on understandings from their first language in order to support them to learn an additional language. This existing understanding acts as an 'anchor' to further learning of and through additional languages (Bligh, 2014). Cummins (1980) refers to this as common underlying proficiency (CUP), which includes basic interpersonal communication skills (BICS) and cognitive academic language proficiency (CALP).

BICS refers to social and conversational language and the surface skills of listening and speaking, including observing non-verbal behaviours and reactions, voice cues and imagery. These are often learnt through playful social participation with speakers of the same language (Bligh, 2014). CALP relates specifically to the language of the academic classroom, where non-verbal cues are typically absent and literacy demands are much higher. This therefore includes the necessary knowledge and skills required to work academically in a classroom and the ability to think in and use language as a tool for learning (Bligh, 2014).

The model is represented by two icebergs that are separated above the surface of the water. The peak of each iceberg represents a language, and despite appearing different above water, they merge into one below the surface. It is the CUP, which is found below the surface, that enables bilingual learners to function in more than one language. However, if a pupil is lacking CUP in one language, then it is likely that they will find it difficult to learn another language.

It is therefore clear that language and communication interventions in a second language will be ineffective if a pupil has not met the required CUP threshold in their first language. This has clear implications for the content and structure of intervention programmes. It demonstrates that interventions must be appropriate and responsive to the needs of individual pupils in relation to the explicit and meaningful development of BICS and CALP. For example, offering pupils the opportunity to practise verbal conversations is not cognitively demanding and, as such, will support the development of BICS. This is because this activity allows pupils to practise conversational language and listening and speaking skills. In addition, scientific investigations will be cognitively demanding and promote the development of CALP. This is because scientific investigations expose pupils to subject-specific vocabulary and the knowledge and skills required to work and think academically.

EXTENDED THINKING

+ What are the disadvantages of removing pupils from class for intervention work?

+ What are the advantages and disadvantages of assigning the label of SEND to pupils?

CASE STUDY

SUPPORT FOR PUPILS WITH SEND

WHOLE SCHOOL

A secondary school has a large number of pupils with SEND. The teachers had recently completed some training on evidence-based strategies to support pupils with SEND. The following strategies were used in lessons, though not all in one lesson:

+ writing frames, partially completed examples, knowledge organisers, essay prompts, bookmarks, structure strips, sentence starters;

+ reminders of what equipment is needed for each lesson, and classroom routines;

+ scaffolding discussion of texts and promoting prediction, questioning, clarification and summarising;

+ worked examples with the teacher modelling self-regulation and thought processes – for example, a teacher might teach a pupil a strategy for summarising a paragraph by initially 'thinking aloud' while also identifying the topic of the paragraph to model this process to the pupil; they might then give the pupil the opportunity to practise this skill;

+ using visual aids and concrete examples to promote discussion and links in learning;

+ chunking the task through provision of checklists or instructions on a whiteboard, or providing one question at a time – this helps to reduce distractions and avoid overloading working memory;

+ using prompt sheets to help pupils evaluate their progress; these can also have ideas for further support;

+ allocating temporary groups so teachers can set up opportunities for collaborative learning – for example, opportunities to read and analyse source texts, complete graphic organisers, carry out a skill independently, remember a fact or understand a concept;

+ pre-teaching key vocabulary or subject content;

+ using a visualiser to model worked examples;

+ using technology applications, such as online quizzes;

+ using speech generating apps to enable note-taking and extended writing.

CRITICAL QUESTIONS

+ Can you add to these strategies?

+ Which of these strategies might benefit all pupils?

SUMMARY

This chapter provided an overview of the SEND Code of Practice. It also provided some strategies that can support adaptive teaching. These include chunking, worked examples and pre-teaching. The chapter introduced critical debate about the practice of differentiation. We argued that differentiation can widen the ability gap between different groups of pupils, and therefore setting pupils different tasks or placing pupils on different curricula should be the exception and not the norm.

CHECKLIST

+ Differentiation widens the ability gap.

+ Adaptive teaching requires teachers to raise their expectations of pupils.

$\longrightarrow$

+ Adaptive teaching does not place an artificial limit on what learners can achieve.

+ Adaptive teaching involves modifying teaching or tasks so that pupils can achieve their full potential.

+ Learners with SEND or EAL often make the least progress because they spend the most time being supported by teaching assistants.

FURTHER READING

Deunk, M I, Smale-Jacobse, A E, de Boer, H, Doolaardand, S and Bosker, R J (2018) Effective Differentiation Practices: A Systematic Review and Meta-analysis of Studies on the Cognitive Effects of Differentiation Practices in Primary Education. *Educational Research Review*, 24(1): 31–54.

Hattie, J (2009) *Visible Learning: A Synthesis of Meta-analysis Relating to Achievement*. London: Routledge.

Mould, K (2020) EEF Blog: Five Evidence-based Strategies to Support High-quality Teaching for Pupils with SEND. [online] Available at: https://educationendowmentfoundation.org.uk/news/five-evidence-based-strategies-pupils-with-special-educational-needs-send (accessed 28 August 2022).

✚ CHAPTER 8

THE CURRICULUM AS THE PROGRESSION MODEL

CHAPTER OBJECTIVES

After reading this chapter you will understand:

+ what is meant by 'progress';

+ how to design a curriculum to ensure that pupils make progress;

+ the relationship between the curriculum progression framework and assessment.

INTRODUCTION

This chapter introduces you to the concept of the curriculum as the progression framework. In recent times, teachers have often used national benchmarks to make judgements about pupils' progress. Teachers may have relied on statutory assessments at the end of key stages to determine how much progress pupils have made as they move from one key stage to the next. However, these judgements about progress are not reliable. This is because statutory assessments do not assess the whole domain of a subject. In this chapter, we unpick what we understand by progress, and we link this to the curriculum. We provide examples of how to design curriculum frameworks that enable pupils to demonstrate progress, and we explain the relationship between curriculum progression and assessment.

WHAT DO WE UNDERSTAND BY PROGRESS?

Progress is simply knowing, remembering and doing more in a subject. Subject leaders take responsibility for designing a subject curriculum that enables pupils to meet the ambitious end points of the national curriculum. These broad goals are stated in the national curriculum but are often not broken down further. Subject leaders must therefore identify the component knowledge that pupils need to learn to achieve the ambitious goals of the national curriculum. As pupils progress through the subject curriculum, they develop more knowledge of the subject, and their knowledge should become deeper. Pupils make progress when they learn the curriculum as intended. When they know more, remember more and can do more of the subject, they are effectively making progress. Therefore, it is accurate to say that progress cannot always be determined through a numerical score or grade assigned to the pupil. It can be a qualitative judgement, but it should always be linked to the knowledge that is outlined in the curriculum progression framework.

Knowing more about a subject might mean knowing more subject facts or understanding specific subject concepts. Teachers will need to deliberately plan how to support pupils to *remember* the knowledge they are learning. *Doing more* in a subject might mean being able to apply the knowledge that has been gained to solve problems, or being able to demonstrate the required disciplinary knowledge to work as a scientist, historian or geographer, for example.

130

THE CURRICULUM AS PROGRESSION

A well-sequenced curriculum should gradually develop pupils' knowledge of the subject content. The national curriculum is not a progression framework because it only identifies the composite knowledge that pupils need to achieve at the end of Key Stage 3 and Key Stage 4. The aspects of component knowledge that enable pupils to achieve the composite knowledge in the national curriculum are the building blocks of progress. As pupils progress through the curriculum, they start to know more about the subject. They gradually start to learn each aspect of component knowledge, and their knowledge builds. Knowing and remembering more of the curriculum is a reliable indicator that pupils are making progress because it shows that pupils are mastering increasingly complex subject content. However, progress is only assured if the curriculum is correctly sequenced in the first place.

The sequencing of component knowledge should result in modification of schemas as pupils progress through the subject curriculum. Content needs to get more challenging so that it requires pupils to think hard about the subject. It is not sufficient to design a subject curriculum where pupils study different topics as they move through the curriculum. The sequencing of content should provide opportunities for revisiting subject content and deepening pupils' understanding of that content. This means that they are developing a more advanced understanding of the content, and learning that occurs later in a sequence may not easily 'fit in' with what pupils already know. The new learning needs to be accommodated, and schemas that have already formed may need to be modified to accommodate the new knowledge. Progress is therefore knowing more, remembering more and being able to do more of the subject curriculum.

SUPPORTING PUPILS TO REMEMBER MORE

Pupils do not automatically remember the knowledge they are taught in lessons. Even if they do remember the knowledge at the end of a lesson, there is no guarantee that they will remember the subject content in a week's time, a month's time or six months' time.

Remembering the subject content is a key factor in determining whether pupils have made progress. New subject content is processed in the working memory and transferred to the long-term memory. However, for knowledge to become automatic, pupils need to work with that subject content on a regular basis, and therefore knowledge that is stored in the long-term memory must be retrieved and reprocessed in the working memory many times before pupils achieve automaticity.

Teachers can use a range of retrieval activities in lessons to support the development of automaticity in relation to component knowledge. These might include:

+ having a short quiz at the start of a lesson to test pupils' knowledge of the previous lesson;

+ providing opportunities for pupils to complete labels on diagrams;

+ asking pupils to list the pertinent points from a previous lesson;

+ asking pupils to complete a mind map to record pertinent facts;

+ using multiple-choice-style low-stakes assessments;

+ asking a pupil to explain subject content to another pupil;

+ using regular quizzes during a unit of work to assess component knowledge.

CRITICAL QUESTIONS

+ Why is retrieval so important?

+ If a pupil is making progress, what does this mean?

+ How does pupil progress relate to the curriculum as a progression framework?

THE PROBLEM WITH BLOOM'S TAXONOMY

Bloom's taxonomy (1956) identifies various levels of skills, arranged in a hierarchy. It positions *knowledge* and *understanding* at the lowest levels within the hierarchy, and *application* at a higher level, thus assuming that application is more complex than knowing or understanding something. This is deeply problematic because some knowledge is extremely complex and some forms of application are very easy to do. Therefore, it does not necessarily follow that application requires a higher level of thinking than knowing or understanding something. Bloom's taxonomy is therefore not helpful in determining levels of challenge within a classroom.

KNOWLEDGE AND SKILLS

The subject curriculum often identifies intended knowledge that pupils need to learn. Typically, this might be a subject fact or subject concept that pupils need to know and understand. In addition, the subject curriculum might specify skills that pupils need to have. However, the distinction between knowledge and skills is not helpful. This is because to execute a skill, it is necessary to first have secure underpinning knowledge. As an example, pupils need good vocabulary knowledge to be able to execute the skill of reading for meaning. In addition, pupils also need good knowledge of the alphabetic code to decode new words. Pupils need to have knowledge of graphemes and phonemes to be able to spell unfamiliar words, or knowledge of alphabetical ordering to be able to demonstrate the skill of locating words in a dictionary. When we are demonstrating the skill of driving a car, we need knowledge of the Highway Code to be able to drive effectively.

These examples illustrate that it is actually very difficult and often unhelpful to separate out knowledge and skills. Skills are dependent on knowledge, and therefore the subject curriculum should simply specify the knowledge that pupils need to be able to meet the ambitious end points of the national curriculum.

EXTENDED THINKING

+ What are the limitations of using statutory assessment tests to assess pupils' knowledge?

+ What are the limitations of assessing pupils' subject knowledge against age-related expectations?

CASE STUDY

SEQUENCING IN CURRICULUM DESIGN

WHOLE SCHOOL

Arif is a geography subject leader. He was in the process of developing a new curriculum plan for geography at Key Stage 3 and Key Stage 4. He first looked at the national curriculum to identify the national curriculum goals that pupils are expected to attain at the end of each key stage. Arif produced a grid and wrote the goals in the final column of the grid. Each goal was separated by a horizontal line. He then worked backwards from each goal to identify the component knowledge the pupils need to learn in each year to achieve the goal. Each year was demarcated using a vertical line. Arif checked the sequence of the components to ensure that knowledge deepened as pupils progressed from one year to another, and he edited the plan where appropriate. He then produced a final version of the plan.

CRITICAL QUESTIONS

+ Would you follow a similar process to the geography leader?

+ What might you do differently?

SEQUENCING IN SUBJECT CURRICULUMS

Some examples of sequencing in subject curriculums are given below.

CURRICULUM SEQUENCING IN ENGLISH

One of the ambitious end points of Key Stage 3 is for pupils to be able to *'participate in formal debates and structured discussions, summarising and/or building on what has been said'* (DfE, 2014, p 17).

CRITICAL QUESTIONS

+ What component knowledge do pupils need to be able to take part in discussions and debates?

+ How might you sequence this knowledge within a unit of work?

+ How can discussions and debates be integrated across the whole curriculum.

CURRICULUM SEQUENCING IN MATHEMATICS

One of the ambitious end points of Key Stage 3 in geometry is for pupils to 'derive and apply formulae to calculate and solve problems involving: perimeter and area of triangles, parallelograms, trapezia, volume of cuboids (including cubes) and other prisms (including cylinders)' (DfE, 2014, p 46).

CRITICAL QUESTIONS

+ What component knowledge do pupils need to understand area?

+ How might you sequence the component knowledge across several units of work to enable pupils to achieve this national curriculum goal?

CURRICULUM SEQUENCING IN SCIENCE

One of the ambitious end points of Key Stage 3 is for pupils to know about 'the rock cycle and the formation of igneous, sedimentary, and metamorphic rocks' (DfE, 2014, p 63). This content might be taught in a single unit of work that introduces pupils to the following component knowledge:

+ what rocks are;

+ porous rocks;

+ igneous rocks;

+ sedimentary rocks;

+ metamorphic rocks;

+ the rock cycle;

+ weathering.

CRITICAL QUESTIONS

+ If you were designing this curriculum, would you change it or follow this progression framework?

+ How would you ensure that knowledge of the subject content is revisited over time?

+ What knowledge would you assess, and when would you assess?

CURRICULUM SEQUENCING IN HISTORY

One of the ambitious end points of Key Stage 3 history is that pupils must learn how to 'use historical terms and concepts in increasingly sophisticated ways' (DfE, 2014, p 95). It is important that pupils are not left to deduce historical knowledge by exploring source materials. Teachers need to teach historical knowledge explicitly and directly, and pupils should investigate source material with good content knowledge that is secure. One of the problems of inquiry-based learning is that it often requires pupils to construct their own knowledge through the process of interacting with source materials. The danger of this is that pupils might be learning the wrong information or developing misconceptions. Although pupils do need to develop knowledge of how historians investigate the past (disciplinary knowledge), they should not be left to deduce historical facts if they only have a partial understanding of the historical concepts and facts. Teachers should therefore ensure that the substance of history (substantive knowledge) is taught directly and reinforced through effective curriculum sequencing so that substantive historical concepts are taught and revisited through different topics.

At Key Stage 3, the concept of 'revolution' might be revisited through different topics to build on and deepen pupils' understanding of the concept (see Figure 8.1).

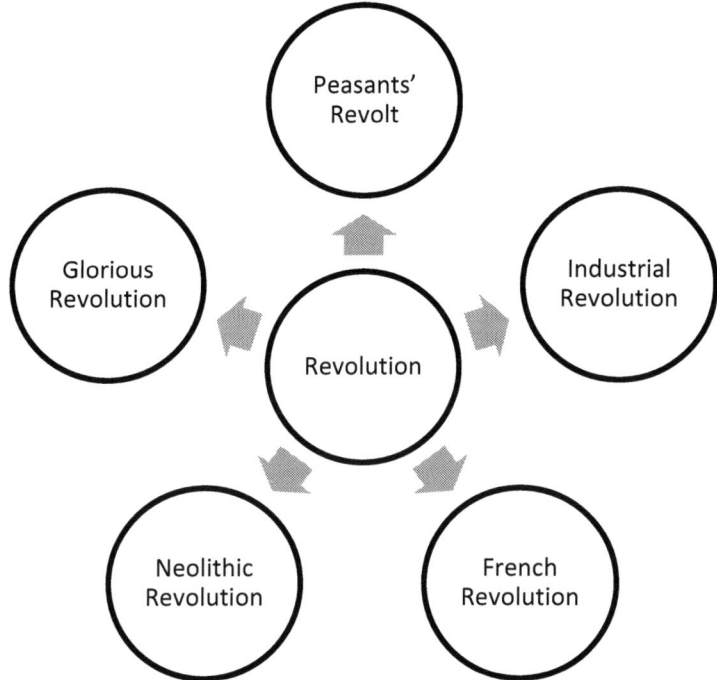

Figure 8.1 Component knowledge for the concept of revolution

CRITICAL QUESTIONS

+ What are the substantive concepts that pupils need to learn in history at Key Stages 3 and 4?

+ How might an assessment framework be developed in relation to these substantive concepts?

CURRICULUM SEQUENCING IN COMPUTING

One of the ambitious end points of Key Stage 3 computing is to '*understand a range of ways to use technology safely, respectfully, responsibly and securely, including protecting their online identity and privacy; recognise inappropriate content, contact and conduct and know how to report concerns*' (DfE, 2014, p 87).

A curriculum sequence might be developed in a unit of work to iden-tify component knowledge that underpins this national curriculum goal. This component knowledge might include the following:

+ online dangers;

+ data protection and right to privacy;

+ illegal content;

+ reporting concerns.

CRITICAL QUESTIONS

+ How might this content be further broken down?

+ How might you ensure that knowledge builds and deepens as pupils progress through the component knowledge?

CURRICULUM SEQUENCING IN GEOGRAPHY

One of the ambitious end points of Key Stage 3 geography is to 'under-stand physical geography relating to: geological timescales and plate tectonics; rocks, weathering and soils; weather and climate, including the change in climate from the Ice Age to the present; and glaciation, hydrology and coasts' (DfE, 2014, p 92). This composite knowledge might be taught through a series of lessons as follows:

+ the Ice Age;

+ how glaciers form;

+ glacial erosion;

+ glacial landforms.

CRITICAL QUESTIONS

+ If you were designing this curriculum, would you change it or follow this progression framework?

+ How would you ensure that knowledge of the subject content is revisited over time?

+ What knowledge would you assess and when would you assess?

CURRICULUM SEQUENCING IN MUSIC

One of the ambitious end points of Key Stage 3 music is to '*improvise and compose; and extend and develop musical ideas by drawing on a range of musical structures, styles, genres and traditions*' (DfE, 2014, p 102).

CRITICAL QUESTIONS

+ What component knowledge is required for pupils to meet this national curriculum goal?
+ How would you sequence this component knowledge to ensure that pupils make progress?
+ How would you revisit the component knowledge over time to ensure that pupils retain the knowledge?

CURRICULUM SEQUENCING IN PHYSICAL EDUCATION

One of the ambitious end points of Key Stage 3 physical education is to '*perform dances using advanced dance techniques within a range of dance styles and forms*' (DfE, 2014, p 104).

CRITICAL QUESTIONS

+ What are the 'threads' that hold the dance curriculum together?
+ How might you use these threads to sequence a dance curriculum?
+ What styles of dance do pupils need to learn?

CURRICULUM SEQUENCING IN CITIZENSHIP

One of the ambitious end points of Key Stage 3 citizenship is to know about '*the functions and uses of money, the importance and practice of budgeting, and managing risk*' (DfE, 2014, p 83). This national curriculum goal is underpinned by the component knowledge shown in Figure 8.2.

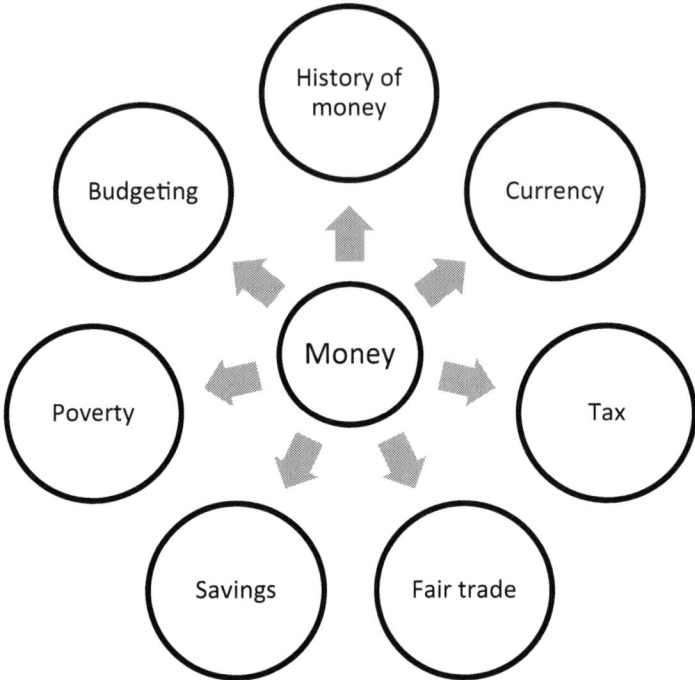

Figure 8.2 Component knowledge for the concept of money

CRITICAL QUESTIONS

+ How might you sequence this component knowledge across a unit of work?

+ What knowledge would you assess?

+ When would you assess it?

CURRICULUM SEQUENCING IN ART AND DESIGN

One of the ambitious end points of Key Stage 3 art and design relates to pupils' knowledge of the '*history of art, craft, design and architecture, including periods, styles and major movements from ancient times up to the present day*' (DfE, 2014, p 81).

CURRICULUM SEQUENCING IN DESIGN AND TECHNOLOGY

One of the ambitious end points of Key Stage 3 design and technology is for pupils to '*understand and apply the principles of nutrition and health*' (DfE, 2014, p 88). This is the composite knowledge that pupils need to learn. The following is an example of how the subject curriculum in design and technology might be sequenced to enable pupils to achieve the goals of the national curriculum.

NUTRITION

Table 8.1 provides a possible learning sequence across Key Stage 3 and, within two units, to show what the deepening of knowledge might look like in relation to nutrition.

Table 8.1 A possible learning sequence for nutrition

Learning sequence	Questions to deepen knowledge
1. Carbohydrates	+ What are carbohydrates? + What are food sources? + How does your body use carbohydrates? + What is the chemical structure of carbohydrates?
2. Fats	+ What are the sources of fats? + What is the function of fat in the body? + Which fats can be harmful to the body and why if they are consumed in excess?
3. Proteins	+ What are proteins? + What are the food sources of proteins from animals? + What are the food sources of proteins from plants? + What are amino acids?

$\longrightarrow$

Table 8.1 (Continued)

Learning sequence	Questions to deepen knowledge
4. Vitamins	+ What are the water soluble vitamins?
	+ What are the fat soluble vitamins?
	+ Which food sources provide vitamins?
5. Minerals	+ What minerals can you name?
	+ Why are minerals important to the body?

HEALTH

The following is a possible learning sequence across Key Stage 3:

+ the importance of physical health;

+ looking after your physical health;

+ the relationship between physical and mental health;

+ malnutrition;

+ obesity.

CRITICAL QUESTIONS

+ How might you design a unit of work in design and technology using the principles of spaced or distributed practice?

+ How might you use retrieval practice within a unit of work on carbohydrates?

CASE STUDY

A CURRICULUM FOR DESIGN AND TECHNOLOGY

WHOLE SCHOOL

Yasmeen is a design and technology subject leader. She was in the process of designing the curriculum and was focusing on the following ambitious goal from the national curriculum: Pupils should be taught to *'understand the source, seasonality and characteristics of a broad range of ingredients'* (DfE, 2014, p 90).

Yasmeen identified that pupils needed to learn about the source of foods. She wanted them to learn that some food is grown, some is caught and some is reared. She identified that pupils need to learn about the manufacture of wheat into bread and the role of processes such as freezing, cheese and yoghurt production, and heating in food production. Yasmeen also wanted the pupils to understand types of meat, fish and dairy and the role of seasons in food availability.

CRITICAL QUESTIONS

+ Did Yasmeen omit any component knowledge from her curriculum plan?

+ Choose one specific unit within this curriculum (eg bread production). What component knowledge do pupils need to learn within this unit? How would you order it into a logical sequence?

EVIDENCE-BASED PRACTICE

Generating an answer or procedure, or retrieving information, even if no feedback is given, leads to better long-term recall than simply studying, though not necessarily in the short term (Coe et al, 2014).

SUMMARY

This chapter introduced the concept of the curriculum as a progression framework. It emphasised the importance of designing a curriculum that provides pupils with increasingly more knowledge as they learn the curriculum, so that they can achieve the ambitious end points of the national curriculum. The chapter linked the curriculum progression framework to assessment and emphasised that teachers must assess component knowledge and not just the broad goals of the national curriculum.

CHECKLIST

+ The curriculum is the progression.

+ When pupils know more, remember more and can do more in the subject they are making progress.

+ Pupils make progress when they learn the intended curriculum.

+ The curriculum for each subject should enable pupils to learn the goals of the national curriculum.

+ The component knowledge that underpins the national curriculum goals is the curriculum rather than the national curriculum per se.

FURTHER READING

Didau, D (nd) Why 'Using the Curriculum as a Progression Model' Is Harder than You Think. [online] Available at: https://learningspy.co.uk/assessment/why-using-the-curriculum-as-a-progression-model-is-harder-than-you-think/ (accessed 28 August 2022).

Mr Vallance Teach (nd) Curriculum as the Progression Model: What Are We Really Talking About? [online] Available at: https://mrvallanceteach.wordpress.com/2021/06/27/curriculum-as-the-progression-model-what-are-we-really-talking-about/ (accessed 28 August 2022).

Newmark, B (nd) The Secret of Great Curriculum Design in Secondary School. [online] Available at: www.teachwire.net/news/the-secret-of-great-curriculum-design-in-secondary-school/ (accessed 28 August 2022).

Singh, H (nd) Designing a Secondary School Curriculum that Prepares Pupils for the World. [online] Available at: https://teaching.blog.gov.uk/2019/07/15/designing-a-secondary-school-curriculum-that-prepares-pupils-for-the-world/ (accessed 28 August 2022).

✚ CHAPTER 9

THE ROLE OF SUBJECT LEADERS IN THE CURRICULUM

CHAPTER OBJECTIVES

After reading this chapter you will understand:

+ the role of the subject leader in curriculum design;
+ the role of the subject leader in curriculum implementation.

INTRODUCTION

This chapter outlines the role of the subject leader in relation to curriculum design. Examples of breaking down the national curriculum goals into component knowledge are provided. Curriculum intent, implementation and impact are discussed, and there is an emphasis on curriculum design that meets the needs of pupils with SEND and disadvantaged pupils from the outset.

THE ROLE OF THE SUBJECT LEADER

Subject leaders in secondary schools have multiple responsibilities. However, the most significant responsibility they hold is to ensure there is a sequenced curriculum that progressively increases pupils' knowledge of the subject. There are two important points to emphasise here. First, the national curriculum is not strictly a curriculum. It is a document that states what pupils need to learn at the end of Key Stages 3 and 4. This is the composite knowledge pupils need to know at the end of each key stage. It does not specify the component knowledge that pupils need to learn to reach those ambitious end points of the national curriculum. The components of knowledge are smaller chunks of knowledge that pupils need to learn at specific times, and in a specific sequence, to be able to learn the composite knowledge specified in the national curriculum. The national curriculum cannot therefore be viewed as a curriculum because it does not break the composite knowledge down into smaller components and it therefore does not provide any guidance on how component knowledge should be sequenced. Second, an examination syllabus is not a curriculum for the same reasons that the national curriculum is not strictly a curriculum. Examination syllabi detail broad ambitious end points that pupils need to learn at the end of Key Stage 4 and Key Stage 5. This composite knowledge is not broken down into component knowledge, and there is no indication of how component knowledge should be sequenced to form a coherent curriculum. Subject leaders, in collaboration with their subject teams, therefore have an important task to execute. They must design a clearly sequenced curriculum that sets out sequentially the component knowledge that pupils need to learn. The curriculum plan should also specify the ambitious end points of the national curriculum (ie the composite knowledge) that pupils need to learn.

EXTENDED THINKING

+ Are the goals of the national curriculum ambitious enough? Explain your response to this question.

THE IMPORTANCE OF CURRICULUM

The curriculum is the substance of education. It focuses on *what* pupils need to learn rather than *how* they will learn it. Too much emphasis on the *how* in recent years has resulted in insufficient emphasis on the *what.* There has been an overemphasis on designing three- or four-part lessons that include elements such as lesson starters, plenaries and mini-plenaries. Observations of lessons have therefore focused on the *how* rather than the what. Teachers have been criticised for not doing a lesson starter, a mini-plenary or a plenary. Some teachers have been criticised for not using technology in their lessons or not including other school 'non-negotiables', such as peer or self-assessment, in lessons. This emphasis on the *how* rather than the *what* is not helpful because it has resulted in teachers 'box-ticking' by making sure that their lessons include the elements the senior leadership team have specified as non-negotiables.

What really matters of course is not whether teachers are following a recipe but whether pupils are learning the intended curriculum. It does not matter if teachers do not use a starter. They may wish to use a starter to consolidate some aspect of prior knowledge, but they do not have to use a starter in every lesson. Similarly, they do not have to use a mini-plenary or a plenary, and they do not have to use technology, particularly if it does not help pupils to learn the intended curriculum. There is no requirement for teachers to use self- and peer assessment in every lesson or to show good examples of work on the visualiser. Subject leaders need to shift the focus from the *how* to the *what*.

We recognise that what we are stating here will require a major shift in some schools. Subject leaders and senior leaders should no longer be grading teachers' lessons, because it is not possible to make a judgement on the quality of education based on a single lesson observation. Ofsted no longer grade lesson observations for this reason. In the past, teachers have been told that their lessons are not outstanding because they omitted to use a starter or they ran out of time to do a plenary. This happened regardless of whether pupils actually learned the intended curriculum.

This new emphasis on whether pupils are learning the intended curriculum is refreshing because it provides teachers with a high degree of professional autonomy to reclaim their teaching. It also gives permission for teachers to design lessons that focus on helping pupils to learn the intended curriculum rather than on developing lots of creative activities which do not add value. Asking pupils to spend time in lessons doing card-sorting activities and diamond nine tasks can reduce the pace of the lesson and result in pupils not learning the intended curriculum. Problem-based learning tasks can play an important role in education. However, pupils need subject knowledge to be able to engage effectively in problem-based learning tasks. If they do not have substantive knowledge of the subject, pupils can experience cognitive load when they are required to complete problems. Asking pupils to spend time researching knowledge by themselves can result in pupils developing misconceptions and not learning the intended curriculum. Asking pupils to analyse historical sources can lead to cognitive load if they do not have the substantive historical knowledge required to enable them to successfully complete the historical inquiry task. Pupils can quickly experience cognitive load in science if they are asked to undertake a scientific investigation without the substantive scientific knowledge required to enable them to understand what they are observing. Completing a shape hunt in mathematics will not support pupils' understanding of the properties of shapes. These examples illustrate how creative pedagogies can sometimes detrimentally impact on pupils' ability to learn the intended curriculum. Teachers should therefore select pedagogical approaches that support pupils to learn the intended curriculum. In lessons that appear to be quite repetitive (eg overlearning a particular subject fact), teaching can be considered effective if it helps pupils to learn the intended knowledge. Of course, teachers must also consider pupils' motivation in lessons, but focusing on creative and engaging activities is not helpful if those activities do not help pupils to learn the intended curriculum.

CURRICULUM INTENT

Intent, implementation and impact were addressed in Chapter 1. This section is a reminder. Intent refers to the planning that takes place before the curriculum is delivered. Typically, this might include a vision statement for the curriculum and the curriculum planning. The curriculum plan should demonstrate how the component knowledge will be sequenced to ensure that the ambitious end points of the national curriculum are met. Curriculum plans should therefore also show the national curriculum expectations at the end of Key Stage 3 and Key Stage 4 as well as the smaller aspects of component knowledge that are taught over time to enable pupils to achieve the ambitious targets in the national curriculum.

CURRICULUM IMPLEMENTATION

Implementation refers to the delivery of the curriculum plan. It includes approaches to both pedagogy and assessment that enable pupils to learn the intended knowledge specified in the curriculum plan. It is usefully understood as the curriculum in action. Explicit teaching involves chunking subject content into smaller components, guiding pupils' practice and gradually releasing control (fading) so that pupils develop mastery and fluency (Ashman, 2019). The principles of explicit teaching contradict those of inquiry-based learning. In inquiry-based learning, pupils find out their own information to answer a question, with varying amounts of teacher support (Pedaste et al, 2015). Leaving pupils to discover knowledge for themselves is a risky pedagogical approach because it can result in cognitive load and also lead to pupils developing misconceptions. However, it may sometimes be an appropriate pedagogical tool in the teacher's toolkit.

Teachers often focus on motivating pupils in lessons and adopt the assumption that increasing motivation will improve academic achievement. However, research demonstrates that academic achievement is a predictor of motivation (Garon-Carrier et al, 2016; Bouffard et al, 2003; Harter, 1981), while intrinsic motivation does not predict academic achievement (Barker, 2019). If teachers want pupils to be motivated, they must therefore focus on improving academic achievement in classrooms, and evidence demonstrates that explicit direct instruction has the greatest impact on academic outcomes (Barker, 2019).

Explicit modelling plays an important role in promoting pupils' understanding, and the approach of 'I do' (the teacher models the subject content), 'we do' (the teacher and pupils work together on a task or problem) and 'you do' (the pupils work independently) is often effective because teacher scaffolding is built into this model and gradually removed (fading). According to Barker, '*If we're looking to improve motivation, then we need to start with competence and instil a sense of success in our students*' (2019, p 114). Tangible rewards that are intended to act as motivators are unlikely to improve achievement and can lead to extrinsic rather than intrinsic motivation.

Pupils also need time to practise working on subject content in lessons. Without this opportunity, pupils do not develop fluency and mastery of subject content. In addition, regular repetition of subject content during a lesson can help to ensure that pupils develop the intended knowledge.

Assessment is also a crucial aspect of implementation. We are not referring here to the use of marks, grades or statutory assessment tests. We are referring to the formative assessment strategies teachers use in lessons to check pupils are learning the knowledge that is intended. Strategies include:

+ checking that prior learning is secure at the start of the lesson;

+ using questioning to check pupils' understanding of the subject content;

+ building in quick quizzes, including multiple-choice quizzes, to check pupils' understanding;

+ checking that pupils have understood the subject content before moving on to the next stage of the lesson;

+ providing pupils with verbal feedback in the lesson and noticing and addressing misconceptions;

+ using a hinge question.

Hinge questions are questions that assess pupils' understanding of subject content at a fixed point in the lesson. The teacher asks a question and requires a whole-class response. This might be a choral response (all pupils answer the question out loud at the same time) or a written answer. If approximately 80 per cent of the class have understood the subject content, the teacher can move on to the next stage of the lesson. They will need to make a note of which pupils have not understood the subject content and provide them with additional support during the lesson to enable them to catch up. This might be done when the other pupils start a task. If more than 20 per cent of the class have not understood the subject content, it might be useful for the teacher to go over the content again with the whole class before moving on to the next stage of the lesson.

IMPACT

The impact of the curriculum is evaluated by the progress pupils make. However, the concept of progress often means different things to different people, so it is important to be clear about how Ofsted use this term. In recent years, schools have measured pupils' progress using test scores and national benchmarks. However, it is important to remember that national benchmarks and statutory assessments are not useful indicators of what pupils know within a subject. This is because they do not assess the full breadth of knowledge within a subject. They assess part of a subject domain but not the entire breadth of knowledge that pupils need to know. Progress is therefore currently evaluated on the basis of what pupils know and remember from the intended curriculum. Therefore, pupils are making progress when they are learning the intended curriculum and when they know and remember more of that curriculum. This means that schools cannot always quantify progress in ways that they have done previously.

Subject leaders therefore need to start thinking about assessment at the point when they design the subject curriculum. The intended curriculum is the progression that pupils are expected to follow and therefore the curriculum should sequence knowledge so that it is sequential and cumulative. As pupils learn the curriculum their knowledge should build so that it becomes deeper and more sophisticated. A well-designed subject curriculum should therefore result in schemas being modified and this should lead to an alteration in pupils' thinking. Learning the intended knowledge in the curriculum is an indication that pupils are making progress. As they progress through the curriculum, they know more about the subject and they remember what they have been taught.

In recent years examination results have often been used as proxies for a good-quality education. It was assumed that if pupils achieve good results in statutory tests, the quality of teaching must have been good. However, this is not necessarily the case. As stated above, statutory assessments do not assess everything that pupils need to know about a subject. Therefore, it cannot be assumed that good examination results are a reliable indicator that pupils have good subject knowledge. In addition, the emphasis on assessment results in recent years has led to curriculum narrowing and gaming. In some schools, the curriculum at Key Stage 4 has been introduced a year earlier, resulting in pupils not getting their full Key Stage 3 entitlement. In other schools, gaming has been evident where pupils are repeatedly asked to practise past examination questions and papers to improve examination results. Another example of gaming is where curriculum time for non-examined subjects is squeezed and timetabled time for examination subjects is increased, or where curriculum content that appears in examinations is prioritised over curriculum content that may not be tested. These approaches have led to pupils not gaining the full breadth of knowledge they need to learn within subjects, and subject leaders must make sure these practices are eradicated.

If the curriculum is designed to enable pupils to achieve the ambitious goals of the national curriculum, it follows that a well-designed curriculum should enable pupils to achieve subject qualifications and therefore progress to their next steps. If pupils do not achieve qualifications, this raises questions about the quality of the subject curriculum itself.

CRITICAL QUESTIONS

+ What do you understand by impact?
+ How do you know if the impact of your curriculum is good or poor?

EXTENDED THINKING

+ Should impact always be based on pupils' performance in examinations? Explain your response to this question.

EVIDENCE-BASED PRACTICE

Christine Counsell (2020) argues that examination results are a proxy that conceals curriculum quality. She argues that a grade 4 at GCSE represents a very low baseline and is not an indicator that pupils have deep knowledge of a subject. If a pupil has achieved a grade 4, there are aspects of the curriculum that are not secure or that they have not experienced.

PLANNING AN AMBITIOUS CURRICULUM

Subject leaders often claim to have an ambitious subject curriculum, but often when they are asked to explain why the curriculum is ambitious, they focus on the *how* rather than the *what*. For example, it is often assumed that a challenging *activity* is an indicator of a challenging curriculum. In the past, teachers may have used theoretical models such as Bloom's taxonomy to plan more challenging activities for pupils. This model assumes that knowledge and understanding require lower-order thinking, while tasks which require application and analysis require higher-order thinking. However, this is not necessarily the case. Some aspects of knowledge may be very challenging for pupils to grasp, and some tasks that require pupils to demonstrate the skill of application may be less challenging than the knowledge pupils need to learn.

Therefore, we need to think differently about ambition and challenge. The ambition and challenge should be in the curricular goals that we expect pupils to achieve, not in the activities we ask pupils to do in classrooms. Some activities might be repetitive and appear to lack challenge, but they may support pupils to know and remember challenging subject content. Subject leaders must therefore be able to demonstrate that the subject curriculum meets – and, in some cases, exceeds – the ambition of the national curriculum. This is how we determine whether a curriculum is challenging.

Subject leaders also need to consider challenge for pupils who are disadvantaged or those with SEND. Teachers must ensure that all pupils are working towards the same curricular goals, regardless of their social backgrounds or other circumstances. Leaders should have the same curricular expectations for all pupils to ensure that all pupils have equality of opportunity. It is important for us to be clear about what we mean by this. Of course, some pupils will be working at vastly different stages of development. Some pupils will be further along a curriculum pathway than others. The critical point is that all pupils should be following the same pathway and working to the same curricular goals unless there are very exceptional circumstances requiring some pupils to follow an alternative curriculum. If pupils are working at an earlier stage along a curriculum plan, teachers should provide additional intervention, practice and opportunities for overlearning so that they can catch up with their peers. In reality, some pupils may always be several steps behind other pupils, but teachers should not assume that they are not capable of catching up, with appropriate intervention. Teachers should take all the necessary steps to close the gap between pupils at different stages of development within a subject, and subject leaders need to ensure there is a strategy in place to enable pupils to catch up with their peers. They should not simply accept that there is an achievement gap and that pupils can progress along a curriculum pathway at a steady pace. Rapid intervention, teaching to automaticity and then further rapid intervention will have the effect of reducing the achievement gap.

It is also important that leaders do not assume pupils with SEND have low ability. Pupils with SEND, like all pupils, will rise to the expectations of their teachers. Too often, pupils with SEND are subjected to a culture of low expectation. This results in them underachieving and experiencing poor long-term outcomes. Leaders must therefore raise their expectations of all pupils and think about challenge in relation to curricular goals, not pedagogy.

CRITICAL QUESTIONS

+ What is your understanding of an ambitious curriculum?

+ How would you address the needs of disadvantaged pupils in the process of curriculum design?

IDENTIFYING COMPONENT KNOWLEDGE

Component knowledge refers to the smaller chunks of knowledge that pupils need to learn before they can achieve the national curriculum end points. One example is taken from chemistry at Key Stage 3 (see Chapter 8 for further examples). The national curriculum requires pupils to learn about a simple atomic model. To learn this, pupils need to know the work of John Dalton and understand the following.

+ All matter is comprised of tiny definite particles called atoms.

+ Atoms can be neither created nor destroyed.

+ Atoms are indivisible and indestructible.

+ An atom is a ball-like structure.

+ It has a central nucleus.

+ An atom is a complex arrangement of negatively charged electrons arranged in defined shells about a positively charged nucleus. This nucleus contains most of the atom's mass and is composed of protons and neutrons (except for common hydrogen which has only one proton).

+ It has electrons.

+ It has protons.

+ It has neutrons.

+ The number of electrons in a neutral atom is equal to the number of protons. The mass number of the atom is equal to the sum of the number of protons and neutrons in the nucleus.

This is not an exhaustive list, but it is a useful starting point when thinking about component knowledge. The component knowledge listed here is not specified in the national curriculum. Subject leaders need to identify the components that will enable pupils to achieve the ambitious goals in the national curriculum. They also need to make decisions about sequencing the components. In this example, it might be useful to know something about the work of John Dalton before moving on to look at the structure of an atom. It may also be useful to introduce pupils to each component part of an atom (nucleus, protons, neutrons and electrons) before focusing on the structure of an atom. The component knowledge – not the national curriculum – forms the curriculum that pupils will learn.

CASE STUDY

DESIGNING SUBJECT CURRICULUMS

WHOLE SCHOOL

Subject teams in a secondary school developed a carefully designed and well-sequenced subject curriculum by breaking down the goals in the national curriculum. The curriculum plan identified the knowledge that pupils needed to learn, and there were opportunities to revisit specific concepts over time.

All subjects include subject-specific concepts that pupils need to understand. In history, these concepts include revolution, empire, democracy and peasantry as well as broader concepts like cause and consequence, change and continuity, similarity and difference, significance, evidence, and interpretation. None of these concepts can be divorced from the substance of history. They should be integrated into specific units of work and revisited. The history subject leader identified key knowledge from the national curriculum that pupils needed to understand. These concepts were embedded into specific units and were revisited in different units to deepen pupils' understanding of these terms.

SEQUENCING COMPONENT KNOWLEDGE

This chapter and Chapter 5 have discussed the importance of accurate sequencing of component knowledge. Effective sequencing of knowledge ensures that the curriculum makes sense to pupils. It enables pupils to form schemas. These schemas are modified as pupils progress through the curriculum. This happens when their understanding deepens and the original schemas no longer work. The initial schemas that are formed are important for a foundational understanding of the subject content, but as pupils learn more about the subject, the schema may need to be modified. The simple atomic structure that pupils learn about in chemistry at Key Stage 3 is important because atoms are abstract and pupils need a simple way of visualising what they look like. This helps them to cope with abstract subject content. However, as pupils progress through the subject curriculum, they learn that this structure is too simplistic, and they develop a more sophisticated understanding of atomic structure which would not have made sense to them if they had studied it earlier.

CRITICAL QUESTIONS

+ Why is correct sequencing of component knowledge important?

+ When schemas are revised, what is the impact of this on working memory?

DELIVERING THE SUBJECT CURRICULUM AS INTENDED

Once the component knowledge has been specified in the curriculum plan, subject leaders need to ensure that the curriculum is being implemented as intended. They need to be sure pupils are learning the component knowledge that the curriculum plan identifies. This is more important than using specific pedagogical approaches in lessons. Subject leaders should not be checking that teachers are delivering three- or four-part lessons, that they are using lesson starters, mini-plenaries and plenaries. This information is not the overriding concern of subject leaders. Essentially, what they need to know is whether pupils are learning the curriculum as intended. How they learn that curriculum should largely be down to teachers' own professional judgement.

QUALITY ASSURING THE SUBJECT CURRICULUM

One way that subject leaders can check that the curriculum is being delivered as intended is to talk to pupils about what they are learning and to take a look in pupils' exercise books. Subject leaders can visit lessons to check that pupils are learning the knowledge specified in the curriculum at the right time. They can talk to pupils about their understanding of the subject content, and they can question them about the knowledge they gained in the previous lesson or the previous term. When monitoring pupils' books, it is often more helpful to do this with pupils or with the subject teachers than to do it in isolation. Subject leaders must be sure pupils with SEND and disadvantaged pupils are also learning the intended curriculum, so these pupils should usually be part of the sample of pupils that leaders talk to.

SUPPORTING SEND AND DISADVANTAGED PUPILS

SEND and disadvantaged pupils should be the subject leaders' focus when designing the curriculum. Rather than adapting the curriculum to meet the needs of SEND or disadvantaged pupils, subject leaders and subject teams should design the curriculum from the outset with these pupils in mind. If the curriculum is designed with these pupils in mind from the outset, it will not need adapting and it will meet the needs of all pupils. This is a different way of thinking about adaptive teaching.

CASE STUDY

CURRICULUM DESIGN FOR PUPILS WITH SEND

WHOLE SCHOOL

A school decided that the best way to support pupils with SEND was to ensure that all pupils had the opportunity to learn the same curriculum and work towards the same national curriculum goals. Some pupils progressed more quickly through the curriculum than others, but to ensure that pupils with SEND could catch up and keep up, additional support lessons were planned, which provided opportunities for pupils with SEND to practise components to automaticity. Pupils with SEND were therefore introduced to the same subject content repeatedly so that they could overlearn the content.

EVIDENCE-BASED PRACTICE

Kirschner et al (2006) defined learning as a change in the long-term memory. They stated:

If nothing has changed in long-term memory, nothing has been learned. Any instructional recommendation that does not or cannot specify what has been changed in long-term memory, or that does not increase the efficiency with which relevant information is stored in or retrieved from long-term memory, is likely to be ineffective.

(Kirschner et al, 2006, p 77)

SUMMARY

This chapter outlined the important role of the subject leader in curriculum design. There is not a singular approach to curriculum design, and leaders across the school or trust should work together to develop a consistent approach. The chapter provided useful examples of how to break down composite knowledge into components, and subject leaders need to think carefully about how to use a similar approach in their subjects.

CHECKLIST

+ Intent is everything that happens before the curriculum is delivered. It is not just the vision statement for the curriculum, but also the curriculum plan itself.

+ Implementation refers to pedagogy and formative assessment during curriculum delivery.

+ Impact is knowing more, remembering more and being able to do more in the subject.

+ The broad national curriculum goals are often referred to as composite knowledge.

+ Composite knowledge is broken down into smaller components of knowledge.

FURTHER READING

Nelson, T (nd) Ofsted and Subject Leadership – Key Questions. [online] Available at: www.focus-education.co.uk/blog/ofsted-and-subject-leadership/ (accessed 28 August 2022).

Sealy, C (2020) The ResearchED Guide to The Curriculum: An Evidence-informed Guide for Teachers. Woodbridge: John Catt Educational.

+ CHAPTER 10

DEVELOPING A MENTAL HEALTH CURRICULUM

CHAPTER OBJECTIVES

After reading this chapter you will understand:

+ what mental health is;

+ the causes of mental ill health in young people;

+ how to design a mental health curriculum.

INTRODUCTION

In 2017, approximately 850,000 children and young people had a clinically diagnosable mental health disorder (DfE and Department of Health [DoH], 2017) and the mental health crisis has worsened due to the effects of the Covid-19 pandemic. Since the arrival of Covid-19, the prevalence of mental ill health has risen substantially to one in six young people.

The 2017 Green Paper Transforming Children and Young People's Mental Health Provision (DfE and DoH, 2017) outlines the important role of schools in addressing mental health. This suggestion was contentious for two main reasons: first, the role of schools is primarily to educate young people through teaching the curriculum and preparing pupils for examinations; and, second, teachers and other educators are not qualified mental health practitioners. Although these arguments are sound, it is also the case that young people spend a significant amount of time in school and teachers are therefore likely to see young people who are displaying warning signs. In addition, as schools are part of young people's daily lives, it makes sense to provide support and intervention to young people in school rather than in National Health Service clinics. Teachers therefore need guidance on how to support young people's mental health through the curriculum and through working in partnership with young people.

CRITICAL QUESTIONS

+ Do you agree that mental health should be part of a school's remit? Justify your response.

+ Why do you think the government requires schools to extend their remit through addressing mental health?

WHAT IS MENTAL HEALTH?

It is a myth that mental health simply relates to mental *ill* health. Mental health operates along a spectrum from being mentally healthy to being mentally ill (see Figure 10.1). Mental health is a dynamic characteristic. It changes in response to one's daily experiences and circumstances. With appropriate support and intervention, the mental health of an individual can fluctuate from a state of mental ill health to a state of being mentally healthy.

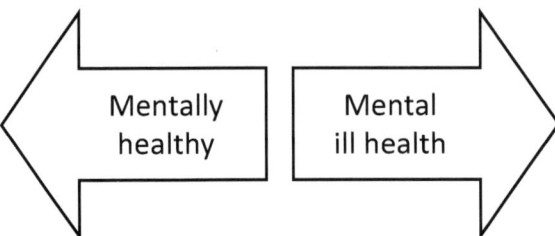

Figure 10.1 The spectrum of mental health

According to the World Health Organization, mental health is 'a state of well-being in which the individual realizes his or her own abilities, can cope with the normal stresses of life, can work productively and fruitfully, and is able to make a contribution to his or her community' (2004, p 59). This definition is useful because it does not describe mental health 'disorders' and is therefore not adopting a deficit perspective on mental health. It describes a mentally healthy individual and therefore suggests that an individual with mental ill health might be unable to cope with the usual demands of daily life.

CRITICAL QUESTIONS

+ What do you think about the use of the word 'disorder' to describe mental health?

+ If you had to write your own definition of mental health, what would this be?

CAUSES OF MENTAL ILL HEALTH

The causes of mental ill health are complex and multifaceted. The biopsychosocial model of health demonstrates how mental health is affected by overlapping biological, social and psychological factors (Figure 10.2).

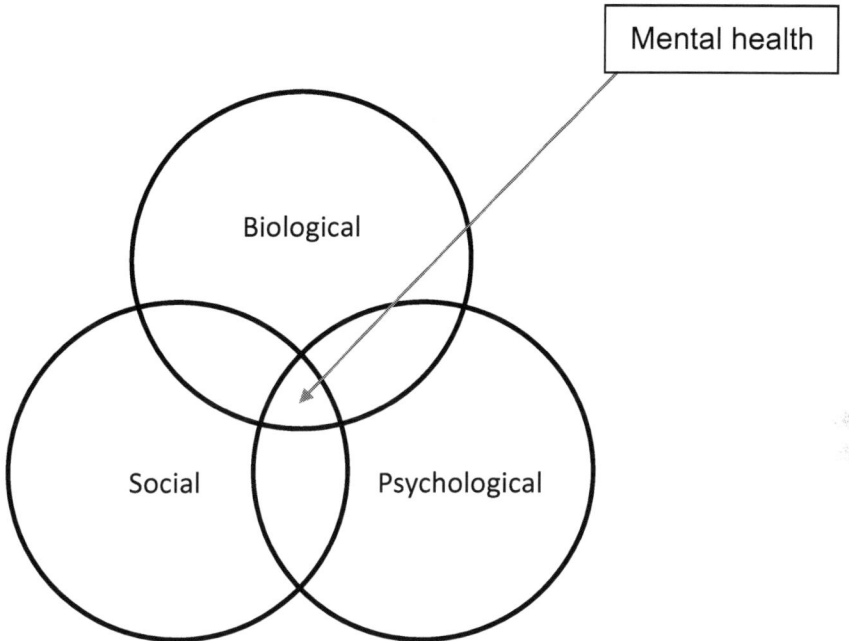

Figure 10.2 Biopsychosocial model of health

An example of a biological factor is a disability. Young people with dis-abilities are more likely to experience mental ill health. Social factors include poverty, family characteristics and bullying. Young people who experience adverse childhood experiences (eg abuse, neglect, parental conflict or criminality) are more likely to experience poor mental health, and there is a strong relationship between social deprivation and mental health. School-related factors including bullying and examination stress can also contribute to mental ill health. Psychological factors might include resilience or self-esteem. Pupils with low resilience and poor self-esteem are less likely to adapt when they experience transitions. Self-esteem and resilience act as buffers to the damaging effects of negative transitions, and these are crucial characteristics to develop in young people. Self-esteem is not a stable/fixed characteristic in individ-uals, so interventions can improve it. However, the use of interventions to raise self-esteem are unlikely to be effective on their own. Self-esteem improves in tandem with academic capability. In Mruk's (1999) model of self-esteem, self-competence (capability) is one of the dimensions of overall self-esteem. Therefore, when self-competence improves, so too does self-esteem. Resilience is also not a straightforward characteristic. In line with Roffey (2017), we adopt a socio-ecological perspective on resilience. It is not solely an innate characteristic. It is fuelled by access to positive social relationships and, for young people, access to a positive school culture.

Adolescence is a particularly difficult time because it is a phase in the life course where individuals experience multiple transitions, including academic, biological, social and psychological transitions. Many young people will explore their identities during adolescence, and this process can result in poor mental health. Meyer's (2003) model of minority stress demonstrates how LGBTQ+ young people may experience additional stressors due to anticipating negative reactions to their identities. The effect of this is that some young people experience internalised homophobia (self-stigma) and may choose to conceal their identity (Meyer, 2003). This results in internal psychological distress.

A WHOLE-SCHOOL APPROACH TO MENTAL HEALTH

A whole-school approach to mental health and well-being is outlined by Public Health England (2021). The model includes eight strands, described below.

1. Leadership: school leaders should champion mental health and make it a strategic priority.

2. School ethos and environment: creating a positive school environment allows pupils and staff to thrive and supports good well-being.

3. Curriculum: schools should provide young people with a mental health curriculum that is designed to educate them about mental health.

4. Pupils as partners: schools should develop innovative approaches to working in partnership with pupils so that they can lead mental health initiatives.

5. Staff development and well-being: school leaders should provide training for all staff so that they can identify mental ill health and

are empowered to have conversations with young people about their mental health. School leaders should also develop initiatives to improve staff well-being by reducing unnecessary workload and by creating positive school cultures.

6. Identification and intervention: schools should develop a system or process for identifying mental ill health in young people – for example, by introducing universal mental health screening for all students. Universal, group and individual evidence-based interventions should be provided to support pupils' mental health. An example of a universal intervention for all pupils is a mental health curriculum.

7. Working in partnership with parents: schools should ensure that parents are empowered to support their children's mental health more effectively through information sharing and workshops that raise parents' awareness of mental health. Schools may also need to consider how to support parental mental health – for example, through signposting parents to appropriate services.

8. Referral: schools should have a policy and systems to facilitate referrals to specialist services for pupils with the most enduring and complex mental health needs.

CRITICAL QUESTIONS

+ How might schools address universal screening for all pupils?

+ What aspects of the whole-school approach should school leaders prioritise?

+ When might it be appropriate to provide group or individual interventions?

DESIGNING A MENTAL HEALTH CURRICULUM

Designing a mental health curriculum is not an easy task. Schools might decide to purchase an off-the-shelf curriculum. However, the curriculum will still need to be adapted to address the issues pupils are experiencing. The mental health curriculum should aim to develop pupils' 'mental health literacy'. This is an official term, first used in 1997 by Jorm et al. According to Jorm et al (1997, p 182), mental health literacy consists of several components, including: *'the ability to recognise specific disorders; knowing how to seek mental health information; knowledge of risk factors and causes, of self-treatments, and of professional help available; and attitudes that promote recognition and appropriate help-seeking'*.

School leaders need to design a curriculum that deepens pupils' knowledge as they progress through secondary school. The curriculum also needs to consider pupils' prior learning at primary school. Schools need to consider not only *what* to teach but *how* to teach mental health content. Mental health is undoubtedly a sensitive topic and pupils may have personal experiences of mental ill health. Some pupils might find some of the content challenging.

CRITICAL QUESTIONS

+ How can schools sensitively introduce mental health content to pupils?

+ Why is it important for all pupils to learn about mental health?

One strategy that teachers might want to adopt is the technique of distancing. Distancing is an approach where teachers may discuss a topic without drawing on pupils' personal experiences – for example, by using fictional case studies of young people to illustrate a specific issue. However, pupils might want to discuss their personal experiences of mental health. It is therefore important that teachers establish a safe space in lessons by reinforcing some key ground rules. For example, pupils need to be informed that they must not discuss other pupils' experiences outside of the lesson, and pupils need to be assured that anything they say will be kept confidential unless the teacher feels that the young person might be at risk. If pupils raise potential safeguarding concerns in lessons, teachers should communicate with them about why specific information needs to be shared, who it needs to be shared with and exactly what information will be shared with a third party.

Figure 10.3 provides an example of how you might structure a mental health curriculum for pupils in Year 9.

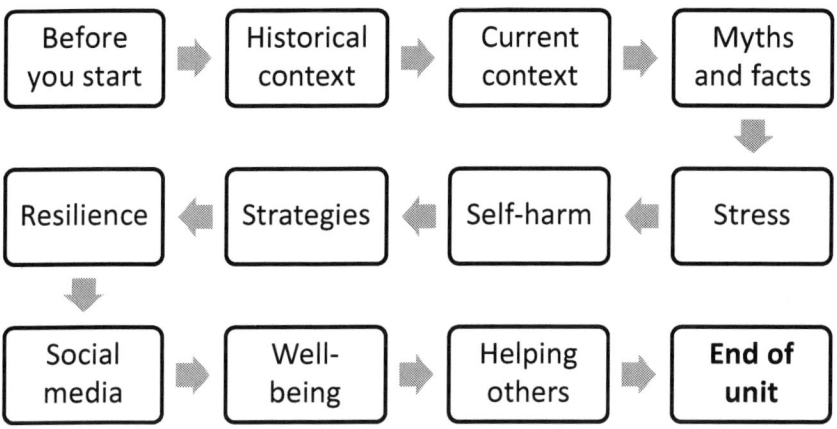

Figure 10.3 Mental health curriculum for Year 9

BEFORE YOU START THE CURRICULUM

It is useful to get a baseline in relation to pupils' prior knowledge of mental health before you deliver the curriculum. One approach is to develop a set of statements that are either true or false and ask pupils to sort each statement into one of these categories. The curriculum should be designed to address each of the statements, and in the final session you can ask the pupils to revisit the statements and update their responses. Alternatively, you might want to give the pupils a mental health literacy questionnaire to assess their prior knowledge of mental health. Each response is scored to produce an overall mental health literacy score. The same questionnaire can be used in the final lesson to see if there is an improvement in pupils' mental health literacy.

HISTORICAL CONTEXT

This lesson introduces pupils to the historical context in relation to mental health. Pupils explore how people with mental illnesses were treated in the past and the reasons why they were treated like this. In the lesson, pupils might learn about stigma, mental health institutions and the medicalisation of mental health.

CURRENT CONTEXT

In this lesson, pupils learn about mental health statistics, the current emphasis on breaking down stigma and organisations that young people can access if they need support. This lesson provides an opportunity to discuss the causes of mental ill health in modern society.

MYTHS AND FACTS

Pupils are presented with a set of myths and facts related to mental health, and their task is to work together in pairs to sort them into the two categories. Each statement is discussed in depth.

STRESS

In this lesson, pupils explore what is meant by stress, drawing on their personal experiences. It is important for pupils to recognise that stress is not always unhealthy. They must recognise that a certain level of stress is inevitable in daily life and that individuals require a degree of stress in their lives because it helps them stay focused and achieve goals and it supports motivation. Through discussion, pupils can be supported to understand the difference between healthy and unhealthy stress. Stress becomes unhealthy when it prevents us from functioning and making a positive contribution in society. Pupils can learn about the harmful effects of stress and strategies to manage stress.

SELF-HARM

This lesson should provide an opportunity to explore misconceptions about self-harm. Pupils need to learn that self-harm can take a variety of forms and occurs across people of all ages. Pupils need to understand that self-harm can be dangerous. They also need to recognise that individuals do not self-harm to draw attention to themselves, but rather it is usually in response to some form of trauma or emotional distress and is often a way of coping with emotional pain. Pupils need to learn about where to get support and strategies to seek support from others.

STRATEGIES

In this lesson, pupils learn about strategies for managing their own mental health, including the importance of social connection, physical activity, the outdoors, mindfulness, listening to music and other practices that promote self-care. Crucially, pupils need to be supported to recognise when their own mental health is starting to decline so that they can take immediate action. They need to understand that a decline in mental health is often temporary and not permanent, and that mental health can return to a positive state quite quickly. The relationship between mental and physical health is important, and pupils should be encouraged to reflect on how physical activity can alter their mood. It is important for pupils to learn about the benefits of a healthy diet and exercise on mental health as well as the positive benefits to mental health of giving service to others for free through volunteering.

RESILIENCE

Pupils should learn about the concept of resilience by reflecting on how well they 'bounce back' from difficult situations. Examples might include bouncing back from a low score in an examination, learning from feedback or bouncing back from a defeat in a team game. However, bouncing back from adversity is only one dimension of resilience. Individuals who demonstrate resilience are able to reach out to others and ask for help when their mental health is in decline. Pupils need to know how to ask for help and where to go if they need support. They also need to understand that access to support from friends, peers, teachers and parents can also support their resilience. Resilience is therefore not something that is independent of the social contexts in which individuals operate. Teachers might use a range of activities to explore resilience, and pupils can be introduced to a model of resilience.

SOCIAL MEDIA

The relationship between social media and mental health is now well-documented. This lesson can explore a range of themes including:

+ the benefits of social media;

+ the relationship between social media and mental health;

+ online bullying;

169

+ healthy and unhealthy screen time;

+ social media and sleep deprivation;

+ peer pressure;

+ fake images and body image;

+ the risks associated with following online influencers;

+ the concept of digital citizenship;

+ how to get support.

WELL-BEING

In this lesson, pupils can learn about the different dimensions of well-being, including physical, social, emotional, psychological and spiritual well-being. Pupils can be given short case studies to illustrate different types of well-being, and they could be asked to assign each scenario to the appropriate category.

HELPING OTHERS

In this lesson, pupils learn about how to be a good listener. They learn about the importance of demonstrating empathy, making eye contact and not interrupting. Role play can be used to provide pupils with an opportunity to practise effective listening.

CASE STUDY

DELIVERING A MENTAL HEALTH CURRICULUM WITH EXTERNAL SUPPORT

YEAR 8

School leaders worked with a local sports organisation to design a mental health curriculum for pupils in Year 8. The football club delivered the sessions and pupils enjoyed listening to footballers who came in to school to talk about their own lived experiences of mental ill health. Sports coaches from the football club were also involved in delivering some of the curriculum.

CRITICAL QUESTIONS

+ What are the advantages of this approach to delivering the curriculum?
+ What other types of organisation might you approach to deliver this curriculum?

AFTER YOU HAVE DELIVERED THE CURRICULUM

In the final session, to enable the teacher to check the impact of the mental health curriculum on pupils' knowledge and understanding, pupils can be given the same assessment that they were provided with at the start of the teaching sequence.

CRITICAL QUESTIONS

+ Do you agree with this sequence of lessons?
+ What other content would you include in a mental health curriculum?

EVIDENCE-BASED PRACTICE

Over a quarter (26 per cent) of young women aged 16–24 report having a common mental health problem in any given week. This compares to 17 per cent of all adults (McManus et al, 2016).

Personal well-being decreases as children move from primary to secondary school, and this fall continues through secondary school. This fall is more pronounced for girls than for boys (Crenna-Jennings, 2021). There is an increase in levels of psychological distress through adolescence. From age 14, girls have higher psychological distress scores than boys, and as they move into late adolescence, girls have a greater rise in psychological distress than boys (Crenna-Jennings, 2021).

CRITICAL QUESTIONS

+ Why do you think mental ill health is prevalent in the 16–24 age bracket?

+ What factors might account for mental ill health in girls?

WORKING IN PARTNERSHIP WITH PUPILS

Many schools have developed the role of pupil mental health ambassador or champion. This role provides an opportunity for pupils to lead on mental health and be positive agents of change. Some schools raise the profile of the role by asking pupils to apply for the role and undertake a short interview. Schools can decide how to deploy the pupil leaders, but one approach is for pupil mental health champions to adopt the role of 'peer listener'. Older pupils can be deployed to support younger pupils through a programme of peer listening.

CRITICAL QUESTIONS

+ How can schools develop inclusive approaches for working in partnership with pupils?

+ What are the advantages and disadvantages of peer mentoring interventions?

+ What other roles might the pupil mental health champions adopt?

EXTENDED THINKING

+ Are clinical interventions (eg counselling, cognitive behaviour therapy and talking therapy) appropriate for all young people experiencing mental ill health?

+ How might the issue of mental health be addressed systemically rather than at the level of the individual?

CASE STUDY

MENTAL HEALTH AMBASSADORS

YEAR 10

A secondary school developed a description for the role of mental health ambassador in Year 10. Pupils applied for the role and were interviewed. Those who were successful completed a training course in mental health and safeguarding. They provided peer mentoring for younger pupils through a peer-listening initiative. Pupils who needed support were matched to an ambassador who listened to their concerns.

CRITICAL QUESTIONS

+ What are the advantages of peer mentoring schemes?
+ What are the potential disadvantages?

EVIDENCE-BASED PRACTICE

Black or Black British people are more likely than white British people to experience a common mental health problem in any given week (23 per cent compared to 17 per cent) (McManus et al, 2016). Bullying has strong and lasting effects on young people's mental and emotional health through adolescence (Crenna-Jennings, 2021). Young people's mental and emotional health scores are worse for those in families with lower income (Crenna-Jennings, 2021).

CRITICAL QUESTIONS

+ Why do you think mental ill health is more prevalent among Black or Black British people?
+ How can schools address this through the curriculum?

SUMMARY

There is evidence to show that the attitudes of young people can be changed more easily than the attitudes of adults. The mental health curriculum in secondary schools should break down the stigma associated with mental ill health. It should develop pupils' mental health literacy, and it should teach pupils how to get help when they need it. The damaging effects of social media is a serious issue facing schools. Despite education, there is evidence to suggest that pupils are continuing to use technology in damaging ways outside of schools, which impacts detrimentally on their mental health. Schools cannot address this issue alone, and parents and social media companies must also shoulder some responsibility. The main thing for schools to address is ensuring that there is a comprehensive mental health curriculum which addresses internet use.

CHECKLIST

+ Mental health is broader than mental ill health and includes being mentally healthy.

+ All schools must provide pupils with a mental health curriculum.

+ The mental health curriculum is not a single episode. It should be designed to ensure progression in knowledge as pupils move through the curriculum.

+ Specific groups are more likely to develop mental ill health.

+ The mental health curriculum should be taught through subjects as well as being taught discretely.

FURTHER READING

Mentally Healthy Schools – www.mentallyhealthyschools.org.uk/

MindEd – www.minded.org.uk/

Young Minds – www.youngminds.org.uk/

✛ CHAPTER 11

LGBTQ+ INCLUSION IN THE CURRICULUM

CHAPTER OBJECTIVES

After reading this chapter you will understand:

+ how to integrate LGBTQ+ content into subjects;

+ strategies for involving pupils in curriculum design.

INTRODUCTION

Embedding LGBTQ+ content into the curriculum is a proactive way of educating pupils about gender and sexual diversity. An effectively designed LGBTQ+ curriculum can support the development of positive attitudes in pupils and foster good relationships between different groups of people. This meets the public sector equality duty, which forms part of the Equality Act 2010. Through embedding LGBTQ+ inclusion in the curriculum, the incidents of homophobic, biphobic and transphobic (HBT) bullying in school should decrease.

A carefully designed curriculum that promotes LGBTQ+ inclusion will help to shape the development of positive attitudes among pupils towards people with non-normative gender identities and sexualities. LGBTQ+ inclusion should be embedded into RSHE and health education, and across all subject areas. This will help to make LGBTQ+ identities visible.

Examples of effective practice are listed below.

+ All national LGBTQ+ celebration and awareness events are embedded in the academic year.
+ LGBTQ+ identities are visible in the curriculum.
+ The lived experiences of LGBTQ+ people are addressed through the curriculum.
+ RSHE addresses the sexual and health needs of LGBTQ+ pupils.
+ RSHE addresses same-sex relationships.
+ RSHE address the nuances of gender identity, including gender fluidity.
+ Health education addresses the specific mental health needs of pupils who identify as LGBTQ+.
+ The digital curriculum addresses the specific risks associated with online activity for LGBTQ+ pupils.

EMBEDDING LGBTQ+ INCLUSION

Traditionally, schools and colleges have sought to promote LGBTQ+ inclusivity through curriculum drop down days, extracurricular events and themed assemblies. However, in recent years, schools and colleges have begun to embed LGBTQ+ inclusion throughout their core curriculum. This reflects a cultural shift in the promotion of LGBTQ+ inclusion whereby standalone activities are seen as insufficient in promoting and developing a culture of LGBTQ+ inclusion.

When introducing or developing an LGBTQ+-inclusive curriculum, senior leaders will often create an institutional policy or offer advice and guidance for teaching staff to provide clarity, consistency, certainty and confidence. In doing so, senior leaders must ensure that they consider the impact of any curriculum reform on teachers' workload. In doing so, it is often valuable to consult with staff and create opportunities to provide reassurance. All members of school staff with teaching or planning responsibilities must understand that introducing an LGBTQ+-inclusive curriculum does not require a new curriculum or scheme of learning. Instead, staff must recognise that adjusting and adding to an existing provision is enough to provide a curriculum that effectively promotes and develops LGBTQ+ awareness.

When updating and adjusting the current curriculum offer, it is useful for staff to consider the approaches and strategies used by colleagues from other schools. This can help to develop staff confidence, and it minimises the impact of any curriculum change on staff workload. Where possible, it is also valuable to provide opportunities for teaching staff to meet and collaboratively exchange ideas both within and across subject areas. Table 11.1 provides suggestions for integrating LGBTQ+ content into the curriculum for different subjects.

Table 11.1 Integrating LGBTQ+ content in the curriculum

Subject	Suggestions for an LGBTQ+-inclusive curriculum
Art and design	+ Provide opportunities for pupils to illustrate and explore their own identity within their artistic creations. + Examine how LGBTQ+ topics have been represented within the subject and how this may have developed through time and across cultures. + Study LGBTQ+ artists and the contributions they have made to the subject area. + Create opportunities for pupils to create art works that celebrate the diversity of the human population.

→

Table 11.1 (Continued)

Subject	Suggestions for an LGBTQ+-inclusive curriculum
Business and economics	+ Use a variety of case studies in data response and essay-based questions – for example, refer to a gay or lesbian couple within the context of business ownership, as in: David and Jason are married and have opened their own organic coffee shop. + When practising calculations, provide opportunities for pupils to access LGBTQ+ statistics. + Explore the impact of legislation on workplace culture and diversity. + Discuss the economic impact of discrimination in relation to an economy's development. + Promote the work of LGBTQ+ entrepreneurs and their contributions to the field of business. + Introduce the concept of the 'pink pound' and discuss its value as a contribution to the world economy.
Citizenship	+ Discuss LGBTQ+ rights within the context of the legal environment – for example, in relation to the Equality Act. + Provide opportunities for pupils to discuss the consequences of bullying and hate crime against individuals and communities. + Explore cultural perceptions of LGBTQ+ inclusion and the developments in awareness and tolerance. + Explain how and why relevant laws are created, introduced and enforced, and how these protect those within minority communities.
Computing	+ Explore how gender stereotypes create a barrier to participation in science, technology, engineering and mathematics (STEM) subjects and careers. + Promote the work of LGBTQ+ computer scientists and reflect on their contributions to the subject area.
Design and technology	+ Explore how gender stereotypes create a barrier to participation in design and technology careers. + Promote the work of LGBTQ+ engineers, technologists and designers and reflect on their contributions to the subject area.

Table 11.1 (Continued)

Subject	Suggestions for an LGBTQ+-inclusive curriculum
	+ Allow pupils to analyse the gendering of different products and discuss the stereotypes underpinning design decisions.
Drama	+ Provide opportunities for pupils to experience LGBTQ+ playwrights, scenes and themes. + Explore how drama has been used to represent LGBTQ+ identities, and identify how these representations have developed or changed through time and across cultures. + Highlight instances of bullying and hate crime through drama. + Ensure taught activities represent diversity and promote difference through their focus on characters and families.
English	+ Develop pupils' understanding of gender-neutral pronouns; link these to the choices an individual has made about their gender identity and the role of pronouns in respecting these choices. + Ensure that debates and writing activities are based on LGBTQ+ topics; provide opportunities for pupils to create persuasive writing pieces on the importance of same-sex marriage or the right for LGBTQ+ couples to adopt. + Explore authors' representations of masculinity and femininity and the role of stereotypes within texts. + Study the work of LGBTQ+ authors and discuss how the identity of these authors may have shaped their literary creations. + Reflect on the work of LGBTQ+ authors and their contributions to the subject area. + Compare representations of LGBTQ+ characters and explore how these differ across time periods and cultures. + Use creative writing to rewrite traditional stories avoiding the use of gender pronouns and introduce main characters with LGBTQ+ identities.

⟶

Table 11.1 (Continued)

Subject	Suggestions for an LGBTQ+-inclusive curriculum
Geography	+ Discuss the role of migration within the context of LGBTQ+ people and their experiences. + Examine the impact of LGBTQ+ identity on international tourism, and explore how this has changed over time. + Review LGBTQ+ legislation in different countries and any impact this has on a country and its ability to develop. + Explore the contributions of LGBTQ+ people to the subject area.
History	+ Explore how LGBTQ+ equality has evolved over time and examine the achievements of campaigners and activists from previous decades. + Study the contributions of historical LGBTQ+ figures and their role in promoting tolerance and acceptance. + Discuss the sexuality of suffragettes such as Emmeline Pankhurst and why historians have chosen to ignore this. + Compare the legal and political factors impacting the lives of LGBTQ+ people over time and across different countries. + Explore how the Nazis treated minority groups and those with LGBTQ+ identities. + Use examples of the love letters sent between soldiers and their boyfriends and discuss the risks they took in doing so.
Mathematics	+ Use a variety of case studies in problem-based questions; for example, refer to a gay or lesbian couple when calculating the cost of a wedding, or to a transgender parent in a scenario about a child's pocket money. + For data collection and analysis topics, provide opportunities for pupils to calculate and interpret LGBTQ+ statistics. + Explore how gender stereotypes create a barrier to participation in STEM subjects and careers.

Table 11.1 (Continued)

Subject	Suggestions for an LGBTQ+-inclusive curriculum
	+ Promote the work of LGBTQ+ mathematicians and reflect on their contributions to the subject area.
Media	+ Explore the representation of LGBTQ+ topics in the media and examine how these have changed and evolved over time and across cultures.
Modern languages	+ LGBTQ+ rights in other countries.
Music	+ Discuss and highlight examples of LGBTQ+ musicians and the contribution they have made to the subject area. + Explore how music can be used to represent assumptions about gender and love. + Examine how music is influenced by the context in which it is created – for example, explore how LGBTQ+ issues have influenced genres of music over time and in different cultures and societies. + Analyse the role of music as an instrument for social change and as a tool for the expression of feelings and experiences.
Physical education	+ Provide opportunities for pupils to discuss the role of equality within sport. + Encourage pupils to debate LGBTQ+-themed topics – for example, the Olympics being hosted in countries that criminalise homosexuality; whether there really are no LGBTQ+ footballers in the premier league. + Identify and promote the sporting successes of LGBTQ+ role models; sharing the stories of LGBTQ+ athletes (eg Tom Daley) can raise awareness and promote acceptance. + Challenge homophobia and gender stereotypes; deconstruct pupils' perceptions about specific sports being masculine or feminine. + Promote LGBTQ+ inclusion through rainbow laces and kit design.

→

Table 11.1 (Continued)

Subject	Suggestions for an LGBTQ+-inclusive curriculum
Psychology	+ Debate and examine the role of love and marriage within the context of relationships and evolutionary explanations. + Discuss famous and historical LGBTQ+ psychologists and their contributions to psychology. + Explore mental health in relation to LGBTQ+ people. + Discuss psychological perspectives on gender identity.
Religious education	+ Introduce pupils to examples of LGBTQ+ people being open and honest about their identity within the context of their faith. + Explore different views on love and marriage and how these are interpreted within and by different religions and faiths. + Provide examples of religious leaders who have sought to promote and develop understanding and acceptance of those with LGBTQ+ identities.
Science	+ Explore how gender stereotypes create a barrier to participation in STEM subjects and careers. + Use inclusive case studies and examples to illustrate scientific concepts – for example, discuss the role of IVF in LGBTQ+ relationships. + Explore the work of LGBTQ+ scientists and their contributions to the discipline.
Sociology	+ Explore family structures and units, and how these have changed over time. + Explain gender roles and stereotypes, and how these have been challenged in recent years. + Discuss the social and cultural influences on tolerance and awareness.

Developing an inclusive curriculum is crucial if the needs and identities of all pupils are to be represented, accepted and understood. An inclusive curriculum ensures that all pupils feel included, and this alleviates anxieties and allows pupils to focus on their learning. Through discussing the role of significant past or present LGBTQ+ people within a specific subject area, pupils can understand the valuable contributions made by those within the LGBTQ+ community. This develops pupils' awareness of LGBTQ+ role models and can raise aspirations and support pupil performance.

CRITICAL QUESTIONS

+ How might you address LGBTQ+ content within your subject?

+ Which significant LGBTQ+ individuals have influenced your subject?

INCLUDING LGBTQ+ IN THE RSHE CURRICULUM

All maintained secondary schools must provide RSHE as part of the basic curriculum. The revised guidance for RSHE (DfE, 2019b) became statutory in September 2020. It is mandatory for all secondary schools to provide RSHE.

It is important for schools to teach young people that different types of relationships are equally valid. Young people need to learn about same-sex marriage and the differences between marriage and civil partnerships. Within the context of same-sex relationships, schools might wish to include units of work on parenting within same-sex relationships, including same-sex adoption and fostering. It is critical that all pupils learn about power within relationships, including the abuse of power within same-sex relationships. Pupils need to learn that domestic abuse can take place in all types of relationships and that perpetrators of domestic abuse are not always male. It is important to teach young people how to recognise the early signs of domestic abuse and to understand that physical abuse is not the only form of domestic abuse.

ADDRESSING BULLYING THROUGH THE RSHE CURRICULUM

All pupils need to know what constitutes bullying and how to respond to it when they see it, and that bullying of individuals with protected characteristics contravenes the Equality Act 2010. The following students may be at risk of HBT bullying:

+ pupils who confide about their gender identity or sexuality to a friend who they have misjudged, and subsequently find that they have been outed without their consent;

+ pupils who have lesbian, gay and same-sex parents, and students who have parents who identify as transgender;

Anyone irrespective of their actual gender identity or sexuality can experience HBT bullying:

+ male students who do not demonstrate 'masculine' characteristics;

+ female students who do not demonstrate 'feminine' characteristics;

+ heterosexual male or female students who others think of as gay or lesbian;

+ pupils who have LGBTQ+ siblings;

+ boys who are perceived to be overly 'academic'.

The following are signs of HBT bullying.

+ The pupil is reluctant to join in activities.

+ The pupil is often the target of jokes.

+ The pupil is reluctant to go to certain places or work with certain individuals.

+ The pupil has bruising or other signs of injury, including self-harm.

+ There are sudden changes in the pupil's mood or behaviour, such as withdrawal from others or being unusually quiet.

+ The pupil may demonstrate emotional responses that are not typical for them.

+ The pupil's attendance may start to decline.

+ The pupil's academic profile may start to decline.

+ There may be changes in the pupil's physical appearance, such as changes in weight.

+ The pupil may be unusually tired due to sleeplessness.

+ The pupil may prefer to stay in school at break time.

All staff should be supported to recognise the signs of HBT bullying. Bullying does not have to be witnessed by a staff member to be identified. If a member of staff suspects that a pupil is being bullied, the staff member can ask them if there is anything they want to talk about. The pupil may not be 'out', so it is obviously important not to directly ask them if they are experiencing HBT bullying. Pupils should be reassured that they can talk to adults confidentially. In cases where adults need to refer cases for more specialist support, the member of staff should explain to the pupil why information needs to be shared, who it will be shared with and what will happen next. Teachers should take steps to seek students' consent before passing on information to parents. However, although consent should be sought, teachers should not lie, deceive or mislead parents and if the student is at risk of harm a referral should be made and it might be necessary to inform parents.

Homophobic language includes phrases like 'that's so gay' or 'you're so gay'. Young people may excuse this language as harmless banter, but there are two key issues for schools to address here. First, often the word 'gay' is being used as a synonym to replace 'rubbish' – 'those trainers are so gay' can mean the same as 'those trainers are rubbish'. The association of 'gay' with 'rubbish' is dangerous because it can result in the marginalisation of LGBTQ+ people. Second, regardless of whether language was intended as harmful banter, if it is perceived as homophobic, biphobic or transphobic by the person it is aimed at, it should be addressed as a homophobic, biphobic or transphobic incident. All schools should therefore have a zero-tolerance policy on the use of HBT language, and this should be reinforced through clear, visible notices displayed around the school. All staff should be prepared to challenge the inappropriate use of language and banter. This can be done calmly and in a non-confrontational way by explaining to young people why it is wrong, hurtful and damaging. Educating young people is more effective than using punishment. It is important to remember that many young people will be exposed to inappropriate language and banter at home and may have internalised it. If use of HBT language has never been challenged, young people may not understand why it is wrong. Helping young people to understand why they must not use terms based on prejudice is essential, and preferable to resorting to punishment.

Schools play a critical role in educating pupils about prejudice and help to reshape any prejudiced attitudes. It is important to help young people to understand the harmful effects of prejudice and discrimination on individuals and on society as a whole. This is difficult work because in some cases schools are directly challenging parental, community or religious values. However, it is crucial work because young people need to understand that prejudice is not tolerated in society, FE or HE, or employment. In order to function successfully as a productive member of society, young people need to learn to adjust any HBT behaviours. However, adjusting behaviours is insufficient; schools need to support young people to believe that prejudice and discrimination are wrong so that HBT behaviours do not occur in contexts outside of school.

Outside of school, pupils may experience online bullying. Schools should educate pupils to block the accounts of perpetrators and to take screenshots when bullying happens online. These can be used as evidence. Those who experience cyberbullying need to be encouraged to talk to friends, parents or teachers about their experiences. Schools play a key role in ensuring that young people know they should not feel ashamed or embarrassed if they experience bullying. Schools should also highlight the importance of seeking help by talking to others. Pupils who experience bullying should be encouraged to resist replying to negative comments because this can fuel the situation. The digital curriculum should provide all pupils with the digital literacy skills they need to keep themselves safe online. In addition, it should introduce pupils to the concept of digital citizenship. Young people need to be taught how to be good digital citizens. They need to learn that behaviour that is not tolerated in the real world is also not acceptable in the online world. Good digital citizens treat others online with respect, compassion and empathy – behaviours that also constitute good citizenship offline.

Encouraging both sides to meet and talk together can be effective. Restorative approaches support all those involved. The person who was bullied is supported by a mediator to explain to the perpetrator how the bullying has affected them. They can talk about the impact of the bullying on their feelings, their mental health and their daily life. The person who did the bullying should be supported to listen to this account and then explain why they chose to bully the other person and what they have learned from listening to their account. They can also be supported by a mediator to explain how they will modify their behaviour in the future. The approach is designed to provide reassurance to the pupil who was bullied that there will not be a repeat incident so that they feel safer.

CRITICAL QUESTIONS

+ What are microaggressions, and how might teachers address these?

+ What examples of microaggressions might be evident in the classroom?

EXTENDED THINKING

+ How might intersectional identities result in multiple forms of oppression and marginalisation?

CASE STUDY

TOPICS IN THE RSHE CURRICULUM

WHOLE SCHOOL

One multi-academy trust in the Midlands recently launched its RSHE curriculum for Key Stages 3, 4 and 5. Each of the seven year groups focuses on a specific curriculum topic: bullying, sexuality, identity, relationships, friendships, personal safety and risky behaviour. The trust maps each of these curriculum topics to an external speaker, charity or agency whose input provides an opportunity to expose pupils to real-life scenarios and expertise from sector-specific specialists. For example, Year 10 focuses on sexuality, and these sessions are supported by a local charity that provides advice and guidance on sexuality and the process of coming out. This allows pupils of all sexualities to receive personalised advice and support with any issue they wish to discuss or explore through interactive workshops and debates. This annual programme gives pupils an opportunity to connect with role models, seek advice and gather information relating to sexuality or gender identity. There is also an opportunity for pupils to request private one-to-one support should they feel that they wish to further their conversation or seek confidential advice.

EMBEDDING LGBTQ+ INTO THE HEALTH EDUCATION CURRICULUM

The statutory guidance for RSHE also includes guidance on the content of health education programmes in secondary schools. Health education will be made compulsory in all state-funded schools. To ensure that health education is LGBTQ+ inclusive, schools should focus on the following:

+ the importance of stable and committed same-sex relationships;

+ the emotional changes that young people experience when they are coming to terms with their gender identities or sexualities;

+ the link between emotional health, physical health and mental health, including how to manage anxiety and depression, the dangers of self-harm, substance misuse and eating disorders – the role of physical activity and social connectivity in improving mental health should be addressed.

Schools will need to carefully map out the content to be covered in national curriculum subjects, RSHE and health education to ensure that subjects complement each other and do not duplicate information.

PUPILS LEADING ON CURRICULUM DESIGN

Many secondary schools have an LGBTQ+ pupil group that provides a safe space for LGBTQ+ pupils and their allies. The LGBTQ+ pupil group can play an important role in ensuring that the curriculum addresses LGBTQ+ inclusion. Schools can involve LGBTQ+ pupils in designing the RSHE curriculum to ensure that it addresses the following aspects:

+ sexual orientation and gender identity, including pronoun use;

+ coming to terms with sexual orientation and gender identity;

+ same-sex marriage and civil partnerships;

+ keeping safe online;

+ sexually transmitted infections;

+ domestic abuse in same-sex relationships.

In addition, schools can involve LGBTQ+ pupils in researching ways of embedding LGBTQ+ issues into other subject content. The LGBTQ+ pupil group can meet with subject leaders or heads of department to review schemes of work to ensure that the curriculum is LGBTQ+ inclusive. It is important that LGBTQ+ pupils can see that their identities are visible in the taught curriculum. This helps to establish a sense of belonging.

RUNNING AN LGBTQ+ PUPIL GROUP

Developing an LGBTQ+ pupil group is an effective way of empowering pupils. The group can provide LGBTQ+ pupils with a safe, informal space to gain mutual support. However, effective LGBTQ+ pupil groups achieve far more than providing members with mutual support; they advance LGBTQ+ inclusion, challenge prejudice and discrimination and change attitudes. It is important to allow non-LGBTQ+ pupils to join the group, because this creates a powerful message that the group is inclusive and has support from the heterosexual pupil body. These pupils can act as LGBTQ+ allies, and their membership of the group helps to demonstrate that the group is not separate from the rest of the school community.

The group may be initiated by a staff member, or it may be completely pupil-led. When developing the group, it is useful to refer to the guidance that Stonewall has published. Stonewall (2018) sets out what should happen in the first meeting.

+ Establish the aims, focus and aspirations of the group. The group members will need to decide what exactly they want the group to achieve within a specific timescale and how they are going to achieve this.

+ Ensure that the group is pupil-led right from the start.

+ Gain support from the senior leadership team. One way of achieving this is for a member of the leadership team to voice their commitment to the group in the first meeting.

+ Allow non-LGBTQ+ pupils to join the group.

+ Name the group. The pupils will need to decide on a name and logo for the group so that the group has a brand.

+ Consider how the group will be advertised.

+ Create ground rules. One of the most important things to establish in the initial meeting is that the group provides a confidential space for members to discuss their concerns. In addition, disagreements between members of the group should be kept outside of the group and not brought into meetings.

+ Create a plan for the year. Members will need to decide what they want to achieve over the course of the year. Decisions will need to be made about what activities the group will develop to address key calendar dates. These include LGBTQ+ History Month, Anti-Bullying Week and Mental Health Awareness Week.

The pupil members should be empowered to take responsibility for making decisions in relation to the above points. It is important that the group has a visible presence in the school and is not hidden away. One way of achieving this is to assign a space for the group to display their achievements and to advertise key events. The pupil members need to decide if there will be a chair and deputy chair and, if so, how they will be elected. This is a good way of teaching pupils about democracy and addressing one of the fundamental British values. The group also needs to decide how often meetings will be held and whether minutes of meetings will be recorded. Fundamentally, the group needs to be given opportunities to organise events. The pupil members need to be kept busy by working on worthwhile projects. This will help them stay motivated.

Members may wish to consider creating a newsletter, leaflets, social media platforms or a website to promote the group and to provide helpful advice for other pupils. Guidance on coming to terms with one's sexual or gender identity as well as advice on coming out is more likely to be taken seriously if it has been written by pupils who have experienced these issues.

It is more effective to distribute different tasks to different pupils so that there is fair allocation of workload. Pupil members will have different strengths. Some will have strengths in oral communication, others in event organising, others in technology, and so on. It is important to draw on different people's talents and experiences.

LGBTQ+ pupil groups may also want to be 'outward-facing'. One way of achieving this is for the group to gain support from community organisations, parents and carers. Some parents may resist the group and be suspicious of its motives. This is a matter for staff members to address. Parents' concerns need to be listened to, but leadership teams should communicate a clear message to parents that the school is committed to equality and has a legal obligation to support the LGBTQ+

pupil body. Pupil members may wish to consider gaining support from parents and carers who are willing to participate in the group.

Senior leadership teams need to consider how they are going to measure the impact of the LGBTQ+ pupil group. Impact can be measured both qualitatively and quantitatively. Examples of impact measures include:

+ quotes from pupil members of the group;

+ more detailed case studies of pupil members – for example, one-page pen portraits;

+ attendance data or achievement data for pupil members;

+ changes in the number of incidents of LGBTQ+ bullying.

Staff members also need to be encouraged to promote the group by signposting pupils who may benefit from being members to the group. Members need to view themselves as agentic individuals who have the power to effect positive change. The group should not be viewed solely as a means of support for pupils. However, this should fall within its remit.

The group is a key element of the whole-school approach to LGBTQ+ inclusion as it represents the 'student partnership' strand. However, it can also influence the curriculum, teaching and learning, and staff development.

CASE STUDY

CHAMPIONS TO ADDRESS HBT BULLYING

YEARS 11, 12 AND 13

A secondary school developed a scheme to train a group of champions to address HBT bullying. The champions were pupils in Years 11, 12 and 13. The champions were recruited via an applications process, and they were interviewed for the role. The champions completed a series of training workshops that covered topics such as what HBT bullying is, how to recognise it and how to respond if they witness it. The champions were encouraged to challenge and report HBT bullying. The champions were also trained in how to challenge bystanders of bullying. To celebrate their achievements, all champions were presented with an award and a certificate at the end of the school year.

EVIDENCE-BASED PRACTICE

The Stonewall *School Report* identified the following.

+ *Nearly half of lesbian, gay, bi and trans pupils (45 per cent) – including 64 per cent of trans students – are bullied for being LGBT at school.*

+ *Half of LGBT pupils (52 per cent) hear homophobic language 'frequently' or 'often' at school, more than a third (36 per cent) hear biphobic language 'frequently' or 'often', and almost half (46 per cent) hear transphobic language 'frequently' or 'often'.*

+ *The majority of LGBT pupils – 86 per cent – regularly hear phrases such as 'that's so gay' or 'you're so gay' in school.*

+ *Nearly one in ten trans pupils (nine per cent) are subjected to death threats at school.*

+ *Almost half of LGBT pupils (45 per cent) who are bullied for being LGBT never tell anyone about the bullying.*

+ *[Less] than a third of bullied LGBT pupils (29 per cent) say that teachers intervened when they were present during the bullying.*

+ *Two in five LGBT young people (40 per cent) have been the target of homophobic, biphobic and transphobic content online.*

+ *Nearly all LGBT young people (97 per cent) see homophobic, biphobic and transphobic content online.*

+ *Two in three LGBT young people (65 per cent) think that online platforms are unlikely to do anything about tackling homophobic, biphobic and transphobic content or incidents when it is reported to them.*

(Bradlow et al, 2017, p 7)

This study sought the views of young people aged 11–19. While the statistics presented above are an improvement on previous data collected by Stonewall, they are still alarming and have serious implications for secondary schools. Schools need to monitor incidents of HBT bullying. Incidents should be recorded and there should be evidence on the documentation to demonstrate how incidents have been addressed. Schools should reflect on incidents of homophobic bullying to review the school provision. It is important that schools learn from incidents of bullying and subsequently implement improvements to the current provision.

According to Stonewall, bullying can lead to school absence, self-harm and attempted suicide (Bradlow et al, 2017). It can therefore have a serious impact on pupils' mental health and result in damage to confidence and self-esteem. Consequently, academic potential is not fulfilled. Some people who identify as LGBTQ+ may develop mental health problems such as depression. If the issues are not addressed during adolescence, they can be long-lasting and affect individuals in adult life. In some cases, individuals who identify as LGBTQ+ go on to develop dependency on drugs or alcohol.

Some LGBTQ+ young people struggle to come to terms with their gender identity or sexuality, while some who are comfortable with their own identity or sexuality fear the reactions of others. This anticipation of negative reactions can lead to internalised psychological distress. If pupils have to come to terms with their identity in secret due to fear of the reactions of friends, family members or teachers, this can result in heightened stress, anxiety and depression. In cases where LGBTQ+ young people have good support networks around them, this can reduce the likelihood of developing mental ill health.

SUMMARY

This chapter explored the importance of teaching pupils about LGBTQ+ issues, including gender and sexual diversity. The benefits of an effectively designed LGBTQ+ curriculum were discussed, and this was set within the context of the Equality Act 2010. Strategies and approaches to embedding LGBTQ+ inclusion across the secondary curriculum were examined, and the chapter detailed the key elements of an inclusive RSHE curriculum. The chapter also summarised the contribution that health education can make to promoting inclusive attitudes about people with non-normative gender and sexual identities.

CHECKLIST

+ Building LGBTQ+ content into the curriculum helps LGBTQ+ pupils to experience a sense of belonging.

+ Involving LGBTQ+ pupils and their allies in curriculum design is empowering.

+ Teaching all pupils about diverse identities helps to address the Equality Act 2010.

FURTHER READING

Meyer, I H (2003) Prejudice, Social Stress, and Mental Health in Lesbian, Gay, and Bisexual Populations: Conceptual Issues and Research Evidence. *Psychological Bulletin*, 129(5): 674–97.

Stonewall (2017) *Creating an LGBT-inclusive Curriculum: A Guide for Secondary Schools*. London: Stonewall.

✚ CHAPTER 12

RELATIONSHIPS, SEX AND HEALTH EDUCATION

CHAPTER OBJECTIVES

After reading this chapter you will understand:

+ the statutory guidance for RSHE;

+ approaches for teaching sensitive topics.

INTRODUCTION

This chapter addresses some of the key aspects of content in the RSHE curriculum. The content of the statutory guidance has changed since it was first written in 2000, and the latest guidance includes new content that reflects the issues that are prevalent in society. These include domestic abuse, issues of consent and pornography. LGBTQ+ content is also a key component of the RSHE curriculum. It is important to emphasise from the outset that parents do not have a right to withdraw their child from the RSHE. The right to withdraw only applies to sex education. Much of the content of this curriculum also addresses the school's legal duties in relation to the Equality Act 2010. Some aspects of the health education curriculum may also be addressed through the science curriculum.

EXTENDED THINKING

+ Do you agree that parents should have the right to withdraw their child from sex education? Justify your answer.

TYPES OF RELATIONSHIP

The statutory guidance (DfE, 2019b) states that pupils should know that there are different types of committed, stable relationships. Pupils should therefore be taught about heterosexual relationships, same-sex relationships, marriage, civil partnership, co-habiting and other relationship types. Essentially, regardless of the type of relationship, it is important that pupils understand how relationships can contribute to mental well-being. Pupils should be taught to understand that there are different types of families, including families with same-sex parents, foster or adoptive parents, and single parents. Some children may be raised by siblings or other members of the extended family. Pupils need to understand that regardless of family structure, there are things that healthy families share in common. These include valuing time together, caring for one another, supporting each other emotionally and/or financially, respecting each family member and demonstrating love and commitment.

CRITICAL QUESTIONS

+ How have views on relationships changed in recent decades?

+ To what extent are commitment and stability important in relationships?

+ Why do you think the government wants pupils to learn about the importance of committed, stable relationships?

HEALTHY RELATIONSHIPS

Healthy relationships, including friendships, are characterised by trust, respect, honesty, kindness, generosity, boundaries, privacy, consent, conflict management and reconciliation. Adolescence can be a difficult time. It is a stage within the life cycle when many young people are exploring their identities and developing their interests, aspirations, values and beliefs. It is common during this stage for friendships to be dissolved and for new ones to be established. It is also a time when young people seek greater independence from their parents. Consequently, peer influence can be greater than parental influence during this stage of development. Adolescence can be a time when young people start to take risks. For many it is a time for developing personal and intimate relationships and therefore a time for sexual experimentation. Taking all of these things into account, adolescence can be a time when friendships and family relationships are tested to their limits.

EXTENDED THINKING

+ If pupils observe and experience unhealthy relationships in family or community contexts, what impact might teaching them about healthy and unhealthy relationships have?

+ How might you address this sensitively?

HEALTHY INTIMATE RELATIONSHIPS

It is important that pupils understand that healthy intimate relationships are underpinned by mutual respect, consent, loyalty, trust and sex.

Pupils need to understand the principles of consent and the law relating to consent. Healthy intimate relationships are usually underpinned by friendship, shared interests and shared viewpoints. However, it is important that pupils recognise that intimate partners may sometimes have different interests and viewpoints, and that mutual respect for different perspectives is always a characteristic of healthy relationships. Although friendship is often a characteristic of intimate relationships, this is not always the case. People can have healthy intimate relationships without establishing a friendship, but mutual respect and consent should always be evident within these relationships.

Young people live in a world where monogamy is not always upheld within intimate relationships. It is important to discuss mutual consent within relationships if these discussions arise. Teaching should promote the benefits of a stable and committed relationship. In addition, the increasing use of online dating platforms has made it easier for people to achieve intimacy with other people without necessarily establishing a 'traditional' relationship with the partners that they meet. Pupils need to understand that this is not necessarily negative, depending on one's beliefs, providing that the principles of consent and mutual respect are upheld within all types of relationship. Pupils should be supported to recognise that casual sexual relationships can be healthy, providing that those involved are aware of the risks and know how to protect themselves from these risks, and that there is always consent and no sexual pressure, coercion or manipulation within these relationships.

CONSENT

Consent is often understood within the context of sexual relationships. However, consent should underpin all healthy relationships, including friendships. A person consents to something if they agree by choice, and they possess the freedom and capacity to make that choice. Consent is underpinned by some key principles, outlined below.

+ *It is the person seeking consent who is responsible (ethically and legally) for ensuring that consent is given by another person, and for ensuring that that person has the freedom and capacity to give their consent.*

+ *If consent is not clear, informed, willing and active, it must be assumed that consent has not been given. If consent is not clearly given, or is given and then subsequently retracted, this decision must always be respected. Since people can change their minds, or consent to one thing but not to something else, the seeker of consent must keep assessing whether consent is clear, informed, willing and active. Consent must be seen as an ongoing process, not a 'one-off'.*

+ *In healthy relationships, both parties respectfully seek each other's consent and know that their decision to give or not give consent will be respected. A person is never to blame if their decision not to give consent or to withdraw consent is not respected.*

(PSHE Association, 2015, p 3)

Within the context of healthy friendships consent must be sought by one person and freely given by another person who has the capacity to provide consent and has been given full information about what they are being asked to do. Capacity to provide consent may be affected by a range of factors, including sexual orientation, gender, socio-economic and cultural background, and SEND. Consent is ongoing and can be withdrawn at any point. If consent is withdrawn, the person who sought the consent must respect this decision.

According to the PSHE Association, '*learning about consent should begin before young people are sexually active, otherwise it is too late*' (2015, p 3). Key definitions are stated below.

Consent *is agreement which is given willingly and freely without exploitation, threat or fear, and by a person who has the capacity to give their agreement.*

Sexual consent *refers to a positive choice to take part in a sexual activity by people who understand the nature and implications of the activity they are agreeing to.*

(PSHE Association, 2015, p 6)

When teaching pupils about consent, it is important to draw on related concepts. These include mutual respect, empathy, personal safety and bullying and abuse. It is also important that pupils are taught about risk. Pupils must recognise that it is important to be curious and adventurous, but at the same time they need to understand how to keep themselves safe. Schools have a responsibility to teach pupils to understand how to manage and mitigate risks. It is therefore crucial for teaching to focus on supporting pupils to take positive and well-considered risks at an appropriate time and with a focus on maintaining personal safety. When teaching about risk and consent, you should reinforce that although people take risks, they are never to blame when others fail to respect their decision to withhold or withdraw consent (PSHE Association, 2015). Furthermore, when teaching pupils about consent and the concepts it links to, it is important to support pupils to understand common myths, assumptions and misunderstandings. To support your teaching, you may find it valuable to draw on real-life examples to illustrate these. For example, although sexual images shared through the internet are widely available, they often depict scenarios where it is not clear that consent has been negotiated (PSHE Association, 2015).

Teachers have a responsibility to consider the needs of their pupils and to ensure that lessons and teaching activities are appropriate and build on pupils' prior knowledge. This enables schools to determine how to teach pupils about consent, and it allows teachers to be responsive to the needs of pupils. However, it is important to ensure that all lessons are effective and meaningfully planned. According to the PSHE Association (2015), all lessons should:

+ be delivered in a safe learning environment;

+ enable pupils to build on and develop existing knowledge;

+ provide opportunities for pupils to ask questions and raise concerns;

+ be taught by teachers with appropriate knowledge and expertise;

+ be taught by teachers who have access to and support from colleagues;

+ be responsive to pupils' circumstances and experiences;

+ highlight unrealistic norms and the implications of these;

+ recognise the influence of social media and the sharing of pornography and images of a sexual nature;

+ be supported through the use of realistic scenarios that are not reflective of teachers' or pupils' personal circumstances.

SEXUAL EXPLOITATION

The legal age of consent is 16. Any sexual activity with a person under the age of 16 is against the law. Child sexual exploitation is when people use their power to sexually abuse children. Sexual abuse covers penetrative sexual acts, sexual touching, masturbation and the misuse of sexual images, such as on the internet or transmitted by mobile phone. Sexual exploitation also occurs within adult relationships when consent is not sought or respected.

When teaching pupils about sexual exploitation, it is important to draw on their prior knowledge of consent and abuse. This is because pupils need to recognise the relationship between sexual exploitation and consent and between sexual exploitation and abuse. Pupils must also understand that sexual exploitation may involve young children and may exist within the digital and online environment. If pupils are not taught about these risks, they are left unprepared and unprotected should they ever be approached by a perpetrator. Pupils must know how to report concerns, and they must understand how to seek support at all times and regardless of whether they are in the school building with access to school staff.

When you teach pupils about sexual exploitation you must consider the needs, circumstances and personal experiences of your pupils. It is important to establish a safe learning space in which pupils feel able to ask questions and share any concerns with you. You should also ensure that pupils understand that the classroom is a non-judgemental space.

CASE STUDY

TEACHING ABOUT ABORTION

YEAR 9

A secondary school addressed the topic of abortion in a unit of work on pregnancy options. Pupils were introduced to the following curriculum content:

+ the human life cycle and how conception occurs, in order to understand how contraception works;

+ the choices in relation to pregnancy (with medically and legally accurate, impartial information on all options, including keeping the baby, adoption, abortion and where to get further help);

+ the emotional impact of pregnancy;

+ the law on abortion;

+ timing of abortion;

→

+ myths about abortion;

+ the emotional impact of abortion;

+ the facts about the full range of contraceptive choices and options available;

+ the facts around pregnancy, including miscarriage;

+ the facts about reproductive health, including fertility and the potential impact of lifestyle on fertility for men and women.

The school addressed the following points.

+ It is important to create a safe space free of stigma.

+ Teachers must not share their own views on abortion. They should just present the facts clearly and respectfully.

Teachers referred to the FSRH and Royal College of Obstetricians & Gynaecologists (2021) document titled 'Abortion and Abortion Care Factsheet' to guide their approach.

GROOMING

Grooming is when a person builds a relationship or develops trust and emotional connectivity with a child so they can manipulate, exploit and abuse them. Pupils must recognise that they can be groomed by people they know and that many perpetrators of sexual abuse are known to the children they target. Pupils need to recognise the importance of being careful and alert with everyone, including those they trust. However, it is also important that pupils do not become unduly anxious and unable to develop trusting relationships with peers and adults for fear of being abused. This can make it incredibly difficult to teach pupils about grooming. However, to support your teaching, it is useful to teach pupils about common signs associated with grooming.

+ Groomers pretend to be your friend and may try to build trust with you over a long period of time.

+ Groomers may use games and jokes to test your boundaries and see how far they can push you without alarming you.

+ Groomers may, over a long period of time, move from social contact, including hugging, to accidental touching and then to intimate touching.

+ Groomers may encourage you to break rules so that they can blackmail you in the future.

+ Groomers may encourage the consumption of drugs and alcohol so that it is more difficult for you to object or react.

+ Groomers may share sexual material to test your reaction.

+ Groomers may ask you to communicate secretly or through apps that do not keep logs and copies of your conversation.

+ Groomers may blame you for their abuse or try to confuse you by telling you that you like the attention.

These scenarios can be used to teach pupils to recognise uncomfortable or dangerous situations. Pupils must also be taught how to respond to these. Within your teaching, you should teach pupils how to recognise the signs of a situation that may become uncomfortable or dangerous.

COERCION

Coercion is the use of various strategies – including intimidation, physical threats or emotional threats – to force someone to do something. Coercion can involve threatening to break a confidence. When exploring this concept, pupils should learn that regardless of what is actually said, agreement sought or given under coercion is not consent. It is also important for pupils to recognise that a refusal to give consent does not require justification to others. Failing to provide consent is a personal choice that should be respected. Forcing someone to do something when consent has not been provided is coercion. Pupils need to be supported to recognise coercion within the context of unhealthy relationships, including intimate relationships and friendships.

HARASSMENT

The term 'harassment' is used to refer to unwanted behaviours that occur with the intention or effect of violating an individual's dignity or creating an environment that an individual finds intimidating, hostile, degrading, humiliating or offensive. Pupils must understand that harassment can occur online and offline, and that it does not need to take place face to face or within a physical space. It is important to emphasise within your teaching that harassment can be between children, between adults or between an adult and a child.

Pupils need to be able to identify the common signs of harassment, including:

+ telling stories and spreading rumours;

+ making lewd comments;

+ making remarks about someone's appearance;

+ name-calling;

+ making comments about family members;

+ unwanted messages;

+ coercion and threats;

+ nonconsensual sharing of material.

Schools have a responsibility to teach pupils to recognise and report sexual harassment. Schools must also ensure that they challenge all instances of sexual harassment. Failure to do so can normalise inappropriate behaviours, and this may provide an environment that leads to sexual violence (DfE, 2015).

RAPE

According to the law, only a man can commit rape as the penetration has to be with a penis. However, both women and men can be raped. Rape can occur within a relationship or within a marriage. The Sexual Offences Act 2003 says that person A is guilty of rape if:

a) *he intentionally penetrates the vagina, anus or mouth of another person (B) with his penis;*

b) *B does not consent to the penetration, and*

c) *A does not reasonably believe that B consents.*

The legal position in England and Wales is that women can carry out sexual assault (or assault by penetration, which carries the same sentencing) but not rape according to the legal definition. Sexual assault is when any male or female intentionally touches another person sexually without their consent.

EXTENDED THINKING

+ What are the arguments for and against including rape in the curriculum?

MYTHS ABOUT RAPE

Pupils may believe several myths about rape, and these need to be challenged. PSHE Association guidance refers to the following myths.

+ *If someone is raped while drunk, they are at least somewhat responsible.*

+ *If someone dresses provocatively, they are asking for trouble.*

+ *Someone who teases someone else deserves anything that then happens.*

+ *If you go back to someone's house, you are saying you want to have sex with that person.*

+ *When people are raped it is because they haven't said 'no' strongly enough.*

+ *Men don't usually intend to force sex on anyone but sometimes they get carried away.*

+ *If someone engages in kissing or intimacy and then lets things get out of hand, it's their own fault if their partner forces them to have sex.*

+ *Many so-called rape victims are actually people who had sex and 'changed their minds' afterwards.*

+ *People are almost never raped by their partners.*

+ *Rape only happens to women.*

(PSHE Association, 2015, pp 60–1)

CRITICAL QUESTIONS

+ What mental image do you hold of a rapist?
+ To what extent is this image based on a stereotype?
+ What sensitive issues might arise when teaching pupils about rape?

DOMESTIC ABUSE

Domestic abuse is an incident or pattern of incidents of controlling, coercive, threatening, degrading and violent behaviour, including sexual violence, by a partner or previous partner. It includes:

+ coercive control;

+ psychological and/or emotional abuse;

+ physical abuse;

+ sexual abuse;

+ financial abuse;

+ harassment;

+ stalking;

+ online or digital abuse.

When you are teaching pupils about domestic abuse, it is important to consider that some of your pupils may have had experiences of living in situations that have involved domestic abuse. Some pupils may also live in households that are currently affected by domestic violence. Throughout your teaching, you should signpost support services and emphasise that pupils can discuss their concerns with any member of school staff. Teachers should promote positive relationships in the classroom that are built on trust and safety, and this will support pupils to discuss any concerns they may have in relation to the topic.

CRITICAL QUESTIONS

+ What might be the signs of the early stages of domestic abuse within a relationship?

+ What impact might domestic abuse have on the person who was abused?

+ What sensitive issues might arise when teaching pupils about domestic violence?

BEHAVIOUR WITHIN RELATIONSHIPS

Pupils need to understand what constitutes healthy behaviour within relationships, including friendships. It is particularly important that pupils understand that coercion, manipulation, exploitation and violent forms of behaviour are not acceptable within relationships. Pupils also need to understand that controlling behaviours are also not acceptable. It is important that pupils know that healthy relationships are based on trust, respect, kindness, consent, honesty and boundaries.

SEXUAL PRESSURE

Sexual pressure can be applied through a variety of tactics. These include:

+ coercion: using physical, psychological or emotional threats to make a person engage in sexual activity;

+ manipulation: gaining agreement for sexual activity by increasing someone's vulnerability;

+ exploitation: exploiting someone's vulnerability by offering support, shelter, food, money, alcohol or drugs in return for sexual activity.

If consent is sought through these tactics, then it is assumed that consent has not been given and pupils need to recognise that sex without consent is illegal. Providing pupils with a range of scenarios for them to read and asking them to decide if sexual pressure has been applied or not is a useful way of supporting pupils to understand sexual pressure. Pupils also need to be taught a range of strategies for resisting sexual pressure. The statements below are useful for pupils to know.

+ *No thank you.*

+ *I don't want to.*

+ *I've changed my mind.*

+ *I need you to stop.*

(PSHE Association, 2015, p 40)

These statements are more effective than phrases where young people attempt to justify themselves in situations where they are exposed to sexual pressure. For example, '*I don't want to do this anymore because ...*' invites the person applying the pressure to respond. It is far better to make a direct statement than to invite a response.

LEGAL RIGHTS AND RESPONSIBILITIES

Pupils need to understand the implications of the Equality Act 2010. This legislation protects individuals from unfair treatment and promotes a fair and more equal society. It safeguards individuals with protected characteristics from direct or indirect forms of discrimination and harrasment. The protected characteristics include age, disability, gender reassignment, race, religion or belief, sex, sexual orientation, marriage and civil partnership and pregnancy and maternity.

SEXUAL BULLYING

Sexual bullying is any bullying behaviour, whether physical or non-physical, that is based on a person's sexuality or gender. It is when sexuality or gender is used as a weapon (by a person of any sexuality or gender) towards another person. Sexual bullying can be conducted online or offline and can include:

+ sexualised name-calling;

+ verbal abuse;

+ criticising sexual performance or behaviour;

+ ridiculing physical appearance, spreading rumours about someone's sexuality or sexual experiences they have had or not had;

+ unwanted touching and physical assault.

Sexual bullying is behaviour which is repeated over time and intends to hurt someone by using that person's gender, sexuality or sexual (in)experience to hurt them.

Sexual harassment refers to unwanted behaviours which are of a sexual nature. These may include, but are not limited to:

+ behaviour which seeks to intimidate you or violate your dignity;

+ behaviour which seeks to degrade, humiliate or embarrass;

+ behaviour which seeks to create an uncomfortable, hostile or offensive environment.

It is important to understand that an individual does not need to have previously objected to someone's behaviour for it to be legally considered as unwanted. Furthermore, the law states that unwanted behaviours can constitute sexual harassment even if the effect was not intended.

The term sexual violence refers to any kind of unwanted sexual act or activity. Sexual violence includes rape, but there are also many other types of sexual violence. These include sexual assault, sexual harassment, female genital mutilation and sexual abuse.

Sexual harassment and sexual violence are both forms of sexual bullying. It is important that pupils are aware of this. However, it is also important that pupils are taught the difference between the two and schools play an important role in developing pupils' understanding of these types of abuse. There are a range of charitable organisations that seek to support schools to teach pupils about sexual bullying. It is worth contacting local charities to determine the support that is available. These organisations can often provide you with a range of printed resources or materials and may be able to contribute their advice and expertise through visiting speakers and outreach work.

EVIDENCE-BASED PRACTICE

Ofsted's report on sexual abuse in schools, *Review of Sexual Abuse in Schools and Colleges* (Ofsted, 2021), found the following.

+ *Children and young people [reported] that sexual harassment and online sexual abuse are prevalent in their daily lives.*

+ *For some children, the incidents are so commonplace that they see no point in reporting them.*

+ *Girls [reported] that sexual harassment and online sexual abuse, such as being sent unsolicited explicit sexual material and being pressured to send nude pictures ('nudes'), are much more prevalent than adults realise.*

+ *90% of girls, and nearly 50% of boys, said being sent explicit pictures or videos of things they did not want to see happens a lot or sometimes to them or their peers.*

+ *Children and young people [reported] that sexual harassment occurs so frequently that it has become 'commonplace'. For example, 92% of girls, and 74% of boys, said sexist name-calling happens a lot or sometimes to them or their peers.*

→

+ *[Abuse takes place in] unsupervised spaces outside of school, such as parties or parks without adults present, although some girls [reported] they also experienced unwanted touching in school corridors.*

+ *Children and young people were rarely positive about the RSHE they had received. They felt that it was too little, too late and that the curriculum was not equipping them with the information and advice they needed to navigate the reality of their lives.*

(Ofsted, 2021)

MENTAL WELL-BEING

Pupils should be taught about ways of improving well-being, including the importance of forming social connections and the role of physical activity, community participation and voluntary service in improving mental health.

Young people also need to be taught to recognise common types of mental ill health, including anxiety, depression and self-harm. A well-designed mental health curriculum supports pupils to recognise mental ill health in themselves and others. It facilitates young people's understanding of resilience and provides them with useful strategies to adopt if they experience specific forms of mental ill health. Additionally, pupils should learn how to support others by developing empathy and skills in sensitive, deep listening. Male pupils need to understand the importance of expressing their feelings and emotions rather than conforming to traditional gender stereotypes.

HEALTH AND FITNESS

Both the physical and mental health benefits of engaging in physical activity for adults as well as children and young people are well documented and widely and internationally accepted (Hyndman et al, 2017; McMahon et al, 2017). Physical activity improves fitness and well-being. Pupils need to understand the benefits of a healthy lifestyle through exercise and good nutrition, and they need to understand the link between inactivity, ill health and disease. It is important that pupils do not develop obsessions about body image and diet and that they understand it is acceptable occasionally to eat foods that have a high fat and high sugar content.

SUBSTANCE MISUSE

Young people in secondary schools will be aware of drugs. Drug, alcohol and tobacco use may be prevalent in their homes and communities, and some pupils may already be experimenting with these. It is important that pupils understand the relationships between substance use, mental health and disease, including the link between tobacco use and lung cancer. They need to be taught about the physical and psychological consequences of addiction, including alcohol dependency. Pupils should be taught the facts about legal and illegal drugs and ways of giving up smoking.

Teaching about substance misuse can be challenging, particularly if pupils already have an addiction or if substance use is evident within their families and communities. Teachers should focus on the facts by highlighting the associated health risks. It is important to create a positive climate which supports pupils to openly disclose their addictions. If the climate is non-judgemental, pupils will be more likely to reach out for support. Providing pupils with small-group support sessions through which they can learn to break unhealthy habits is an effective way of helping them. They will often be well aware of the associated risks of substance misuse, but they may need practical solutions to break the habits they have formed.

HEALTH AND PREVENTION

Pupils should understand the importance of good oral hygiene and of regular self-examination and screening. It is important that pupils understand how to check specific body organs, including the genitals and breasts, to identify possible disease. Pupils also need to understand the importance of immunisation, vaccination and good-quality sleep. Pupils need to understand the link between social media use and sleep quality, and the effects of sleep deprivation. In addition, they should be taught about the importance of maintaining personal hygiene.

BASIC FIRST AID

Pupils should be taught how to provide basic treatment for common injuries, life-saving skills and how to administer cardiopulmonary resuscitation. They also need to understand the role of defibrillators and to identify when one might be needed. The school needs to provide a programme of first aid training, delivered by an external organisation.

CHANGING ADOLESCENT BODY

Pupils need to understand the key facts about puberty and the changing adolescent body, including menstrual well-being. They need to know the main changes which take place in the adolescent body and the implications of these for emotional and physical health.

SOCIAL MEDIA

Evidence suggests that social media use can result in young people developing conditions such as anxiety, stress and depression (RSPH, 2017). There are various reasons for this, and this section explores the contributing factors. Research has found that four of the five most-used social media platforms make young people's feelings of anxiety worse (RSPH, 2017).

EVIDENCE-BASED PRACTICE

Research suggests that young people who use social media heavily (ie those who spend more than two hours per day on social networking sites) are more likely to report poor mental health, including psychological distress (Sampasa-Kanyinga and Lewis, 2015). Cyberbullying is a significant problem affecting young people. Evidence suggests that seven in ten young people experience cyberbullying (RSPH, 2017).

CYBERBULLYING

Cyberbullying exists in a variety of forms. It can include the posting of hurtful comments online, threats and intimidation towards others in the online space, and posting photographs or videos online that are intended to cause distress. This is not an exhaustive list. Cyberbullying is fundamentally different to bullying, which takes place in person. A person who experiences cyberbullying may find it difficult to escape, because it exists within their personal and private spaces, such as their homes and bedrooms. Additionally, the number of people witnessing cyberbullying can be extremely large given the potential of social media posts to be shared across hundreds, thousands or even millions of people. For the person experiencing cyberbullying, this can be extremely humiliating and result in loss of confidence and self-worth. Humiliating messages, photographs and videos can be stored permanently online, resulting in the individual experiencing the bullying repeatedly every time they go online. Individuals who experience cyberbullying can experience depression, anxiety, loss of sleep, self-harm and feelings of loneliness (RSPH, 2017).

SOCIAL MEDIA AND BODY IMAGE

Social media has also been associated with body image concerns. Research indicates that when young girls and women in their teens and early twenties view Facebook for only a short period of time, they have more body image concerns compared to non-users (Tiggeman and Slater, 2013). Young people view images of 'ideal' bodies and start to make comparisons with their own bodies. This can result in low body esteem, particularly if young people feel that their own bodies do not compare favourably to the 'perfect' bodies they see online. Young people are heavily influenced by celebrities and may desire to look like them. If they feel that this is unattainable, it can result in depression, body surveillance and low body confidence. Young people can then start to develop conditions such as eating disorders.

The issue of body image is not just a female issue. Young males are also vulnerable and influenced by the muscular, toned bodies they see online. We now live in an age when boys and men are taking increasing interest in their appearance and viewing images of muscular, toned bodies can result in them putting their bodies through extensive fitness regimes. Boys are also vulnerable to developing eating disorders.

The opportunity for people to use digital editing software to edit their appearance in photographs can also result in young people developing a false sense of beauty. It is worrying that there is a rise in the number of young people seeking to obtain cosmetic surgery (RSPH, 2017), and the popularity of 'selfies' in recent years has resulted in an increase in images which portray beauty and perfection. These images can have a negative impact on body esteem and body confidence.

SOCIAL MEDIA AND SLEEP

Research demonstrates that increased social media use has a significant association with poor sleep quality in young people (Scott et al, 2016). It seems that young people enjoy being constantly connected to the online world. They develop fear of missing out, which is associated with lower mood and lower life satisfaction (Pryzbylski et al, 2013). This can result in young people constantly checking their devices for messages, even during the night, resulting in broken sleep. Sleep is particularly important during adolescence and broken sleep can result in exhaustion and lack of opportunity for the brain to become refreshed. Lack of sleep quality can have a range of detrimental effects, but it can also impact on school performance and behaviour.

SOCIAL MEDIA, SELF-HARM AND SUICIDE

The link between social media use, self-harm and even suicide is particularly worrying (RSPH, 2017). The fact that young people can access distressing content online that promotes self-harm and suicide is a significant cause for concern. This content attempts to 'normalise' self-harm and suicide and can result in young people replicating the actions that they are exposed to.

ILLEGAL ONLINE ACTIVITY

Pupils need to understand the law in relation to sharing online content. Creating or sharing explicit images of a child is illegal, even if the person doing it is a child themselves. A young person under the age of 18 is breaking the law if they:

+ *[take] an explicit photo or video of themselves or a friend;*

+ *[share] an explicit image or video of a child, even if it's shared between children of the same age;*

+ *[have, download or store] an explicit image or video of a child, even if the child gave their permission for it to be taken.*

(NSPCC, nd)

Schools play a crucial role in supporting pupils to understand the laws that relate to online activity. It is essential that pupils are able to determine what is considered legal and what is not. To support pupils' understanding, it is valuable to deliver an activity that provides pupils with a selection of legal and illegal scenarios in relation to online activity, which they sort into these two categories.

CASE STUDY

TEACHING ABOUT PORNOGRAPHY

YEAR 9

A secondary school considered carefully how to address the topic of pornography. They identified the following considerations.

+ The classroom needs to be a safe space where teachers feel comfortable teaching and the pupils feel comfortable learning.

+ In lessons it is important to establish ground rules about respecting others' views and avoiding making assumptions or asking personal questions.

+ The school does not want to normalise viewing porn given there will be some in class who have never seen it. However, it is important not to be ambivalent or positive in the messaging around porn given the extensive research that identifies the harmful effects of porn.

+ It is important not to shame those who have seen porn, as this might alienate members of the class.

The curriculum was designed to develop pupils' understanding of the way in which online pornography is pushed by the industry, including the way algorithms graduate towards harder content – so-called 'dark nudges'. The curriculum focused on three main strands:

1. making sure pupils recognise the harms that porn can do;

2. minimising use among pupils who choose to view porn;

→

3. making sure pupils know how to seek help if they need it.

Pupils were given a set of myths and facts about pornography. They were asked to work in pairs to discuss these, and then they were asked to sort them accordingly.

Teachers used the advice in the PSHE Association's (nd) document titled 'Addressing Pornography through PSHE Education'.

CRITICAL QUESTIONS

+ Do you agree that schools should address pornography in the curriculum? Justify your response?

+ Do you agree that Year 9 is the correct age to teach this content? Justify your response.

SUMMARY

This chapter addressed aspects of the relationships, sex and health education curriculum. It is important that curriculum content addresses the real issues that are evident in society. However, it is also important to recognise that some pupils will have personal experiences of the content being taught, and therefore content needs to be addressed using a sensitive and non-judgemental approach.

CHECKLIST

+ Parents can withdraw their child legally from sex education only.

+ The issue of consent does not start in the secondary curriculum. It starts in the primary relationships education curriculum in relation to consent in friendships.

+ Faith schools are allowed to teach the faith perspective in relation to topics such as abortion or same-sex relationships. However, they must also introduce pupils to a range of different perspectives. They cannot indoctrinate pupils into a faith perspective.

FURTHER READING

Department for Education (2021) What Do Children and Young People Learn in Relationship, Sex and Health Education. [online] Available at: https://educationhub.blog.gov.uk/2021/11/30/what-do-children-and-young-people-learn-in-relationship-sex-and-health-education/ (accessed 28 August 2022).

Emmerson, L (2019) New Abortion Factsheet for Teachers. [online] Available at: www.sexeducationforum.org.uk/news/news/new-abortion-factsheet-teachers (accessed 28 August 2022).

Fox, J (2022) Advice on How to Address the Topic of Pornography in the Classroom. [online] Available at: https://teaching.blog.gov.uk/2022/04/18/advice-on-how-to-address-the-topic-of-pornography-in-the-classroom/ (accessed 28 August 2022).

IPPF (nd) Teaching about Consent and Healthy Boundaries – a Guide for Educators. [online] Available at: www.ifpa.ie/sites/default/files/documents/Reports/teaching_about_consent_healthy_boundaries_a_guide_for_educators.pdf (accessed 28 August 2022).

✚ CHAPTER 13
INNOVATING THE CURRICULUM

CHAPTER OBJECTIVES

After reading this chapter you will understand:

✚ the process of designing an innovative curriculum;

✚ how to involve key stakeholders in curriculum design.

INTRODUCTION

Redesigning a whole-school curriculum is a complex task for school leaders. This chapter outlines some approaches for redesigning the curriculum in partnership with key stakeholders. It covers aspects that subject leaders need to address, and it suggests solutions for addressing staff resistance.

Curriculum development and innovation is a process that takes time. School leaders are advised to develop a three-year implementation plan so that the process is gradual rather than rapid. It is important to recognise that there will be many positive aspects of the existing curriculum which can be incorporated into the revised curriculum. Changing everything is not necessary and could result in significant additional workload for staff. Changing everything at once is likely to be overwhelming for staff, and therefore a gradual process of implementation is preferable.

WHAT DO WE MEAN BY AN INNOVATIVE CURRICULUM?

The term 'innovation' means different things to different people. In the context of curriculum development, we interpret this term in the following ways:

+ a curriculum that addresses societal challenges, including mental health, climate change and environmental sustainability;

+ a curriculum that prepares pupils for the world of work;

+ a curriculum that ensures that pupils develop deeper knowledge as they progress through it, thus revising the way they think about subject content;

+ a curriculum that engages and motivates pupils through nurturing the development of creativity;

+ a curriculum that prepares pupils for life in a global society as a global citizen;

+ a curriculum that embeds technological innovation;

+ a curriculum that introduces pupils to the latest thinking and cutting-edge research in the subject;

+ a curriculum that has inclusion and social justice at its heart;
+ a curriculum that promotes debate.

CRITICAL QUESTIONS

+ Do you agree with these points?
+ Can you add any additional aspects that would make a curriculum innovative?

PRESENTING A RATIONALE FOR CHANGE

Senior leaders need to involve staff from the outset in redesigning the curriculum. It is important that a clear rationale that justifies the need for change is articulated to staff. Leaders need to explain how the proposed changes to the curriculum will improve outcomes for pupils. It is important that these outcomes are not just reduced to examination results. The initial consultation with staff should address three key questions.

1. How good is the current subject curriculum?
2. What is working well?
3. What do we need to change?

It is important to recognise that any change is likely to cause some anxiety among staff. They may have been teaching the current subject curriculum for several years and be worried that any changes to the curriculum will lead to additional workload and take them out of their comfort zone. It is important to give staff an opportunity to share their concerns and to offer them reassurance at this point.

The *Education Inspection Framework* (Ofsted, 2019b) has elevated the status of the curriculum in schools. Inspectors are interested in the school's rationale for its curriculum, the knowledge that pupils are taught and how well this is sequenced to provide pupils with a coherent learning experience. In previous inspection frameworks, there was more focus on examination outcomes than on what pupils are taught.

This has led, in some instances, to pupils receiving a narrow curriculum and experiencing superficial learning as teachers have focused on teaching to the test. The renewed emphasis on the curriculum in school inspections is important and one of the reasons why school leaders need to review the curriculum. However, that is not the only reason. We live in a society that is rapidly changing. Society is addressing significant social, economic and environmental issues, and schools need to make sure that pupils have the appropriate knowledge and skills to thrive in the twenty-first century. The pace of technological development has been rapid, and schools need to ensure that pupils can adapt to future developments. A static curriculum does not ensure that pupils are prepared to address current and future challenges. The curriculum must be exciting, dynamic and contemporary so that pupils are well-positioned to be twenty-first-century global citizens. These arguments might support the rationale for change in the curriculum.

Developing a new whole-school curriculum should not result in completely abandoning the current curriculum. There will be many aspects of the current curriculum that are working well. The starting point in curriculum development is to identify what is working well and therefore needs to be preserved. Staff will also be able to identify what is not working well – that is, the topics, themes or units of work that they do not enjoy teaching and which may not be providing pupils what they need. Although teachers do have to teach things that they may not like, generally if teachers enjoy what they are teaching and are passionate and excited about it, then they teach well.

The starting point is therefore to open a discussion about what is working well and what is less effective. However, it must also be acknowledged that the national curriculum already specifies the minimum knowledge that pupils need to be taught. Schools cannot ignore this; they must view the national curriculum as a minimum curriculum requirement. Schools are free to go beyond the requirements of the national curriculum by designing a curriculum that serves the needs of their pupils and the communities which they serve. In some subjects, the guidance in the national curriculum is less prescriptive, in terms of both curriculum content and when that content needs to be taught. This provides an opportunity for school leaders and their staff to think about how to sequence the curriculum, when to teach content, how to build on it throughout the key stages and when to revisit content. Much greater attention needs to be given to the sequencing of subject-specific content so that pupils develop a secure understanding of these subjects.

EVIDENCE-BASED PRACTICE

It is highly likely that some teachers will resist a leader's decision to review or redesign the curriculum. This is problematic because resistance to change can be one of the most difficult barriers to overcome when implementing change. The theorists Kotter and Schlesinger (1979) suggest four reasons why staff may resist change:

+ self-interest;

+ low tolerance for change;

+ making a different assessment of the change that is needed;

+ misunderstanding the change or change rationale.

Crucially, most teachers do not resist change for cynical or negative reasons. Without this understanding, it can often be too easy to assume that resistance is an act of opposition or defence. That said, in some cases, teachers may resist change because of their own self-interest. They may fear that their own status or security is being threatened and respond in such a way as to protect their own interests over those of the school. In these cases, it is important to demonstrate to teachers how the curriculum change may benefit them and the pupils. This could be in relation to the provision of additional opportunities for both teachers and pupils as well as a positive impact on well-being and morale and a reduction in workload for teachers.

Teachers may also resist change because they have a low tolerance for change. These colleagues may prefer the status quo. This may occur because stability is valued or previous attempts to implement change have been unsuccessful. For example, an earlier redesign of the curriculum may have lost momentum despite significant investment in terms of time. In these cases, it is important to emphasise that the school is taking on board the lessons that have been learned from previous change initiatives (including mistakes that were made), and that it is committed to the implementation, monitoring and evaluation of any change.

Another reason for resistance to change relates to when teachers carry out their own appraisal of the situation and this results in a different assessment of the change that is required. For example, a member of staff may feel that a specific approach to curriculum design is more suitable for the context of the school than the approach adopted by leaders. Equally, there may be disagreement in relation to curriculum priorities within the social and cultural context of the school. In these cases, it is essential to probe the alternatives and understand why teachers feel that a different approach may be more appropriate. This supports the 'unpicking' of each option, drawing on necessary research, policies and legislation.

Finally, teachers may simply resist change because they do not understand why it is required or they have been misinformed during informal dialogue. They may not be aware of changes to statutory guidance and legislation, or they may not be aware of the need to respond to changes in the social and cultural context of the school and community. In these cases, education and communication play a crucial role. Teachers need to be made aware of why the redesign is required. They should be supported to understand the justification for the change and, where necessary, any supporting policies and frameworks.

DETERMINING CURRICULUM INTENT

Once staff have a clear understanding about what aspects of the curriculum are working well and what needs to change, it is time for school leaders and staff to consider the intent of the curriculum. The following questions support this phase of curriculum development.

+ What do we want our pupils to know?

+ What skills do we want our pupils to develop?

+ What attitudes do we want to instil in our pupils?

The process of determining curriculum content will take several weeks. School leaders may wish to develop a series of workshops with stakeholders to discuss these three questions. One way of approaching this is to plan and implement workshops with each stakeholder group to address these questions. Leaders should consult with staff, pupils, parents and members of the community.

Parents, staff, governors and community members should be given some context at the start of the meeting. This might include a discussion about the *Education Inspection Framework*, the rationale for the change and the importance of developing a curriculum that provides pupils with cultural capital. Stakeholders may not be familiar with this term, and it must be addressed sensitively with parents so that they do not feel that their socio-economic background is being undervalued.

The meetings should be genuine consultations that allow stakeholders to discuss the questions in small groups, mind map their responses and share the outcomes of their discussions with the larger group. It is useful to provide large sheets of paper, pens and sticky notes so that there are tangible outputs from the meetings which can then inform curriculum development. These can be reviewed by the senior leadership team to inform curriculum change.

WRITING A CURRICULUM VISION STATEMENT FOR YOUR SUBJECT

Following the stakeholder meetings, leaders will need to synthesise the views of staff, governors, pupils and the community in a vision statement. There is no mandatory requirement for schools to produce vision statements, and these are only useful if they are implemented in practice.

A vision statement should address the following questions.

+ What *knowledge* and *skills* do our pupils need to develop in order to thrive in the twenty-first century?

+ What *attitudes* and *values* does our curriculum need to promote to enable our pupils to thrive as global citizens?

REVIEWING THE EXISTING CURRICULUM

Although the initial discussion addressed the strengths and areas for development of the existing curriculum, subject leaders must review the curriculum in their subject areas in greater detail. If the school is part of a multi-academy trust, subject leaders from across the trust can work together on reviewing the curriculum with their specific subject(s), particularly if there is an intention to develop a trust-wide approach to the curriculum.

Subject leaders will need to look carefully at the existing curriculum. This review should address the following questions.

+ What knowledge and skills do pupils need to learn in the curriculum?

+ What subject content is a mandatory requirement of the national curriculum?

+ Is the existing curriculum sequenced correctly to ensure that pupils develop secure subject knowledge and skills?

+ How ambitious is the curriculum?

+ How inclusive is the curriculum?

+ How can cultural capital be embedded through the subject?

+ What training might staff need to implement the revised curriculum?

+ What resources might be needed to implement the new subject curriculum?

IDENTIFYING WHAT NEEDS TO CHANGE

By the time subject leaders have completed a curriculum review of the subjects they lead, they will have started to identify what needs to change. This process can only be completed when there is clear understanding of the vision for the curriculum. Subject leaders can start to identify priorities for curriculum development from the subject leader curriculum review, but it is important that the curriculum vision statement for each subject curriculum contributes to the overall agreed vision statement for the school's curriculum.

INVOLVING STAKEHOLDERS

Leaders need to consider how to involve stakeholders in the process of reviewing the curriculum. There are different levels of involvement that leaders could aim for. One level of involvement is to simply inform stakeholders about the changes to the curriculum. However, this model is not inclusive, as it does not allow the views of stakeholders to inform curriculum development. A development from this is to provide opportunities for stakeholders to review curriculum plans after they have been developed. The feedback from stakeholders can then inform subsequent curriculum development. An even higher level of engagement from stakeholders involves their participation, along with staff, in a working group to develop the curriculum. This model is more inclusive because it allows stakeholders to make an active contribution to curriculum development from the start. However, working groups tend not to be effective if they are starting from scratch with a blank sheet of paper. Many of the stakeholders are not experts in the curriculum or even in education. These meetings are more productive if school leaders take an active role by presenting a clear rationale for change and preparing curriculum plans to table at the meetings.

Schools need to decide how to involve pupils in the process. It might not be appropriate for pupils to sit through a lengthy meeting with other key stakeholders. There are other ways of involving pupils in the process of curriculum review which might be more effective. These include:

+ carrying out focus groups with pupils from different year groups to ascertain their perspectives on the curriculum;

+ completing a pupil questionnaire to ascertain pupils' views on the curriculum;

+ developing a separate working group for pupils from different year groups to provide an opportunity for them to work on curriculum development with subject leaders.

If consultation with pupils is taking place separately, school leaders must ensure that the perspectives of the pupils are fed back to the stakeholder meetings.

THE IMPORTANCE OF SEQUENCING

The *Education Inspection Framework* (Ofsted, 2019b) places more emphasis on sequencing than previous frameworks did. Subject leaders must ensure that knowledge and skills within their subjects are taught in the correct order so that pupils' learning is coherent. During the curriculum review of their subject, leaders need to review the current sequencing of knowledge and skills within and across key stages and within specific units of work. Correct sequencing of knowledge and skills will ensure that pupils make progress within the subject.

THE IMPORTANCE OF DEPTH

The subject curriculum should aim to deepen pupils' knowledge of the subject as they learn the curriculum. It should not just move pupils through a series of unrelated topics. As pupils progress through the subject curriculum, schemas that they have already formed should be modified so that there is a change in the way that pupils think about that aspect of subject content.

CASE STUDY

CURRICULUM REVIEW IN DESIGN AND TECHNOLOGY

WHOLE SCHOOL

Subject leaders in design and technology in a multi-academy trust came together to review and develop the subject curriculum. They realised that the current subject curriculum at Key Stage 3 addressed a range of interesting topics, but it did not specifically address the ambitious goals in the national curriculum. They started by identifying the ambitious goals in the national curriculum at Key Stage 3. They then broke each goal down into smaller component knowledge. Several components made up each national curriculum goal. They used sticky notes to record each component. They worked together to sequence each of the components so that pupils' knowledge develops and deepens as they progress through the curriculum. The component knowledge formed the basis of the subject curriculum in design and technology.

CRITICAL QUESTIONS

+ What are the advantages and disadvantages of a multi-academy-trust-wide approach to the curriculum?

+ Why is it important to adopt a collaborative approach to curriculum review?

THE ACID TEST OF THE NEW CURRICULUM

Once the 'new' curriculum has been developed, leaders should evaluate it against the following questions.

+ Does the curriculum fulfil the aims of the curriculum vision statement?

+ How ambitious is the curriculum?

+ Is the curriculum coherently planned and sequenced?

+ How broad and balanced is the curriculum?

+ How inclusive is the curriculum?

CRITICAL QUESTIONS

+ What are the problems with the word 'ambitious' in the context of the curriculum?

+ What problems might arise during the process of developing the intent of the curriculum, and how might these be overcome?

CASE STUDY

CURRICULUM REVIEW IN MUSIC

WHOLE SCHOOL

A model similar to the one outlined in the previous case study was adopted. Music subject leaders worked together to review the music curriculum before passing their proposed plans on to a working group of key stakeholders. Local musicians were represented on the stakeholder group.

Leaders used the national curriculum to identify the ambitious goals of the Key Stage 3 national curriculum for music. According to this process, pupils should be taught to:

+ *play and perform confidently in a range of solo and ensemble contexts using their voice, playing instruments musically, fluently and with accuracy and expression*

+ *improvise and compose, and extend and develop musical ideas by drawing on a range of musical structures, styles, genres and traditions;*

+ *use staff and other relevant notations appropriately and accurately in a range of musical styles, genres and traditions*

+ *identify and use the interrelated dimensions of music expressively and with increasing sophistication, including use of tonalities, different types of scales and other musical devices*

+ *listen with increasing discrimination to a wide range of music from great composers and musicians*

+ *develop a deepening understanding of the music that they perform and listen to, and its history*

(DfE, 2014, p 102)

Each national curriculum goal was broken down into components. Components were sequenced logically to produce a curriculum that deepened pupils' knowledge as they progressed through the music curriculum at Key Stage 3.

EVIDENCE-BASED PRACTICE

Research demonstrates that long-term memory is the central structure of human thinking (Clark et al, 2012). Additionally, evidence suggests that we learn new things in the context of what we already know (Willingham, 2009). Retrieval practice and spaced (or distributed) practice are critical for supporting transfer of information to the long-term memory.

During the process of curriculum development and sequencing, leaders should build in frequent opportunities to revisit prior subject-specific learning and plan opportunities for retrieval.

CRITICAL QUESTIONS

+ Why might staff resist change?
+ How might senior leaders work with staff who block change?

A STAGED APPROACH

Change takes time. The curriculum is the substance of education. Changing everything at once might not be feasible or desirable, and might lead to instability in the school. Planning a staged approach to reviewing the curriculum, perhaps by developing two or three subjects each year, is more manageable. This provides the opportunity to learn from practice and refine future curriculum developments. A sensible approach would be to develop a three-year plan of curriculum development with time built in to the plan for reflection and review.

CELEBRATING GOOD PRACTICE

Any change within schools creates instability because teachers become used to specific ways of working. Some teachers may initially resist change because they are frightened, they are worried about additional workload that the changes may create, and they are not convinced that the planned changes will be successful. It is better to work with those who are enthusiastic. These are the 'change agents' who will support leaders to convince others to adopt the changes. Every opportunity should be taken to celebrate the good practice that is happening in classrooms as a result of the curriculum review. Good work should be showcased. Change agents should be used to convince others. This will help push forward the changes that need to be made.

EVIDENCE-BASED PRACTICE

Force field analysis was developed by Kurt Lewin (1951). Lewin identified that two forces exist within organisations: driving forces and restraining forces. When these forces are equal, there is a state of equilibrium, or status quo. The equilibrium between the forces needs to be altered to bring about change. The theory has direct practical implications for school leaders who are keen to bring about curriculum development. First, it is necessary for leaders to define the change. Second, they need to identify the driving forces and the restraining forces for that change. Leaders then need to create a strategy for strengthening the driving forces, reducing the restraining forces, or both. This will help them to successfully implement the desired change.

SUMMARY

This chapter emphasised the importance of developing an innovative curriculum with key stakeholders. It suggested strategies for collaborating with key stakeholder groups and outlined key considerations for subject leaders.

CHECKLIST

+ An innovative curriculum prepares pupils to address global challenges.

+ An innovative curriculum develops knowledge, skills, attitudes and values.

+ The curriculum should develop the skills that are needed in the twenty-first-century workplace.

+ The curriculum should enable pupils to achieve the ambitious goals in the national curriculum.

+ The curriculum should embed creativity, technological innovation and social justice.

FURTHER READING

Boyle, B and Charles, M (2016) *Curriculum Development: A Guide for Educators*. London: Sage.

Kidd, D (2020) *A Curriculum of Hope: As Rich in Humanity as in Knowledge*. Carmarthen: Independent Thinking Press.

✚ CHAPTER 14

THE ROLE OF STAKEHOLDERS AND SUBJECT ORGANISATIONS

CHAPTER OBJECTIVES

After reading this chapter you will understand:

+ the role of subject leaders, teachers, parents and governors;

+ the importance of subject associations.

INTRODUCTION

This chapter covers the role of key stakeholders, including subject leaders, parents and governors. Schools do not operate in a vacuum. They must demonstrate to key stakeholders that they are effectively discharging their key responsibilities. In addition to the subject curriculum, schools are now required to provide pupils with a rich co-curriculum offer that develops pupils' cultural capital. Subject organisations provide a range of resources to support subject leaders, and this chapter addresses how subject leaders can induct pupils into the subject community.

THE ROLE OF SUBJECT LEADERS

Subject leaders in secondary schools are often referred to as heads of department. As discussed in Chapter 9, they are responsible for curriculum design, teaching and learning and standards within their subject. As such, they are accountable to the senior leadership team.

Subject leaders are responsible for the complex task of designing the subject curriculum. They may do this in collaboration with their subject teams, but they are ultimately responsible for leading the process of curriculum design. Designing the subject curriculum includes breaking down national curriculum goals, then sequencing the components.

EVIDENCE-BASED PRACTICE

Findings set out by the EEF (2020) have implications for subject leaders when designing the curriculum.

+ *The potential impact on pupils of metacognition and self-regulation approaches is high.*

+ *The evidence indicates that explicitly teaching strategies to help plan, monitor and evaluate specific aspects of learning can be effective.*

+ *Teachers can demonstrate effective use of metacognitive and self-regulatory strategies by modelling their own thought processes. For example, teachers might explain their thinking when [modelling new subject content].*

INCLUSIVE CURRICULUM DESIGN FROM THE OUTSET

Subject leaders should approach curriculum design with pupils with SEND and disadvantaged pupils in mind from the outset. Strategies such as chunking and overlearning should be incorporated so that pupils reach automaticity (see Chapter 7). Subject leaders should also consider how to develop pupils' cultural capital (see Chapter 4).

Other key aspects for subject leaders to address at the curriculum design stage is how the curriculum design reflects anti-racist pedagogy and the extent to which it embeds aspects such as race, gender, sexuality and disability. These aspects of inclusion are not specifically identified in the national curriculum, yet are essential components of an inclusive and socially just curriculum. In addition, subject leaders need to consider how to contextualise the curriculum so that it has relevance to pupils' daily lives and their local communities. Delivering the national curriculum is the minimum entitlement, and addressing these aspects enables subject leaders to exceed the requirements of the national curriculum.

EVIDENCE-BASED PRACTICE

Research by the EEF (2021) has implications for curriculum design. It demonstrates that a high level of success should be required before pupils move on to new content. It is crucial to monitor and communicate pupil progress and to provide additional support for pupils that take longer to reach the required level of knowledge.

MONITORING TEACHING THROUGH LESSON VISITS

Subject leaders need to check that the curriculum is being delivered as intended. It is important that any monitoring serves the purpose of improvement and is not designed to place teachers under surveillance. Subject leaders may go into classrooms and talk to pupils about what they are learning, look in pupils' exercise books and observe the pedagogy. When monitoring teaching, it is important that personal beliefs about pedagogy are suspended. There is no one correct way of teaching. When conducting lesson visits, subject leaders should focus on one main question: Is the teaching enabling pupils to learn the curriculum as intended?

234

CASE STUDY

QUALITY OF EDUCATION

WHOLE SCHOOL

Each subject team developed a termly cycle of monitoring to support their evaluation of the quality of education. Monitoring activities included some very short lesson visits and discussion with pupils with their books to check that they were learning the curriculum as intended. These discussions with pupils proved to be more useful than the lesson visits. It became apparent that although pupils could articulate their knowledge of the curriculum in lessons, when questioned about prior learning while working through their books, they had not retained the key knowledge that was identified in the curriculum. This showed the need to adapt the curriculum plan to include more frequent retrieval activities, and the curriculum was redesigned to address the principles of spaced learning.

FORMATIVE ASSESSMENT

Subject leaders need to design a formative assessment strategy to check that pupils are learning the curriculum as intended. The curriculum is the progression framework; therefore if pupils are learning the knowledge that is specified in the curriculum to automaticity, they are making progress. It is important to design an approach to the curriculum that assesses the knowledge specified in the curriculum design.

In recent years, overemphasis on statutory assessment has led to pupils not having deep knowledge of subjects. Subject leaders should focus on assessing components of knowledge. Low-stakes assessment of the component knowledge will enable teachers to identify why pupils are struggling. Multiple-choice quizzes that are automatically marked provide a quick 'temperature check' and will highlight whether specific components of knowledge need to be revisited. End-of-unit assessments that assess component knowledge are useful because they identify which pupils need additional support and what aspects of the curriculum might need to be revisited.

THE ROLE OF TEACHERS

It is the responsibility of teachers to deliver the intended curriculum so that pupils learn the knowledge the school has prioritised. Of course, this is not meant to imply that teachers do not have autonomy in relation to how they teach, but the curriculum specifies *what* pupils need to learn, not *how* they are going to learn it.

The *how* is often the most exciting aspect of teaching. Teachers often like to design their own activities for pupils and find delivering a prescriptive lesson extremely difficult. When teachers have ownership of their teaching, they teach better than when they are expected to work off someone else's script. However, it is important that the chosen pedagogical approaches enable pupils to learn the intended curriculum. The *what* is not negotiable as the curriculum is designed to enable pupils to achieve the ambitious goals of the national curriculum. The *how* is negotiable, but teachers must still ensure that the pedagogical approaches are enabling pupils to learn the curriculum as intended.

THE ROLE OF GOVERNORS

Governors play an important role in holding school leaders to account. They need to be sure that there is a well-designed, well-sequenced and carefully constructed curriculum for pupils in all subjects. Governors might be assigned to specific subjects or faculties across a large secondary school.

CRITICAL QUESTIONS

School governors should meet with subject leaders to ask challenging questions about the curriculum. These might include the following.

+ How has the curriculum been designed to enable pupils to achieve the goals of the national curriculum?

+ How has the curriculum been sequenced?

+ What professional development have you provided to the teachers who teach your subject?

+ How do you assess pupils' knowledge of the curriculum?

+ What are the outcomes of any monitoring that you have done?

+ Do you introduce pupils to resources from subject associations?

+ How do you adapt the curriculum for pupils with SEND?

+ How does your curriculum meet the needs of disadvantaged pupils?

Governors also fulfil a range of other duties. They meet with school leaders to monitor how they are taking steps to reduce workload and protect staff well-being. They need to be sure that the school is providing a rich co-curriculum offer that gives pupils a wide range of enrichment opportunities. They need to ask questions about how pupil premium funding is spent and ascertain whether school leaders can explain the impact of pupil premium interventions. They need to be sure that the school is compliant in exercising its safeguarding duties and that the school is also compliant in relation to the statutory support required for early career teachers. Governors are entitled to have oversight of the school's self-evaluation and improvement plan, and they should ask challenging questions about these to hold school leaders to account. It is the responsibility of governors to ensure that there is no 'slippage' and that standards are being maintained where they are already excellent or improving where they are too low. Governors are also responsible for monitoring the school budget and dealing with complaints.

CASE STUDY

WORKING WITH GOVERNORS

WHOLE SCHOOL

A leadership team in a secondary school asked the governing body to monitor the school's co-curriculum offer. A small team of governors joined in some of the workshops that took place at lunchtime and after school. After this, they met with a group of pupils to collect their perspectives on the school's co-curriculum. They asked questions to ascertain what was working well and what improvements were needed. The pupils identified a range of aspects that were not addressed through the current co-curriculum, and they made some suggestions to improve the timing of some of the sessions. The governors then discussed their findings with the senior leadership team.

WORKING WITH PARENTS

Often parents have little involvement in curriculum matters in a secondary school. However, one aspect that schools are required to address in parental consultation is RSHE. Schools are required to demonstrate that parental consultation has taken place, particularly in relation to sensitive topics such as LGBTQ+ relationships and identities, and abortion. Parents may object on faith grounds to the teaching of specific content, but they do not have a right to withdraw their child from relationships education (though they can withdraw their child from sex education). Schools are required to demonstrate that parental consultation has taken place. School leaders should do the following.

+ Explain the rationale for the curriculum.

+ Listen to parents' feedback.

+ Provide a suitable response.

+ Share examples of teaching resources with parents.

Parents do not have a right to determine curriculum content or veto the curriculum, and they cannot argue that the faith perspective must override other perspectives. Schools can teach a particular faith perspective in relation to abortion and LGBTQ+ content, but they must open the discussion out for debate and explain the law. Teachers are not allowed to transmit harmful personal views to pupils.

EXTENDED THINKING

+ Do you agree that schools should be allowed to teach a specific faith perspective in relation to sensitive topics?

+ What are the problems with framing particular aspects of content as 'sensitive'?

WORKING WITH SUBJECT ASSOCIATIONS

Subject associations provide teachers with access to the latest thinking and research, and they often have a range of resources that teachers can use in lessons. Secondary schools are advised to pay membership fees so that subject leaders can access up-to-date resources in their subject. Through membership, subject leaders can gain access to the latest research, resources, conferences and webinars, and membership of a subject association enables subject leaders to connect with other leaders in the subject. It is important that pupils also know that subject associations exist, and where possible they should be encouraged to join subject networks if membership is free. This enables pupils to see that they are part of a wider subject network and to become a member of the wider subject community.

CRITICAL QUESTIONS

+ How might you draw on subject associations in your teaching?
+ What are the advantages of subject associations?

SUMMARY

This chapter outlined the role of key stakeholders in relation to the school's curriculum. It emphasised the need for schools to ensure that governors and parents are fully informed about the curriculum and argued that parental consultation is necessary for specific aspects of curriculum delivery.

CHECKLIST

+ Subject leaders are responsible for designing a well-sequenced curriculum.

+ Teachers are responsible for delivering the intended curriculum.

+ Pedagogical approaches should enable pupils to learn the intended curriculum.

+ Governors play a key role in holding school leaders to account.

+ Parents should be consulted about curriculum content that is sensitive.

+ Pupils should be supported to view themselves as a member of a subject community.

FURTHER READING

Association for Language Learning – www.all-languages.org.uk/

Association for Physical Education – www.afpe.org.uk/physical-education/

The Association for Science Education – www.ase.org.uk/

The Design and Technology Association – www.data.org.uk/

Geographical Association – www.geography.org.uk/

Historical Association – www.history.org.uk/

Music Teachers' Association – www.musicteachers.org/

National Centre for Excellence in the Teaching of Mathematics – www.ncetm.org.uk/

National Society for Education in Art and Design – www.nsead.org/

PSHE Association – https://pshe-association.org.uk/

UK Literacy Association – https://ukla.org/

✛ CHAPTER 15

THE ACADEMIC AND TECHNICAL CURRICULUM

CHAPTER OBJECTIVES

After reading this chapter you will understand:

+ the range of qualifications available for 16- to 19-year-olds;

+ the importance of careers information, education and guidance in secondary education and FE and training.

INTRODUCTION

This chapter provides an introduction to the complex world of 16–19 education and training. The choice of educational programmes that pupils can be offered is growing, and it is exciting that there is now a wide range of options for pupils to select from. Pupils can follow an academic or technical pathway, and this is largely determined by the careers they are interested in. All programmes must include structured, unpaid work-based learning, and schools and colleges must, in addition, provide opportunities for pupils to undertake non-qualification activity. This chapter provides an introduction to the qualifications that pupils can study and there is also additional information on careers information. This is important for secondary schools because careers education, information and guidance are now part of the *Education Inspection Framework*.

16–19 PROGRAMMES

The Sainsbury Review (Independent Panel on Technical Education, 2016) set out an ambitious vision for technical education for young people and adults. Its proposals were accepted in full by the government. These are summarised below.

+ All pupils funded through the 16–19 funding methodology must be enrolled on a study programme, or T level programme, which typically combines qualifications and other activities, and is tailored to each student's prior attainment and career goals.

+ All study programmes must have a core aim. This will be tailored to the needs of the individual and typically include a substantial qualification (academic or technical) or preparation for employment. The core aim for most pupils will be either: one or more substantial academic, applied or technical qualification(s) that prepare the student for FE or employment; or a substantial work placement to prepare the student for an apprenticeship or other employment.

+ Pupils must complete qualifications in English and mathematics, where they have not yet achieved GCSE grade 4.

+ All study programmes should include work experience and non-qualification activities that complement the other elements of the programme and support the pupil to progress to FE or HE, or to employment.

The 16–19 technical and applied programmes are listed below (Independent Panel on Technical Education, 2016).

+ Applied general qualifications: level 3 qualifications that allow pupils to develop knowledge and skills through applied learning.

+ Tech level qualifications: level 3 technical qualifications that are comparable with A levels and are recognised by employers. They are for post-16 pupils wishing to specialise in a specific industry, occupation or technical role. They equip pupils with specialist knowledge and skills, enabling entry to apprenticeships or other employment.

+ Technical certificates: level 2 qualifications for post-16 pupils wishing to specialise in a specific industry, occupation or technical role where employers recognise entry at level 2. Technical certificates also provide access to tech levels or apprenticeships.

APPRENTICESHIPS

Apprenticeships combine practical training in a job with study. They exist at a range of qualification levels, from level 2 to level 7 (degree and master's level apprenticeships). Typically, 80 per cent of the time is spent in the workplace and 20 per cent is spent in classroom-based learning.

T LEVEL TRANSITION PROGRAMMES

The T Level Transition Programme is a new type of 16–19 study programme, specifically designed to help pupils develop the knowledge, skills and behaviours that will help them to progress to and succeed at a T level. It is targeted at pupils who have the potential to progress to a T level, to provide extra support and preparation.

T LEVELS

T levels are new two-year courses that are taken after GCSEs and are broadly equivalent to three A levels. They are level 3 qualifications. Launched in September 2020, these courses have been developed in collaboration with employers and education providers so that the content meets the needs of industry and prepares pupils for entry into skilled employment, an apprenticeship, or related technical study through FE or HE. T levels are based on the same standards as apprenticeships designed by employers but differ in that an apprenticeship typically provides 80 per cent on-the-job training, which is substantially more than what is provided through a T level. Every T level includes an industry placement with an employer, focused on developing the practical and technical skills required for the occupation. These last a minimum of 315 hours (approximately 45 days) but can be longer. A wide range of T levels already exist, and new programmes are continually being developed. These qualifications prepare pupils to learn about specific sectors of employment, including education, health, science and building services, and they also prepare pupils for entry to degree-level qualifications.

PUPILS WHO ARE NOT READY FOR LEVEL 2 QUALIFICATIONS

Pupils who are not yet ready to begin a qualification at level 2 should be offered a tailored study programme that supports them to progress to education at a higher level or employment, or to prepare in some other way for adult life. Young people aiming for an apprenticeship or other employment, and who are capable of achieving this within six months, may be offered a traineeship.

LEVEL 1 QUALIFICATIONS

Programmes for pupils working towards level 1 qualifications and below aim to prepare them for level 2 but must still include workplace experience and have a core aim.

TRAINEESHIPS

Traineeships are study programmes for young people with qualifications up to and including level 3. They help prepare pupils for an apprenticeship, other sustainable employment where training is on the job, or further learning. They should last for a minimum of six weeks and a maximum of 12 months. Pupils spend a minimum of 70 hours in a work placement.

ACADEMIC ROUTES

A level pupils are expected to follow a minimum of three A levels or an equivalent that counts as substantial qualifications. A levels are level 3 qualifications. A level study programmes should include extension/development or non-qualification activity, such as Extended Project Qualifications, tutorials, work experience, and personal or study skills, and support pupils to progress to employment or HE.

CRITICAL QUESTIONS

+ Why are academic pathways often given more status than technical pathways?

+ What are the benefits of technical pathways?

EXTENDED THINKING

+ What factors might influence a pupil's decision to follow an academic or technical pathway?

CASE STUDY

16–19 PATHWAYS

YEAR 11

A school invited former pupils who had selected a range of pathways when they were 16 to speak with Year 11 pupils. One former pupil had completed a T level and progressed to university. Another had completed an apprenticeship programme at level 4 and continued with a degree-apprenticeship programme at levels 4, 5 and 6. Yet another had completed A levels. The pupils talked about their experiences on their chosen pathways. They talked about why they had chosen that qualification, their experiences of the qualification and what the qualification had enabled them to go on and do after completing it.

CRITICAL QUESTIONS

+ What are the advantages of using former pupils in this way?
+ What pathways were not represented in this event that the school could have included?

PUPILS WITH SEND

Most young people with SEND are capable of sustained employment with the right preparation and support. Supported internships are a structured, work-based study programme for 16- to 24-year-olds with SEND who have an Education, Health and Care plan. The core aim of a supported internship study programme is a substantial work placement, facilitated by the support of an expert job coach.

This model of supported employment is an example of the social model of disability in action. The social model separates impairment and disability as two distinct concepts. Impairment is located within the body and might include cognitive, physical, linguistic or sensory impairment. Within the social model, disability is defined in relation to access to goods and services. The assumption of the social model is that disability is socially created. It is a social construct. This is because individuals with impairments are disabled not by their impairment, but by the failure of society to make the specific adaptations they need to access employment, education, housing and other services. Disablement is therefore about lack of access, not impairment.

One of the key aims of the SEND Code of Practice (DfE, 2015) is to raise outcomes for learners with SEND. More pupils with SEND should be achieving qualifications, entering FE and HE, gaining employment and achieving independent living. In the past, outcomes for learners with SEND have been too low. Far too many do not achieve qualifications, employment or independent living; but with the right support, they can achieve these outcomes. Supported employment schemes are an excellent example of the social model because they demonstrate that with the right support and guidance, individuals with SEND can enter the workplace and lead productive lives.

Work placements for pupils with SEND may need to be planned very carefully, and where possible the pupil should be involved in the planning process. Employers must learn about the specific needs of the pupil and start to plan adjustments to placements to enable the pupil to successfully complete the placement. For autistic pupils, changes to routines and social interaction and collaboration in the workplace may cause considerable distress, so this has to be very carefully managed. However, when placements are managed well, disabled pupils can thrive in the workplace. Autistic employees have many strengths that are valuable to employers. They are rule bound, and they often demonstrate very good attention to detail. Adopting a capability perspective rather than a deficit perspective is the best approach for employers to take. Some pupils with SEND may benefit from a tightly structured daily timetable, regular breaks and technological adaptations. The adaptations will vary across individuals, and it is important to remember that pupils cannot just be 'dropped' into a workplace context and be expected to thrive. Careful planning from the outset will enable pupils to have a positive experience in the workplace.

EXTENDED THINKING

+ What factors lead to poor long-term outcomes for pupils with SEND?

+ How can schools and colleges improve long-term outcomes for pupils with SEND?

WORK EXPERIENCE

Work experience is a key component of 16–19 study programmes. Activities must be planned to take account of pupils' needs and future plans. Work placements may include evening, weekend and college holiday hours if that would give pupils a more realistic experience. Although work experience that includes training in a simulated work environment or social action project can help pupils develop 'softer' skills, providers are expected, wherever possible, to offer a work placement with an employer.

Characteristics of a high-quality work placement are that it:

+ is purposeful, offers challenge and is relevant to the pupil's study programme and career aspirations;

+ allows the pupil to apply the technical and practical skills learned in the classroom/workshop;

+ is managed under the direction of a supervisor to ensure the pupil obtains a genuine learning experience suited to their needs;

+ has a structured plan for the duration of the placement that provides tangible outcomes for the pupil and employer;

+ has clear roles, responsibilities and expectations for the pupil and employer;

+ is followed by some form of reference or feedback from the employer based on the pupil's performance.

DEVELOPMENT FOR EMPLOYERS

Schools and colleges should provide clear guidance to employment providers and mentors about work placements. Pupils are more likely to thrive if they are provided with a work-based mentor who has attended a training session. Training should support mentors to understand their general responsibilities in relation to the Equality Act 2010, safeguarding duties and their specific responsibilities in relation to the placement, including designing an induction programme. Pupils also need to understand their roles and responsibilities in the workplace, and be aware of professional codes of conduct and any tasks that they are required to complete.

CAREERS EDUCATION

All secondary schools and colleges are required to provide pupils with careers education. The DfE (2021) states the following.

+ *High quality careers education and guidance in school or college is critical to young people's futures.* (p 6)

+ *[Careers education and guidance] helps to prepare them for the workplace by providing a clear understanding of the world of work including the routes to jobs and careers that they might find engaging and rewarding.* (p 6)

+ *All schools and colleges [are expected] to use the internationally recognised Gatsby Benchmarks to develop a careers programme.* (p 8)

+ *[Careers education and guidance supports pupils] to acquire the self-development and career management skills they need to achieve positive employment destinations.* (p 6)

+ *Schools and colleges have a responsibility to set students on the path that will secure the best outcome which will enable them to progress in education and work and give employers the highly skilled people they need. That means schools and colleges must act impartially, in line with their statutory duty or contractual requirement, and not show bias towards any route, be that academic or technical. They should promote a full range of technical options.* (p 6)

EVIDENCE-BASED PRACTICE

Research by the EEF (2016) found the following.

+ Careers education works best when it is personalised and targeted to individuals' needs from an early age. This, together with school-mediated employer engagement alongside independent and impartial career guidance, is key to supporting young people's transitions into education, training and employment.

+ Young people who have a good understanding of what they need to do in school to achieve their career ambitions, and who combine part-time work with full-time study, do a lot better economically later in life than their peers.

+ Young people from poorer homes are more likely to be uncertain about the qualifications they need to access their chosen career and get the skills they need.

+ Part-time employment among teenagers is rapidly declining: the proportion of 16- to 17-year-olds in full-time education and working part time fell from 42 per cent in 1997 to 18 per cent in 2014.

THE BAKER CLAUSE

In 2018 the DfE introduced the Baker clause, which requires all maintained schools and academies to ensure that there is an opportunity for a range of education and training *providers* to access all Year 8 to Year 13 pupils for the purpose of informing them about approved technical education qualifications and apprenticeships.

CRITICAL QUESTIONS

+ How might schools and colleges meet the requirements of the Baker clause?

+ What specific education and training providers might you bring into school or college to meet the pupils?

EXTENDED THINKING

+ How can the curriculum prepare pupils for the world of work when it might be reasonably argued that we cannot predict the jobs and associated skill sets that will be needed in the future?

+ Should education be a preparation for the world of work, or should it serve a different purpose?

+ Girls do better at school than boys, but in employment, men are paid more than women. What factors contribute to this?

CASE STUDY

GCSE OPTIONS

YEAR 9

A school hosted an employability conference prior to pupils selecting their GCSE options in Year 9. A range of employers came to the school, and pupils had an opportunity to talk directly with them. The conference included a range of presentations. These included a female CEO of a building services company, a female engineer, a male early years teacher and a disabled CEO of a computer software company.

CRITICAL QUESTIONS

+ How might this event challenge stereotypes?

+ Why do you think it was important to position this event prior to pupils deciding on their GCSE options?

THE GATSBY BENCHMARKS

All schools and colleges must provide a careers education programme that addresses the eight benchmarks set out by the Gatsby Charitable Foundation.

1. *Every school and college should have an embedded programme of career education and guidance that is known and understood by pupils, parents, teachers, governors and employers.*

2. *Every pupil, and their parents, should have access to good quality information about future study options and labour market opportunities.*

3. *Opportunities for advice and support need to be tailored to the needs of each pupil.*

4. *All teachers should link curriculum learning with careers.*

5. *Every pupil should have multiple opportunities to learn from employers about work, employment and the skills that are valued in the workplace. This can be through a range of enrichment activities including visiting speakers, mentoring and enterprise schemes.*

6. *Every pupil should have first-hand experiences of the workplace through work visits, work shadowing and/or work experience to help their exploration of career opportunities and expand their networks.*

7. *All pupils should understand the full range of learning opportunities that are available to them. This includes both academic and vocational routes and learning in schools, colleges, universities and in the workplace.*

8. *Every pupil should have opportunities for guidance interviews with a career adviser.*

(Gatsby Charitable Foundation, nd, p 7)

In addition, the following recommendations are given.

+ *Every secondary school should be required to have a Careers Plan, published on the school's website.*

+ *Every secondary school should be responsible for publishing the destinations of all pupils for three years after their leaving date. The published destination data should be at an aggregated level, showing the main categories of employment, apprenticeship and further and higher education.*

+ *Every school should have a member of their governing body who has a remit to encourage employer engagement and to take a strategic interest in career guidance.*

(Gatsby Charitable Foundation, nd, p 11)

CRITICAL QUESTIONS

+ Which benchmarks might be more challenging to meet?
+ Why is it important to have a set of benchmarks?

NON-QUALIFICATION ACTIVITY

Examples of non-qualification activity are provided below.

+ National Citizen Service is a government-backed, part-residential youth programme that develops the skills and confidence of young people. Young people work in diverse teams of 12 to 15, building skills for work and life, taking on exciting challenges, meeting people from different backgrounds and contributing to their local area.

+ The DfE's Climate Leaders Award, which is due to be launched in autumn 2022, will complement classroom learning and allow pupils to develop their connection with nature and make a contribution to establishing a sustainable future.

+ Duke of Edinburgh Awards develop a range of skills, including problem-solving and teamwork.

+ The Diploma in Sporting Excellence launched in 2022. It is designed for young people aged 16 to 18 who are on the talent pathway for their chosen sport and want to combine it with study towards academic or technical qualifications. Pupils must be nominated by their sport's national governing body and be in 16–19 education.

CRITICAL QUESTIONS

+ What are the benefits of non-qualification activity?
+ What are the barriers to participation and engagement in relation to non-qualification activity?

EVIDENCE-BASED PRACTICE

Weaknesses in the UK's skills base have contributed to a long-standing productivity gap with France, Germany and the United States. The UK performs poorly on intermediate professional and technical skills (UK Commission for Employment and Skills, 2014).

Research demonstrates occupational segregation in our economy. In 2014/15, 8470 women started level 2 apprenticeships in hairdressing, while just 90 women started on the level 2 engineering apprenticeship framework (Skills Funding Agency and Department for Business Innovation and Skills, nd).

SUMMARY

This chapter outlined the range of qualifications for pupils after they leave school. The decision to follow a technical or academic pathway should be an informed decision, but it is the pupil who should ultimately decide. The technical pathways are designed to enable pupils to progress to university study and apprenticeships at a range of levels, and they provide pupils with an excellent opportunity to combine work-based learning and learning in the classroom. This chapter also included key information about careers education, and this should be viewed as a key component of secondary and FE curriculums.

CHECKLIST

+ Pupils can select an academic or technical pathway once they reach the age of 16.

+ All programmes should combine academic study with real workplace experience.

+ All pupils are expected to participate in non-qualification activities.

+ All study programmes must include English and mathematics for pupils who have not achieved grade 4 or above at GCSE.

+ Schools and colleges must provide pupils with careers education, information and guidance.

FURTHER READING

Amazing Apprenticeships – https://amazingapprenticeships.com/

The Careers and Enterprise Company (nd) All the Resources, All in One Place. [online] Available at: https://resources.careersandenterprise.co.uk/all-resour ces-all-one-place (accessed 28 August 2022).

+ CHAPTER 16

DECOLONISING THE SECONDARY CURRICULUM

JUSTIN MALEWEZI JNR

CHAPTER OBJECTIVES

After reading this chapter you will understand:

+ the meaning of decolonising the curriculum, race, ethnicity, Black, unconscious bias, anti-racist pedagogy, racial microaggressions, critical race theory, everyday racism, institutional racism, white privilege, and minority stress;

+ why it is important to challenge racial myths;

+ how to decolonise the secondary curriculum using authentic cultural themes of the colonised;

+ the whole-school approach for race equality.

INTRODUCTION

What great fine artist comes to mind for you? How about a music composer? As a response to these questions, most people, including Black people, have given me names of white people. This is not a coincidence. We have come a long way towards racial equality, but we are not there yet. When it comes to young people in secondary school, it is important that they regard people of all races and ethnicities. For this to happen, we need to 'decolonise' the curriculum. This chapter considers the essential components of decolonising the secondary curriculum. It is written from the perspective of a person of colour, a Black academic and former secondary school teacher. The chapter aims to stimulate debate and raise critical questions. The curriculum should reflect the experiences and identities of people of colour. Pupils need to learn about the adverse effects of British imperialism, including enslavement and racism in all its forms, and recognise the significant achievements of people of colour. Crucially, the curriculum should make visible all identities so that pupils can see that their identities are represented. Making identities visible supports pupils to experience a sense of belonging, raises aspirations and supports positive mental health.

WHAT DOES DECOLONISING THE CURRICULUM MEAN?

According to the NEU (2022) *'decolonisation can mean a process of withdrawal of political, military and governmental rule of a colonised land by its invaders'*. Decolonising the *curriculum* means *'rebuilding a school system that supports all pupils, staff and teachers'* (NEU, 2022). This process has several elements. It should:

+ *[examine] British imperialism and racism, as well as histories and cultures from around the world;*

+ *[promote understanding of the] history of inequalities;*

+ *[promote] a sense of belonging for Black people;*

+ *challenge racism.*

(NEU, 2022)

CRITICAL QUESTIONS

+ What do you understand by racism?
+ How can schools address racism?

EXTENDED THINKING

+ What do you understand by anti-racist pedagogy?

WHAT IS RACE?

My name is Justin Malewezi. I am originally form Malawi in southern Africa. I have dark brown skin and black hair. According to my physical appearance, my race may be categorised as Black. I live in England, where many people have long hair and pink skin. Also, according to their physical appearance, they may be categorised as belonging to the white race. Even though our outward physical appearance is different, beneath our skin, we are all the same. We share the same genetic makeup; therefore, we all belong to one race, the Human Race. The term 'race' has lost its true meaning and is used to describe something else, grouping people according to their outward physical characteristics. Race is therefore a socially constructed concept. In the Equality Act 2010, race can mean colour or nationality. It can also mean ethnic or national origins, which may not be the same as current nationality.

WHAT IS ETHNICITY?

An ethnic group generally refers to a community or group of people with a long, shared history that the group is conscious of as distinguishing it from other groups. There are shared cultural traditions, which may include religion, geographical origin, a common language and literature. We all have an ethnicity. My ethnicity is of the Chewa people of Malawi in southern Africa. Think about what your ethnicity is and the different ethnicities of the children in a classroom.

BLACK AS A POLITICAL TERM

'Black' is a term used to describe the 'race' group of people with dark skin, denoting solidarity between Asian, African and Caribbean people and all people of colour. Initially, it was used by white people as a derogatory term to describe colonised and enslaved Asian and African people. The term was reclaimed in Britain by African Caribbean and Asian communities in the 1970s as part of the struggle against racism, and it is used now as a political term to signify unity.

UNCONSCIOUS BIAS

I grew up in a country in which it was normal to regard white people as being superior to the local Black people. This was due to the residual effects of colonialism. This experience of white people created a categorising system in my brain, which could be used later in life when making decisions about white people. As the mind makes subconscious decisions through pattern recognition, past experiences greatly influence current decisions. This could explain the reason why I subconsciously preferred a white American voice when listening to my audio book. I also had other past experiences of white people, good and bad – both of which can affect my subconscious mind. The important thing is that when it comes to important matters such as race, unconscious influences can lead to poor or biased decision-making. This is called 'unconscious bias'. Being aware of one's own unconscious bias is important. It is more important to slow down the decision-making process in order to bring it to the conscious, hence overriding unconscious bias. After all, our actions are done in full consciousness.

ANTI-RACIST PEDAGOGY

It is fundamental that everyone acts against racism. Teachers have great responsibility in creating a world of racial equality. Children need to know, appreciate and cerebrate people of all races. This is vital especially in communities that are not racially diverse. The children in such communities see people who look like them, and their minds find it difficult to imagine people from other races in common roles. Teachers have to start by looking at their own biases and how to counter them. Then they can put on their anti-racist and cultural responsible lenses to scrutinise and action their teaching and learning. Teachers must also have conversations with children and communities from other races, and find out about their stories and their needs. Then they can develop and implement ideas of how everyone can learn better together in the classroom and beyond. Anti-racist pedagogy, according to Kishimoto (2018), is an organising effort for institutional and social change that is much broader than teaching in the classroom.

RACIAL MICRO-AGGRESSIONS

Racial microaggressions are subtle offensive racial comments which people often make without thinking deeply about what they are saying. I remember picking up my child from his new school one afternoon and finding him surrounded by a group of white children touching his hair and asking him why his hair was like that. Another time, while teaching at a new school, a pupil complimented me that I speak very good English for an African. Yet another time, while being served at a till, as I handed over the money the polite elderly white lady commented that she has always wondered why the inside of the hands of people like me were lighter like hers, and not the rest of the body. Because these comments are micro, one feels like you don't have a reason to be upset, yet they leave a bad feeling that can last for years.

CRITICAL RACE THEORY AND EVERYDAY RACISM

As a young Black person studying A levels in England, I experienced everyday racism. At least once a week while walking to college, a car would slow down to shout abusive racist words at me. I would have my headphones on and look straight ahead, pretending that I could not see or hear them. In class, I would be asked: '*In Africa, do you live with wild animals?*' On the bus, the driver would speak to me very slowly, assuming that I don't speak English. Most people think of racism as these everyday acts of bias or bigotry, yet racism is deeper than that. I once attended a union meeting for Black teachers. We were asked to raise our hands if we had worked in a school longer than most of the white members of staff. Almost every hand was raised. Then we were asked to keep our hands up if we were in senior management. All hands but a few went down. In that meeting, most Black teachers had years of teaching experience yet were not promoted to senior management. This was not an individual issue but a systematic one. Critical race theory

259

states that racism still exists today because we still have systems that are oppressive to minority races. The theory was started in the 1970s by legal scholars and activists as a way of examining laws and power structures through the lens of race.

INTERNALISED RACISM

This occurs because of subliminal messages of racial inferiority and superiority present in society. This can cause people of colour to internalise negative messages about their own abilities and intrinsic worth.

INSTITUTIONAL RACISM

'Institutional racism' is a term used to describe racism when it is normalised in organisations. In Britain, the term was widely used to describe the police following the 1999 Macpherson report as a response to the senseless racially motivated murder of Stephen Lawrence. It was found that the police, as an institution, was racist in the way it dealt with the investigations of the murder case. More recently, the murder of unarmed Black man George Floyd by the police in America sparked worldwide uprising in the form of the Black Lives Matter movement, a campaign for racial equality.

STRUCTURAL RACISM

Structural racism refers to the economic, political, social and cultural structures, actions and beliefs that systemise an unequal distribution of privilege, resources, safety and power in favour of the dominant racial group at the expense of all other racial groups. Examples of this can be found in the overrepresentation of certain minority ethnic groups in poverty, unemployment, and Covid-related deaths.

WHITE PRIVILEGE

White privileges are the advantages in society that are accessible to white people simply because they are white. As a Black person, I do not have the privilege of not worrying about being stopped by the police because of my skin colour. I do not have the privilege of not worrying about living in a neighbourhood without facing discrimination because of my race. Black children do not have the privilege of not worrying about attending school without racial incidences. Perhaps these privileges are easily recognised by those who are not white because of unpleasant incidences.

EVIDENCE-BASED PRACTICE

Scientists have proven it is false that humans can be categorised into different races based on their biology.

There is no evidence that the groups we commonly call 'races' have distinct, unifying genetic identities. In fact, there is more genetic variation within what we think of as races than there is between groups. Despite associations with surface characteristics like skin color, there are no clear boundaries where one racial category begins and another ends.

(Center on the Developing Child, Harvard University, 2021, p 2)

MINORITY STRESS

Meyer's (2003) model of minority stress addresses general stressors. All individuals are exposed to general stressors in life. These stressors might be related to finances, employment, relationships, family and housing. However, Meyer's model identifies two additional stressors that individuals with minority identities experience. These are categorised as distal and proximal stressors.

+ Distal stressors: these are stressors that are external to the individual. They include exposure to discrimination, harassment and prejudice. They are external to the individual, but they result in adverse effects for individuals with minority identities and can result in individuals experiencing mental ill health.

+ Proximal stressors: these are internal stressors. They arise because individuals with minority identities anticipate that they will experience the distal stressors identified above. They can result in individuals self-stigmatising, and they can lead to mental ill health.

Meyer (2003) argues that individuals can mitigate the adverse effects of these stressors by forming collectives: people with similar identities can form groups to gain social support and solidarity, and these groups can provide individuals with minority identities with positive affirmation of identity.

CRITICAL QUESTIONS

+ What distal stressors might people of colour be exposed to?
+ What proximal stressors might people of colour be exposed to?

EXTENDED THINKING

+ Meyer argues that individuals can form collectives of people with similar identities to mitigate the adverse effects of these stressors. What are the problems with this solution?
+ How might the secondary curriculum address issues of discrimination?
+ To what extent should schools be seen as the solution for societal problems (racism)? What does the government need to do to address the systemic issues that result in individuals experiencing mental ill health?
+ People of colour may also experience multiple forms of disadvantage, including poverty and gender inequality. Why is it important therefore to adopt an intersectional perspective?

CHALLENGING THE MYTHS

Myths are often used as barriers to prevent important work being done. Table 16.1 outlines some key myths and provides a response to each.

Table 16.1 Challenging the myths

Myth	Why is this wrong?
Myth 1: We don't have many Black pupils, so addressing racism isn't a priority.	All pupils need to learn about racism and bigotry to prepare them for life in modern society.
Myth 2: We treat everyone the same.	Hierarchies of race and power imbalances result in racism. Treating everyone the same ignores the impact of racism on individuals.
Myth 3: We are focused on 'closing the gap'.	Closing the gap is not a sufficient response. Schools need to understand the impact of racism on Black children and families.
Myth 4: We take a 'zero tolerance' approach to unacceptable pupil behaviour.	Zero tolerance behaviour policies disproportionately harm and segregate Black pupils and working-class pupils with SEND, and lead to increased exclusions for these groups.
Myth 5: We focus on high standards for everyone.	High expectations alone will not eradicate discrimination, especially given that the curriculum in school is based on cultural assumptions driven by white and middle-class norms. Pupils need to learn about British and global history, the power dynamics within racism, bias and racial hierarchies.
Myth 6: Working-class pupils face the biggest challenges.	Racial, class and gender stereotypes can limit pupils' experiences and ambitions

Source: adapted from NEU (nd)

BACKGROUND

I was born in Malawi in southern Africa, a former British colony which received independence in 1964. Twenty years after independence, I attended my primary and secondary education. I remember growing up with a clear distinction between school and home life.

School was the place where we did the hard stuff. The kind of learning that either got us in trouble, if we did not achieve what was expected, or did not get us in trouble, which was a reward. We learned about farming and the rivers of England. We also learned about the history of our country, Malawi. I remember learning that Dr David Livingstone discovered Lake Malawi. During that time, the land was called the Malavi Kingdom, with established governance through Kings and Chiefs. Dr Livingstone asked the local people the name of the lake and they replied 'Nyasa' meaning 'Lake'. He had therefore 'discovered' the lake and named it 'Lake Nyasa', which literally means 'lake lake'. This was in 1851. Forty years later, in 1891, the British government was established, and they called the county Nyasaland, meaning the Land of the Lake. Colonisation involved giving the country a new name. Branding. In 1964 Malawi received independence from British rule. Dr Hastings Kamuzu Banda, the first president of Malawi, renamed the country Malawi, which means 'Flames of Fire'. Decolonisation in Malawi started with the country being rebranded back to its authentic self.

My home life after school was fun. We formed play groups, made our own toys and played until sunset. My favourite toy was the wire car. We made the cars from recycled wire, bottle tops, bicycle tubes and bamboo sticks. In our play groups, we would gather the thrown away materials from different houses, bring them together and construct the cars. The play groups we called 'companies'. We constructed cars for all the members and more. The extra cars we sold to other children, especially the ones who could not make their own. When the cars were finished, we gathered at the field where the soil was exposed. We tied two small sticks pointing down at both ends of a longer stick, which was three times the width of the car, and used this to draw perpendicular lines on the ground. This was our multi-direction single-lane road for the cars. We recreated the city roads and labelled them on the side. Then we would drive around our simulated city, pretending to be grown-ups, dropping our children to school, going to work, shopping and going to the football stadium. We also appointed one car to be a police car just in case someone decided to break the driving rules, which usually happed at the end of play. These complex skills and advanced knowledge that we experienced out of school were not regarded as important at school. Our teachers did not praise us for creating car models from different grades of wire or recreating identifiable geometric shapes that defined the models of the cars, let alone the entrepreneurship of car companies or even the literacy skills of labelling the roads. Instead, we received praise when we spoke good English or quickly recalled historical facts of Great Britain. Even today, it is a common occurrence to hear a parent praising their child for speaking English, calling them *Mzungu*, a word that has two meanings: white person and boss. Although my primary and secondary education was 20 years after colonial rule, Western knowledge and culture still took higher precedence in the curriculum than local knowledge and culture, despite inaccuracies and bias. The process of decolonisation in education would have to involve correcting colonial bias and including the syllabi of the colonised at the same level of significance.

I am now grown up. I am living and working in Britain. I am writing to suggest some ideas for how the British secondary school curriculum can be decolonised. Since the national curriculum is not prescriptive, one might argue that it renders itself free from colonial bias. However, speaking to the migrant children in my local community, I found out that although they appreciated their education, their authentic African identity and culture was rarely experienced at school. Recently I was approached by a white music teacher who was concerned about the authenticity of teaching the African drum. I explained to him the spirituality of the drum in Malawi for the Chewa people, who I belong to. Our conversation grew into an idea of an authentic corroborative pedagogy. We decided that I would acquire footage of the drum being used in Malawi, including interviews with the people using the drum, and these materials would form key knowledge for the pupils. This is what I believe to be decolonising the curriculum, a conversation and efforts aiming to balance and provide authentic knowledge of both cultures.

There are many definitions of decolonisation of the curriculum. In a recent article, Sofia Akel (2020) described the process as rethinking and looking at the curricula without the Europe-centred colonial lens. I agree that decolonisation of the secondary curriculum in Britain should be about the removal of British-centred colonial attitudes but at the same time it should also be about the promotion of ideas and culture of the very same people whose lands were colonised. Decolonising the curriculum should therefore not only be about the removal of colonial Western knowledge but uncovering and including the denied and hidden non-Western knowledge (de Sousa Santos, 2018).

HOW CAN IT BE DONE?

Although much is written about the need to decolonise the secondary curriculum, only a few articles cover how this can be done. Perhaps this is due to the specific nature of the secondary curriculum. Ideas of decolonisation would have to be specific to each subject, hence requiring wide corroboration. Subject literature has appeared, especially in geography and science. Some of the ideas that have been discussed can be used across other subjects. For example, in geography, Nayeri and Rushton (2022) suggest three approaches that can be applied in all subjects. The first is the challenging of misconceptions. This would involve challenging the narratives of British superiority and colonial attitudes. The second is the identification of power inequalities and efforts to balance that power. The third is the reconstruction of the curriculum, with the pupils being empowered to tell the story of what has been left out of the curriculum. Using this as a template and building on my own experience of postcolonial education both in Malawi as a learner and in England as a teacher, I have come up with a model of decolonising the secondary curriculum.

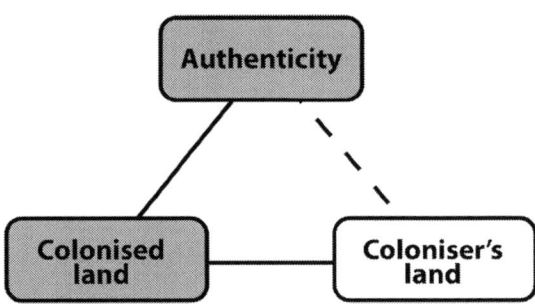

Figure 16.1 Decolonising the curriculum: Malewezi model

This model is based on the previously mentioned conversation with the music teacher. The initial part of the process is to discuss, identify and source authentic (see Figure 16.1) subject-related materials that tell the hidden story of the colonised. Such materials need to address the issues of colonial misconceptions, attitudes and history. Then the learning resources should be provided at the same level as all other material. The following case studies describe relevant projects.

CASE STUDY

DECOLONISING THE ART AND DESIGN CURRICULUM: THE AFRICAN MASK PROJECT

Figure 16.2 *Mzungu* (white man) *Gule Wamkulu* mask, Zambia

This project relates to aspects of the Key Stage 3 art and design national curriculum. Pupils should be taught to:

+ use a range of techniques to record their observations in sketchpads, journals, and other media as a basis for exploring their ideas;

+ use a range of art techniques and media, including painting.

The project also relates to aspects of the Key Stage 3 music national curriculum. Pupils should be taught to:

+ play and perform confidently in a range of solo and ensemble contexts using their voice and playing instruments musically, fluently and with accuracy and expression;

+ improvise and compose, and extend and develop musical ideas by drawing on a range of musical structures, styles, genres, and traditions;

$\longrightarrow$

+ listen with increasing discrimination to a wide range of music from great composers and musicians.

The authenticity of the African mask is in the hidden story surrounding the mask itself. Generally, in Africa, art does not serve an aesthetic purpose, but rather a functional one. The Chewa people in Malawi, Zambia and Mozambique call the mask *Gule Wamkulu*, meaning the honourable dance, and they regard the mask as a sacred object. The Chewa people believe that when people die, their spirit remains on the earth, in the trees of the graveyards near the villages. This is the reason why it is forbidden to cut trees at a cemetery. After the harvest season, the ancestral spirits bring messages to the community. These messages are in the form of advice according to the issues that are present in the community. Members of the *Gule Wamkulu* bring the mask dancers to the village, dancing to several sacred drums, clapping and singing. The character and dance illustrate warning messages that are communicated by the spirits.

Mzungu (white man)

Mwenye (Indian man)

Chadzunda (king)

Gologolo (squirrel)

DESIGN BRIEF

Design and make a mask that illustrates and communicates a message about what concerns you in society. Then compose a song using voice, clapping of hands and African drums to perform an expressive dance communicating your message. You may publish your work in social media under #gulewamkulu.

CRITICAL QUESTIONS

+ How might the music curriculum in secondary schools be decolonised?

+ How might the history curriculum address issues of British imperialism?

+ How might the design and technology curriculum be decolonised? Consider how issues relating to the manufacture of food, clothing and other products might be addressed, including designing and making with food.

CASE STUDY

DECOLONISING THE DESIGN AND TECHNOLOGY CURRICULUM – THE AFRICAN WIRE CAR PROJECT

Figure 16.3 A 13 year-old boy driving a wire car in Lilongwe, Malawi

269

The project would cover aspects of the Key Stage 3 design and technology national curriculum. Pupils should be taught to:

+ use research and exploration, such as the study of different cultures, to identify and understand user needs;

+ develop and communicate design ideas using annotated sketches, detailed plans, 3-D and mathematical modelling, oral and digital presentations, and computer-based tools;

+ select from and use a wider, more complex range of materials, components and ingredients, taking into account their properties;

+ test, evaluate and refine their ideas and products against a specification, taking into account the views of intended users and other interested groups.

The project would cover the following aspect of the Key Stage 3 computing national curriculum: pupils should be taught to design, use, and evaluate computational abstractions that model the state and behaviour of real-world problems and physical systems.

In this example, the process started by discussing, identifying and sourcing an authentic subject-related video that tells the story of the African wire car. It is a story shared with many children in Malawi up to now. As previously mentioned, the national curriculum is not prescriptive, therefore issues of colonial misconceptions, attitudes and history are not initially visible. However, a quick online search for images using 'examples of design and technology resistant material projects' revealed only Western ideas. Most likely, this is due to the teaching focus, resources and examples used in the projects. Therefore, to provide an alternative focus, I sourced a video of a 13-year-old boy driving a wire truck that he made. The video can be found at: www.malewezi. com/wirecar

The pupils can use the key facts that are provided with the video as a starting point for their research. They can then photograph their preferred car models and draw the main outlines that define the shape of the car. To make the wire car, they can follow the following guidance.

1. Making a 90-degree bend	2. Modelling and prototyping
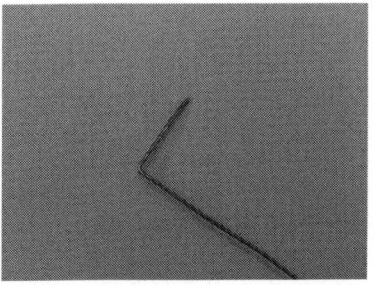	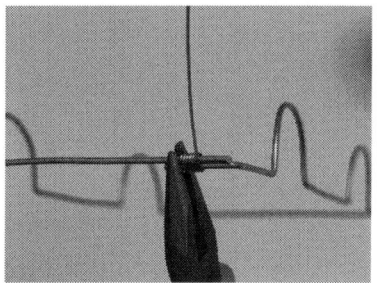
Pupils need to learn how to make a 90-degree bend in wire using small pliers. They also need to learn about safety when using wire.	Pupils need to learn about joining wire by using small grade wire to tightly wind around the two joining pieces.
3. Constructing the chassis	**4. Constructing the body**
	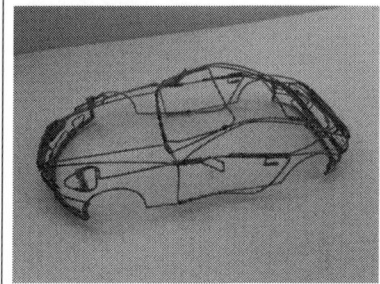
When constructing the car, you start with the chassis as it guides the proportion of the body and fittings for the tyres.	The body is constructed following the sketch lines from the obser-vational drawing.
5. Making tyres	**6. Turning mechanism**

Tyres are made by joining two bottle tops and a thick-cut section of cycle tube. The tyre is then fitted by a fixed wire rod that goes through both ends of the bottle tops.

The front turning mechanism is constructed by joining two wires that are mounted on the wheel. These wires are fixed to the car from the front, and they turn at the back. They are held together by a crossing rod that keeps the wheels aligned. This rod is used to turn the tyres and is powered by a servo motor, which can be programmed through the Crumble controller. This is where the project crosses to the computing curriculum.

7. Back tyres

8. Wiring

As for the back tyres, this example is a one drive system, as one of the back wheel tyres is fixed to a motor and gear system that can be controlled by the Crumble controller.

From here, the computing curriculum picks up the necessary wiring and programming.

The pupils can programme the car for their chosen purpose – for example, they can produce a programme to make the car reverse park automatically. A video of the finished product can be found at: www. malewezi.com/wirecar. At the end of the project, the pupils can evaluate their design and make changes to support fitness for purpose.

The knowledge and skills for this design and technology project reflect an untold story of the past colonised people of Malawi. There are many untold stories that cover the rest of the national curriculum subjects. With the process of sourcing authentic teaching resources, pupils can be offered the opportunity to explore and cerebrate hidden knowledge from other parts of the world. This can only be achieved when the teacher provides the teaching materials with the same emphasis and accessibility as all other materials. Decolonising the national curriculum should involve the provision and promotion of knowledge and skills from many cultures, especially from places that were colonised.

WHOLE-SCHOOL APPROACH

Figure 16.4 shows the whole-school approach, and the elements of this are then discussed.

Figure 16.4 The whole-school approach

LEADERSHIP

Schools should have a race equality policy that specifically outlines how the school will meet its legal duties in relation to the Equality Act 2010 as well as providing a clear policy which outlines how incidents of racial discrimination and harassment will be reported and addressed. Leadership teams should systematically analyse incidents of racism and patterns of exclusion for specific pupil groups. Behaviour policies should be flexible to address the experiences of individuals and pupil groups. In addition, leadership teams should seek to recruit a diverse team of staff, and school leadership teams should seek to recruit a diverse leadership team. School leaders should invest in staff training so that all staff are confident in recognising and addressing racism, and subject leaders and subject teams should be confident in including Black perspectives into the curriculum.

CURRICULUM

The secondary curriculum should address enslavement, colonialism, and the positive contributions of Black people in history and in contemporary society. Schemes of work, lesson plans and resources should reflect life in multicultural Britain. All subjects should address Black perspectives – for example, by teaching pupils about the significant contributions of Black people. The curriculum should educate pupils to challenge stereotypes, and pupils need to be taught about the concept of stigma. The curriculum should also educate pupils about migration and specifically the experiences of migrants entering the UK and the positive effects of migration on Britain.

EMPOWERMENT

Black staff, pupils and parents should confidently be able to talk openly about their experiences and raise concerns. The curriculum should include opportunities for pupils to discuss race, ethnicity, racism and rights. School leaders should also provide a forum for excluded pupils to talk about their experiences. Empowerment can be supported through integrating Black history into the curriculum and discussing the significant achievements of people of colour in all subjects. Pupils in secondary school should learn about the struggle against racism and the implications of the Equality Act 2010 for Black people in education, the workplace and society.

SCHOOL ENVIRONMENT

The school environment includes the physical environment and the emotional environment. The physical environment should include clear anti-racist messages and resources that showcase the significant achievements of Black people. Libraries should include texts by Black authors and poets. The emotional environment should facilitate a sense of belonging, and one way of doing this is through leadership teams ensuring that diversity is represented across the staff team.

STAFF

Black staff are protected against discrimination and harassment under the Equality Act 2010, but it is also important that they are provided with safe opportunities to openly discuss their experiences with the leadership team. All staff should receive training in racism and anti-racist pedagogy, and staff should feel confident in recognising and addressing racist incidents in school.

WELL-BEING

Meyer's (2003) model of minority stress demonstrates that Black people are more likely to experience mental ill health. This is due to the additional stressors they are exposed to – which include bullying, harassment, and discrimination – but also the stress that results from anticipating that they will encounter these stressors. Schools should therefore ensure that well-being teams are trained specifically in how to support Black pupils and staff who might be experiencing poor mental health.

COMMUNITY

Schools should work with their communities by drawing on community resources that will support the decolonisation of the secondary curriculum. These might include working with Black activists, poets, authors and musicians from the community. In addition, where relevant, schools should address Black struggle within the local community. Schools should build effective partnerships with parents so that they feel safe to report any concerns, and festivals and other special days should be marked and celebrated on the school calendar.

CRITICAL QUESTIONS

+ How might the curriculum in business studies address the Equality Act and the importance of diverse leadership teams in business?

+ What do pupils need to learn about the Equality Act?

+ Why is it important that all pupils, not just pupils of colour, should be agents of change?

+ Are there any elements missing from this model of the whole-school approach? What might need to be added?

EXTENDED THINKING

+ What stereotypes should the secondary curriculum address?

EVIDENCE-BASED PRACTICE

A 2020 report from the House of Commons shows the following.

+ *At GCSE level, [Black pupils] on average, have the lowest combined English and maths pass rate of any major ethnic group. [...]*

+ *In England, young people from Black ethnic groups are more likely to go on to higher education than average, but less likely to obtain high grades, enter 'prestigious' universities, end up in a 'highly skilled' job, study further or have career satisfaction.*

(House of Commons, 2020, p 1)

SUMMARY

Decolonisation of the secondary curriculum in Britain should be about the removal of British-centred colonial attitudes and, at the same time, the promotion of ideas and cultures of the very same people whose lands were colonised. It should be about having conversations with Black pupils, parents and communities to find out about authentic cultural themes that can frame the learning of the curriculum. In this chapter, I described the African wire car and the mask dancers of the Chewa people of Malawi, which is a very small part of Africa. More conversations and teaching materials are needed from people of former British colonies. Such materials would need to address the issues of colonial misconceptions, attitudes and history.

CHECKLIST

+ The curriculum should include the significant achievements of Black people.

+ Diverse teams of staff support pupils to experience a sense of belonging.

+ All staff require training on how to identify and challenge racism.

+ Teaching staff require specific training on anti-racist pedagogy.

FURTHER READING

Gandolfi, H E (2021) Decolonising the Science Curriculum in England: Bringing Decolonial Science and Technology Studies to Secondary Education. *Curriculum Journal*, 32(3): 510–32.

Nayeri, C and Rushton, E A C (2022) Methodologies for Decolonising Geography Curricula in the Secondary School and in Initial Teacher Education. *London Review of Education*, 20(1). doi:10.14324/LRE.20.1.04.

✛ CONCLUSION

Throughout this book, we have emphasised that it is not always useful to separate knowledge and skills. This is because pupils need specific knowledge to be able to perform a skill. We have stressed that the curriculum should specify the intended knowledge that pupils need to learn, and by 'knowledge' we mean knowledge of subject principles, concepts and facts as well as the skills that pupils need to learn.

A well-designed curriculum should enable pupils to achieve intended qualifications. The important point here is that good curriculum design should result in pupils gaining the qualifications that they are studying for. A curriculum that is based only on the knowledge assessed in examinations is likely to be a weak curriculum. A strong curriculum provides pupils with breadth and depth of knowledge within a subject. It addresses content that is specified in examination syllabi, but it breaks this knowledge down further into smaller components, sequences those components and covers additional subject content that falls outside the subject specification. A good curriculum plan builds on pupils' existing schemas. As pupils learn more of the subject, their knowledge gets deeper. In a weak curriculum, subject content is not well sequenced, and as they progress through the curriculum, pupils move on to learn new content without securing existing content. By adopting the principles of spaced or distributed learning, subject content is revisited after a gap in time. A curriculum that is designed to revisit content results in schemas being modified, and this is when deep learning occurs. If schemas are not being modified in some way, pupils are not developing deeper knowledge of the subject. And if new learning does not link to prior learning, neural connections and pathways are not formed in the brain.

Curriculum design cannot therefore be divorced from the science of learning and specifically the science of the long-term memory and neuroscience. There has been insufficient emphasis on linking the science of learning to effective curriculum design, but schools are now starting to do this and the result is the development of some excellent research-informed curriculums in schools. The education sector is becoming increasingly interested in evidence-based or research-informed teaching, and curriculum design should form part of this discussion.

Moving forward, have confidence in your curriculum. Be prepared to talk about it confidently, with passion and enthusiasm. It is not a static document, and it should be evaluated at least annually to ensure that it is doing what subject leaders and pupils need it to do.

✚ REFERENCES

Akel, S (2020)

What Decolonising the Curriculum Really Means. [online] Available at: https://eachother.org.uk/decolonising-the-curriculum-what-it-really-means/ (accessed 14 August 2022).

Ashman, G (2019)

The Differentiation Myth. In Barton, C and Bennett, T (eds) *The ResearchED Guide to Education Myths: An Evidence-informed Guide for Teachers* (pp 29–35). Woodbridge: John Catt Educational.

Barker, S (2019)

How Direct Instruction Can Improve Affective Factors. In Boxer, A and Bennett, T (eds) *The ResearchED Guide to Explicit & Direct Instruction: An Evidence-informed Guide for Teachers* (pp 109–16). Woodbridge: John Catt Educational.

Baumert, J, Kunter, M, Blum, W, Brunner, M, Voss, T, Jordan, A and Tsai, Y M (2010)

Teachers' Mathematical Knowledge, Cognitive Activation in the Classroom, and Student Progress. *American Educational Research Journal*, 47(1): 133–80.

Bernstein, B (1971)

Class, Codes and Control. London: Routledge and Kegan Paul.

Bjork, E L and Bjork, R A (2011)

Making Things Hard on Yourself, but in a Good Way: Creating Desirable Difficulties to Enhance Learning. In Gernsbacher, M A, Pew, R W, Hough, L M and Pomerantz, J R (eds) *Psychology and the Real World: Essays Illustrating Fundamental Contributions to Society* (pp 56–64). New York: Worth Publishers.

Bligh, C (2014)

Young Bilingual Learners: A Sociocultural Study into the Silent Period. New York: Springer.

Bloom, B S (1956)

Taxonomy of Educational Objectives, Handbook: The Cognitive Domain. New York: David McKay.

Bouffard, T, Marcoux, M, Vezeau, C and Bordeleau, L (2003)
Changes in Self-perceptions of Competence and Intrinsic Motivation among Elementary School Children. *British Journal of Educational Psychology*, 73(2): 171–86.

Bourdieu, P (1986)
The Forms of Capital. In Richardson, J (ed) *Handbook of Theory and Research for the Sociology of Education* (pp 241–58). New York: Greenwood.

Bradlow, J, Bartram, F, Guasp, A and Jadva, V (2017)
School Report: The Experiences of Lesbian, Gay, Bi and Trans Young People in Britain's Schools in 2017. London: Stonewall.

Center on the Developing Child, Harvard University (2021)
Moving Upstream: Confronting Racism to Open Up Children's Potential. [online] Available at: https://46y5eh11fhgw3ve3ytpwxt9r-wpengine.net dna-ssl.com/wp-content/uploads/2021/05/HCDC_RacismBrief_FINAL3.pdf (accessed 14 August 2022).

Chanfreau, J, Tanner, E, Callanan, M, Laing, K, Skipp, A and Todd, L (2016)
Out of School Activities during Primary School and KS2 Attainment, Centre for Longitudinal Studies, Working paper 2016/1. London: Institute of Education, University College London.

Clark, C (2011)
Setting the Baseline: The National Literacy Trust's First Annual Survey into Reading – 2010. London: National Literacy Trust.

Clark, C and Douglas, J (2011)
Young People's Reading and Writing: An In-depth Study Focusing on Enjoyment, Behaviour, Attitudes and Attainment. London: National Literacy Trust.

Clark, C and Osborne, S (2008)
How Does Age Relate to Pupils' Perceptions of Themselves as Readers? London: The National Literacy Trust.

Clark, C and Poulton, L (2011)
Book Ownership and Its Relation to Reading Enjoyment, Attitudes, Behaviour and Attainment. London: National Literacy Trust.

Clark, C and Rumbold, K (2006)

Reading for Pleasure: A Research Overview. London: The National Literacy Trust.

Clark, R E, Kirschner, P A and J Sweller (2012)

Putting Students on the Path to Learning: The Case for Fully Guided Instruction. [online] Available at: https://files.eric.ed.gov/fulltext/EJ971752.pdf (accessed 10 October 2022).

Clotfelter, C T, Ladd, H F and Vigdor, J L (2010)

Teacher Credentials and Student Achievement in High School: A Cross-subject Analysis with Student Fixed Effects. *The Journal of Human Resources,* 45(3): 655–81.

Coe, R, Aloisi, C, Higgins, S and Major, L E (2014)

What Makes Great Teaching? Review of the Underpinning Research. [online] Available at: www.suttontrust.com/wp-content/uploads/2014/10/What-Makes-Great-Teaching-REPORT.pdf (accessed 28 August 2022).

Coombe, A, and Martin, L (2019)

Using Direct Instruction to Teach Writing: Secondary English. In Boxer, A and Bennett, T (eds) *The ResearchED Guide to Explicit & Direct Instruction: An Evidence-informed Guide for Teachers* (pp 95–107). Melton: John Catt Educational.

Counsell, C (2020)

Better Conversations with Subject Leaders. In Sealy, C and Bennett, T (eds) *The ResearchED Guide to the Curriculum: An Evidence-informed Guide for Teachers* (pp 95–121). Woodbridge: John Catt Educational.

Crenna-Jennings, W (2021)

Young People's Mental and Emotional Health: Trajectories and Drivers in Childhood and Adolescence. [online] Available at: https://epi.org.uk/wp-cont ent/uploads/2021/01/EPI-PT_Young-people%E2%80%99s-wellbeing_ Jan2021.pdf (accessed 28 August 2022).

Cullen, S (2019)

Fading: Removing Teacher Presence in Direct Teaching. In Boxer, A and Bennett, T (eds) *The ResearchED Guide to Explicit and Direct Instruction* (pp 87–94). Woodbridge: John Catt Educational.

Cummins, J (1980)

The Cross-Lingual Dimensions of Language Proficiency: Implications for Bilingual Education and the Optimal Age Issue. *TESOL Quarterly*, 14: 175–87.

Darling-Hammond, L (2000)

Teacher Quality and Student Achievement: A Review of State Policy Evidence. *Education Policy Analysis Archives*, 8(1): 1–44.

Davis, P and Florian, L (2004)

Teaching Strategies and Approaches for Pupils with Special Educational Needs: A Scoping Study. London: Department for Education and Skills.

de Sousa Santos, B (2018)

The End of the Cognitive Empire: The Coming of Age of Epistemologies of the South. Durham, NC: Duke University Press.

Department for Education (DfE) (2014)

The National Curriculum in England: Key Stages 3 and 4 Framework Document. London: DfE.

Department for Education (DfE) (2015)

Special Educational Needs and Disability Code of Practice: 0 to 25 Years: Statutory Guidance for Organisations which Work with and Support Children and Young People who Have Special Educational Needs or Disabilities. London: DfE.

Department for Education (DfE) (2019a)

Character Education: Framework Guidance. London, DfE.

Department for Education (DfE) (2019b)

Relationships Education, Relationships and Sex Education (RSE) and Health Education: Statutory Guidance for Governing Bodies, Proprietors, Head Teachers, Principals, Senior Leadership Teams, Teachers. London, DfE.

Department for Education (DfE) (2021)

Careers Guidance and Access for Education and Training Providers: Statutory Guidance for Schools and Guidance for Further Education Colleges and Sixth Form Colleges. London: DfE.

Department for Education (DfE) and Department of Health (DoH) (2017)

Transforming Children and Young People's Mental Health Provision: A Green Paper, Cm 9523. [online] Available at: https://assets.publishing.service.gov.uk/government/uploads/system/uploads/attachment_data/file/664855/Transforming_children_and_young_people_s_mental_health_provision.pdf (accessed 22 August 2022).

Dixon, R C, Carnine, D and Kameenui, E (1993)

Tools for Teaching Diverse Learners: Using Scaffolding to Teach Writing. *Educational Leadership*, 51(3): 100–1.

Dunlosky, J, Rawson, K A, Marsh, E J, Nathan, M J and Willingham, D T (2013)

Improving Students' Learning with Effective Learning Techniques: Promising Directions from Cognitive and Educational Psychology. *Psychological Science in the Public Interest*, 14(1): 4–58.

Durlak, J A, Weissberg, R P, Dymnicki, A B, Taylor, R D and Schellinger, K B (2011)

The Impact of Enhancing Students' Social and Emotional Learning: A Meta-analysis of School-based Universal Interventions. *Child Development*, 82(1): 405–32.

Education Endowment Foundation (EEF) (2016)

Careers Education: International Literature Review. London: EEF.

Education Endowment Foundation (EEF) (2020)

Metacognition and Self-regulation. [online] Available at: https://educationendowmentfoundation.org.uk/education-evidence/teaching-learning-toolkit/metacognition-and-self-regulation (accessed 4 August 2022).

Education Endowment Foundation (EEF) (2021)

Cognitive Science Approaches in the Classroom: A Review of the Evidence. London: EEF.

Engelmann, S (1992)

War against the Schools' Academic Child Abuse. Garden City, NY: Halcyon House.

Englemann, S and Carnine, D (1982)

Theory of Instruction: Principles and Applications. New York: Irvington Publishing Inc.

Fernald, A, Marchman, V A and Weisleder, A (2013)
SES Differences in Language Processing Skill and Vocabulary Are Evident at 18 Months. *Developmental Science*, 16(2): 234–48.

Fisher, D and Frey, N (2010)
Guided Instruction. Alexandria, VA: ASCD.

FSRH and Royal College of Obstetricians & Gynaecologists (2021)
Abortion and Abortion Care Factsheet. [online] Available at: www.fsrh.org/documents/abortion-and-abortion-care-factsheet-2021/?preview=true (accessed 4 August 2022).

Garon-Carrier, G, Boivin, M, Guay, F, Kovas, Y, Dionne, G, Lemelin, J, Seguin, J R, Vitaro, F and Tremblay, R E (2016)
Intrinsic Motivation and Achievement in Mathematics in Elementary Schools: A Longitudinal Investigation of their Association. *Child Development*, 87(1): 166–7.

Gatsby Charitable Foundation (nd)
Good Career Guidance. [online] Available at: www.gatsby.org.uk/uploads/education/reports/pdf/gatsby-sir-john-holman-good-career-guidance-2014.pdf (accessed 28 August 2022).

Girls Education Challenge (2018)
Thematic Review Extra and Co-curricular Interventions. London: Girls Education Challenge.

Gorard, S (2010)
Education Can Compensate for Society – a Bit. *British Journal of Educational Studies*, 58(1): 47–65.

Gutman, L M and Schoon, I (2013)
The Impact of Non-cognitive Skills on Outcomes for Young People: Literature Review. London: National Foundation for Educational Research and Cabinet Office.

Harter, S (1981)
A New Self-report Scale of Intrinsic Versus Extrinsic Orientation in the Classroom: Motivational and Informational Components. *Developmental Psychology*, 17(3): 300–12.

Higgins, S, Katsipataki, M, Kokotsaki, D, Coleman, R, Major, L E and Coe, R (2013)

The Sutton Trust-Education Endowment Foundation Teaching and Learning Toolkit. London: Education Endowment Foundation.

House of Commons (2020)

Educational Outcomes of Black Pupils and Students. [online] Available at: https://researchbriefings.files.parliament.uk/documents/CBP-9023/CBP-9023.pdf (accessed 4 August 2022).

Hutchinson, J, Reader, M and Akhal, A (2020)

Education in England: Annual Report 2020. London: Education Policy Institute.

Hyndman, B P (2017)

Perceived Social-Ecological Barriers of Generalist Pre-Service Teachers Towards Teaching Physical Education: Findings from the GET-PE Study. *Australian Journal of Teacher Education*, 42(7). doi: 10.14221/ajte.2017v42n7.3

Independent Panel on Technical Education (2016)

Report of the Independent Panel on Technical Education. [online] Available at: https://assets.publishing.service.gov.uk/government/uploads/system/uploads/attachment_data/file/536046/Report_of_the_Independent_Panel_on_Technical_Education.pdf (accessed 23 August 2022).

Jones, K (2019)

Retrieval Practice: Research and Resources for Every Classroom. Woodbridge: John Catt Educational.

Jorm, A F, Korten, A E, Jacomb, P A, Christensen, H, Rodgers, B and Pollitt, P (1997)

'Mental Health Literacy': A Survey of the Public's Ability to Recognise Mental Disorders and their Beliefs about the Effectiveness of Treatment. *Medical Journal of Australia*, 166(4): 182–6.

Joseph Rowntree Foundation (2020)

UK Poverty 2019/20: The Leading Independent Report. York: Joseph Rowntree Foundation.

Kirsch, I, De Jong, J, LaFontaine, D, McQueen, J, Mendelovits, J and Monseur, C (2002)

Reading for Change Performance and Engagement across Countries: Results from PISA 2000. Paris: OECD.

Kirschner, P A, Sweller, J and Clark, R E (2006)

Why Minimal Guidance during Instruction Does Not Work: An Analysis of the Failure of Constructivist, Discovery, Problem-based, Experiential, and Inquiry-based Teaching. *Educational Psychologist*, 41(2): 75–86.

Kishimoto, K (2018)

Anti-racist Pedagogy: From Faculty's Self-reflection to Organizing within and beyond the Classroom, *Race Ethnicity and Education*, 21(4): 540–54.

Kotter, J P and Schlesinger, L A (1979)

Choosing Strategies for Change. *Harvard Business Review*, 57(2).

Lewin, K (1951)

Field Theory in Social Science. New York: Harper and Row.

Lucas, T and Villegas, A M (2013)

Preparing Linguistically Responsive Teachers: Laying the Foundations in Preservice Teacher Education. *Theory into Practice*, 52(2): 98–109.

Macpherson, W. (1999)

The Stephen Lawrence Inquiry. [online] Available at: https://assets. publishing.service.gov.uk/government/uploads/system/uploads/attachment_data/file/277111/4262.pdf (accessed 7 October 2022).

Martinez, A, Coker, C, McMahon, S D, Cohen and Thapa, A (2016)

Involvement in Extracurricular Activities: Identifying Differences in Perceptions of School Climate. *The Educational and Developmental Psychologist*, 33(1): 70–84.

McMahon, E M et al (2017)

Physical Activity in European Adolescents and Associations with Anxiety, Depression and Well-Being. *European Child and Adolescent Psychiatry*, 26: 111–22.

McManus, S, Bebbington, P, Jenkins, R and Brugha, T (eds) (2016)

Mental Health and Wellbeing in England: Adult Psychiatric Morbidity Survey 2014. Leeds: NHS Digital.

Meyer, I H (2003)

Prejudice, Social Stress, and Mental Health in Lesbian, Gay and Bisexual Populations: Conceptual Issues and Research Evidence. *Psychological Bulletin*, 129(5): 674–97.

Moffitt, T E, Arseneault, L, Belsky, D, Dickson, N, Hancox, R J, Harrington, H and Caspi, A (2011)

A Gradient of Childhood Self-control Predicts Health, Wealth, and Public Safety. *Proceedings of the National Academy of Sciences*, 108(7): 2693–8.

Montacute, R and Cullinane, C (2018)

Parent Power 2018: How Parents Use Financial and Cultural Resources to Boost their Children's Chances of Success. London: The Sutton Trust.

Mruk, C (1999)

Self-esteem: Research, Theory and Practice. London: Free Association Books.

National Education Union (NEU) (nd)

Framework for Developing an Anti-racist Approach. [online] Available at: https://neu.org.uk/media/11236/view (accessed 28 August 2022).

National Education Union (NEU) (2021)

Turning the Page on Poverty: A Practical Guide for Education Staff to Help Tackle Poverty and the Cost of the School Day. [online] Available at: https://neu.org.uk/turning-page-guide (accessed 27 August 2022).

National Education Union (NEU) (2022)

Decolonising Education. [online] Available at: https://neu.org.uk/advice/decolonising-education (accessed 27 August 2022).

Nayeri, C and Rushton, E A C (2022)

Methodologies for Decolonising Geography Curricula in the Secondary School and in Initial Teacher Education. *London Review of Education*, 20(1). doi: 10.14324/LRE.20.1.04.

Nieto, S (2000)

Placing Equity Front and Center: Some Thoughts on Transforming Teacher Education for a New Century. *Journal of Teacher Education*, 51(3): 180–7.

NSPCC (nd)

Sharing Nudes and Semi-nudes. [online] Available at: www.nspcc.org.uk/keeping-children-safe/online-safety/sexting-sending-nudes/ (accessed 28 August 2022).

OECD (2015)

Skills for Social Progress: The Power of Social and Emotional Skills. Paris: OECD Publishing.

Office for Standards in Education, Children's Services and Skills (Ofsted) (2019a)

Education Inspection Framework: Overview of Research. Manchester: Ofsted.

Office for Standards in Education, Children's Services and Skills (Ofsted) (2019b)

The Education Inspection Framework. Manchester: Ofsted.

Office for Standards in Education, Children's Services and Skills (Ofsted) (2021)

Review of Sexual Abuse in School and Colleges. [online] Available at: www.gov.uk/government/publications/review-of-sexual-abuse-in-schools-and-colleges/review-of-sexual-abuse-in-schools-and-colleges#executive-summary-and-recommendations (accessed 4 August 2022).

Office for Standards in Education, Children's Services and Skills (Ofsted) (2022)

School Inspection Handbook. [online] Available at: www.gov.uk/government/publications/school-inspection-handbook-eif/school-inspection-handbook (accessed 28 August 2022).

Pedaste, M, Mäeots, M, Siiman, L A, de Jong, T, Van Riesen, S A, Kamp, E T, Constantinos, C M, Zacharia, Z C and Tsourlidaki, E (2015)

Phases of Inquiry-based Learning: Definitions and the Inquiry Cycle. *Educational Research Review*, 14: 47–61.

Peterson, L R and Peterson, M J (1959)

Short-Term Retention of Individual Verbal Items. *Journal of Experimental Psychology*, 58: 193–8.

Pryzbylski, A, Murayama, K, DeHaan, C and Gladwell, V (2013)

Motivational, Emotional and Behavioural Correlates of Fear of Missing Out. *Computers in Human Behaviour*, 29(4): 1841–8.

PSHE Association (nd)

Addressing Pornography through PSHE Education. [online] Available at: https://pshe-association.org.uk/resource/addressing-pornography-pshe-guidance (accessed 28 August 2022).

PSHE Association (2015)

Teaching about Consent in PSHE Education at Key Stages 3 and 4. [online] Available at: https://sexualhealth.cht.nhs.uk/fileadmin/sexualHealth/ contentUploads/Documents/PSHE_Association_guidance_on_teaching_ about_consent_at_key_stages_3_and_4_March_2015.pdf (accessed 28 August 2022).

Public Health England (2021)

Promoting Children and Young People's Mental Health and Wellbeing: A Whole School or College Approach. [online] Available at: www.gov.uk/government/ publications/promoting-children-and-young-peoples-emotional-health-and-wellbeing (accessed 28 August 2022).

Reay, D (2017)

Miseducation: Inequality, Education and the Working Classes. Bristol: Policy Press.

Reid, A (2020)

Cultural Capital, Critical Theory and Curriculum. In Sealy, C and Bennett, T (eds) *The ResearchED Guide to the Curriculum* (pp 41–8). Woodbridge: John Catt Educational.

Rhys, J (2000)

Wild Sargasso Sea. London: Penguin Classics.

Roffey, S (2017)

'Ordinary Magic' Needs Ordinary Magicians: The Power and Practice of Positive Relationships for Building Youth Resilience and Wellbeing. *Kognition und Paedagogik*, 103: 38–57.

Rosenshine, B (2010)

Principles of Instruction. [online] Available at: www.ibe.unesco.org/filead min/user_upload/Publications/Educational_Practices/EdPractices_21.pdf (accessed 28 August 2022).

Rosenshine, B (2012)

Principles of Instruction: Research-based Principles that All Teachers Should Know. *American Educator*. [online] Available at: www.aft.org/pdfs/americane ducator/spring2012/Rosenshine.pdf (accessed 28 August 2022).

Royal Society for Public Health (2017)

#StatusOfMind Social Media and Young People's Mental Health and Wellbeing. [online] Available at: www.rsph.org.uk/static/uploaded/d125b27c-0b62-41c5-a2c0155a8887cd01.pdf (accessed 7 October 2022).

Sadler, P M and Sonnert, G (2016)

Understanding Misconceptions: Teaching and Learning in Middle School Physical Science. *American Educator*, 40(1): 26–32.

Scheerens, J and Bosker, R J (1997)

The Foundations of Educational Effectiveness. Oxford: Pergamon.

Scott, H, Gardani, M, Biello, S and Woods, H, (2016)

Social Media Use, Fear of Missing Out and Sleep Outcomes in Adolescents. [online] Available at: www.researchgate.net/publication/308903222_Social_media_use_fear_of_missing_out_and_sleep_outcomes_in_adolescence (accessed 17 April 2022).

Sealy, C (2020)

Introduction. In Sealy, C and Bennett, T (eds) *The Research Ed Guide to the Curriculum: An Evidence-Informed Guide for Teachers* (pp 13–18). Woodbridge: John Catt Educational.

Sherrington, T (2019)

Teacher-led Instruction and Student-Centred Learning Are Opposites. In Barton, C and Bennett, T (eds) *The Research Ed Guide to Education Myths: An Evidence-Informed Guide for Teachers* (pp 71–82. Woodbridge: John Catt Educational.

Skills Funding Agency and Department for Business Innovation and Skills (nd)

Apprenticeships by Framework, Level and Gender: Starts 2002/03 to 2014/15. [online] Available at: www.gov.uk/government/statistical-data-sets/fe-data-library-apprenticeships (accessed 28 August 2022).

Sleeter, C E (2011)

An Agenda to Strengthen Culturally Responsive Pedagogy. *English Teaching: Practice and Critique*, 10(2): 7–23.

Spielman, A (2019)

Foreword. *Education Inspection Framework 2019: Inspecting the Substance of Education.* [online] Available at: www.gov.uk/government/consultations/education-inspection-framework-2019-inspecting-the-substance-of-education/ (accessed 5 September 2022).

Stipek, D (2010)

How Do Teachers' Expectations Affect Student Learning. [online] Available at: www.education.com/reference/article/teachers-expectations-affect-learning/ (accessed 28 August 2022).

Stonewall (2018)

Student Voice: Setting Up a Student LGBT Group in Secondary Schools and Colleges. London: Stonewall.

Taylor, R D, Oberle, E, Durlak, J A and Weissberg, R P (2017)

Promoting Positive Youth Development through School-based Social and Emotional Learning Interventions: A Meta-analysis of Follow-up Effects. *Child Development*, 88(4): 1156–71.

Tiggemann, M and Slater, A E (2013)

NetGirls: The Internet, Facebook and Body Image Concern in Adolescent Girls. *International Journal of Eating Disorders*, 46(6): 630–3.

Topping, K J (2010)

What Kids Are Reading: The Book-reading Habits of Students in British Schools. London: Renaissance Learning UK.

UK Commission for Employment and Skills (2014)

The Labour Market Story: Skills for the Future. [online] Available at: www.gov. uk/government/publications/skills-and-employment-in-the-uk-the-labour-market-story (accessed 28 August 2022).

Walker, P (2013)

Michael Gove Reveals Surprising Inspiration Behind His Reforms. *The Guardian*. [online] Available at: www.theguardian.com/education/2013/feb/05/michael-gove-inspirations-jade-goody (accessed 5 September 2022).

Walker, M, Sims, D and Kettlewell, K (2017)

Case Study Report: Leading Character Education in Schools. Slough: National Foundation for Educational Research.

Willingham, D T (2007)

Critical Thinking: Why Is It So Hard to Teach? *American Educator*, 31(2): 8–19.

Willingham, D T (2009)

Why Don't Students Like School? A Cognitive Scientist Answers Questions about How the Mind Works and What It Means for the Classroom. Hoboken, NJ: John Wiley and Sons.

Wood, D, Bruner, J S and Ross, G (1976)

The Role of Tutoring in Solving. *The Journal of Child Psychology and Psychiatry*, 17(2): 89–100.

World Health Organization (2004)

Promoting Mental Health: Concepts, Emerging Evidence, Practice (Summary Report). Geneva: World Health Organization.

Young, M (2008)

From Constructivism to Realism in the Sociology of the Curriculum. *Review of Research in Education*, 32(1): 1–32.

Young, M (2013)

Powerful Knowledge: An Analytically Useful Concept or Just a 'Sexy Sounding Term'? A Response to John Beck's 'Powerful Knowledge, Esoteric Knowledge, Curriculum Knowledge'. *Cambridge Journal of Education*, 43(2): 195–8.

Young, M (2014)

Powerful Knowledge as a Curriculum Principle. In Young, M, Lambert, D, Roberts, C and Roberts, M (eds) *Knowledge and the Future Curriculum and Social Justice* (pp 65–88). London: Bloomsbury Academic.

Young, M (2020)

From Powerful Knowledge to the Powers of Knowledge. In Sealy, C and Bennett, T (eds) *The ResearchED Guide to the Curriculum: An Evidence-informed Guide for Teachers* (pp 19–30). Woodbridge: John Catt Educational.

Young, M and Lambert, D (2014)

Knowledge and the Future School: Curriculum and Social Justice. London: Bloomsbury.

✚INDEX

Note: Page numbers in **bold** denote tables.